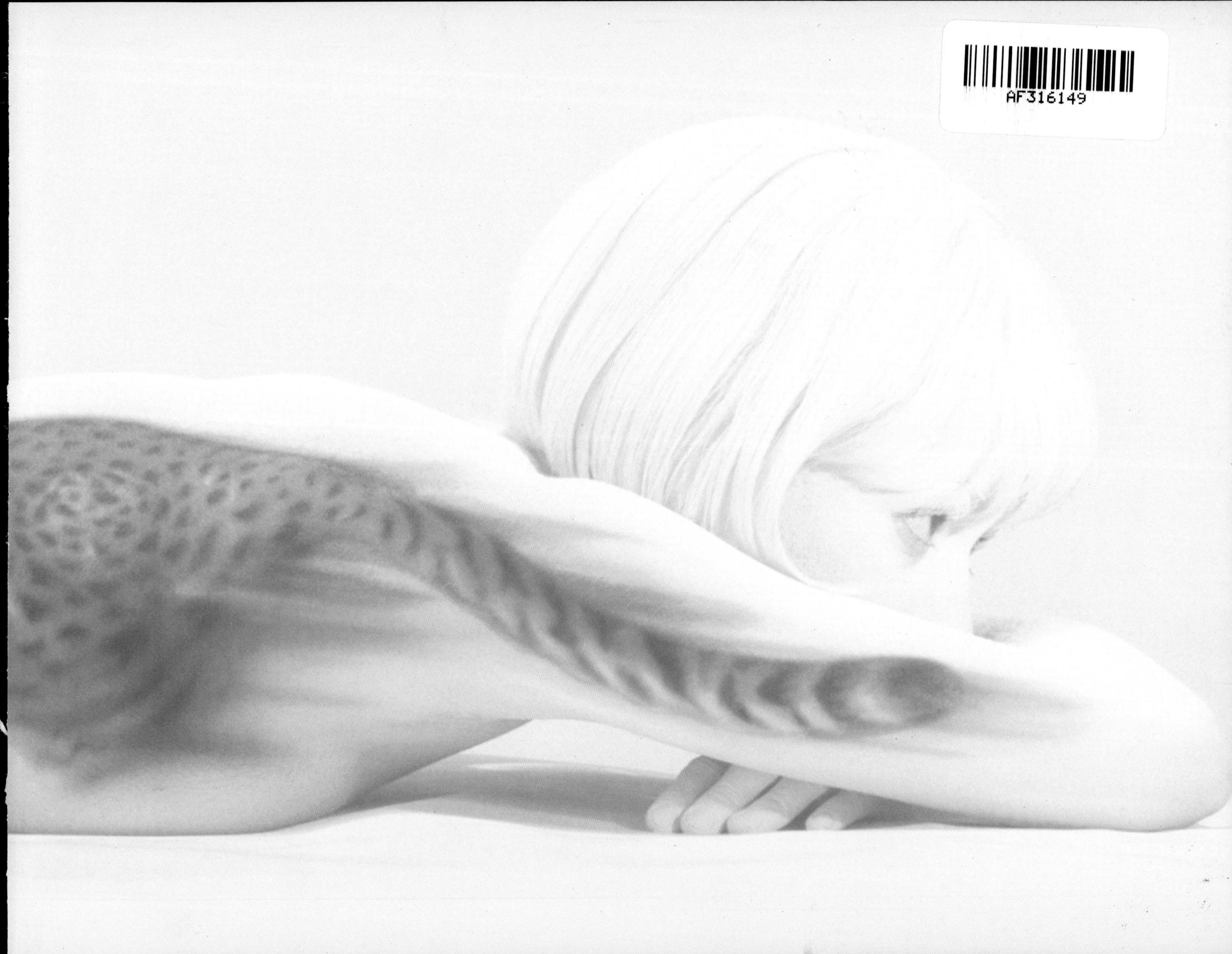
AF316149

PAINTED ALIVE

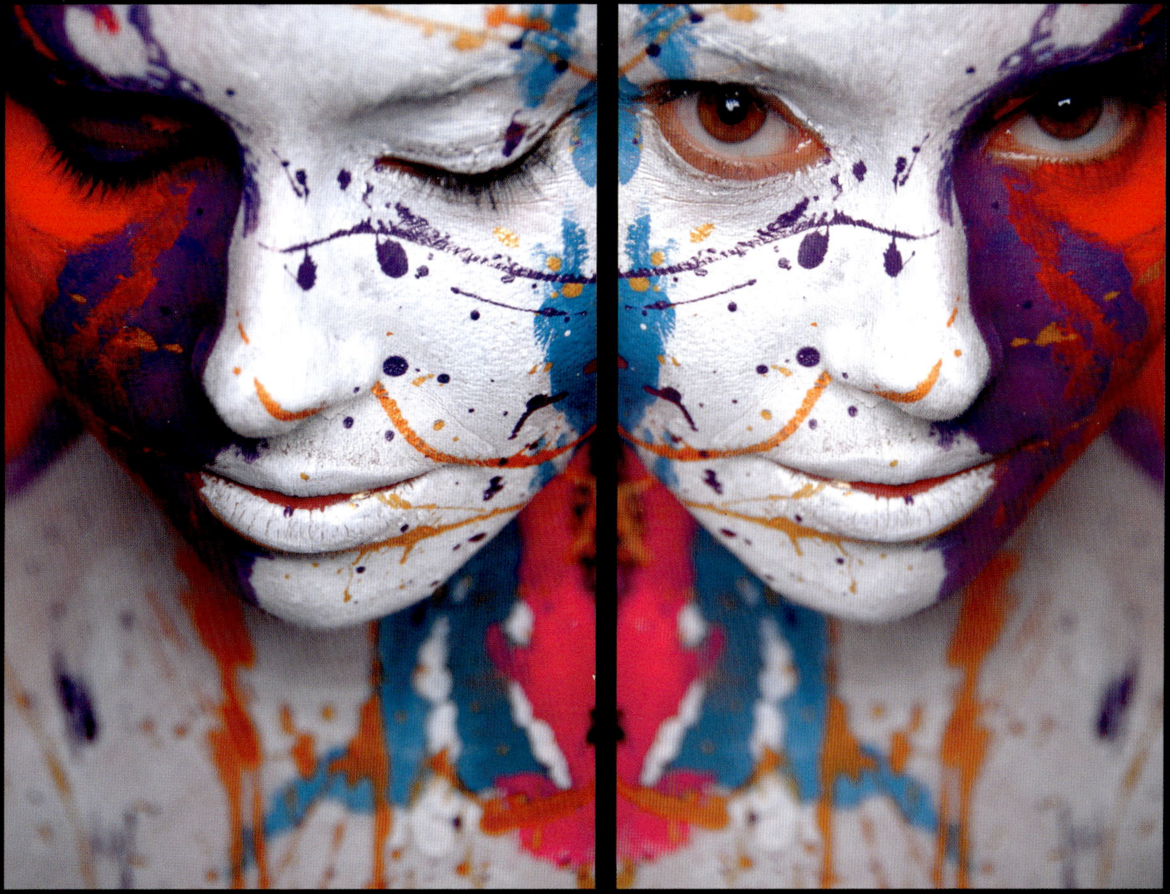

The Fine Art Bodypainting of Craig Tracy

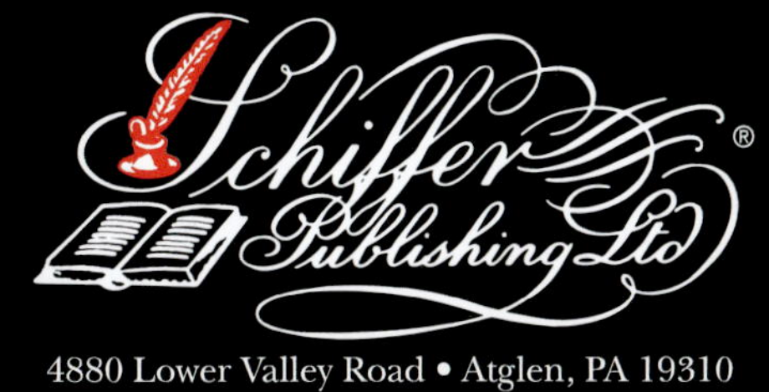

Schiffer Publishing Ltd

4880 Lower Valley Road • Atglen, PA 19310

Schiffer Books are available at special discounts for bulk purchases for sales promotions or premiums. Special editions, including personalized covers, corporate imprints, and excerpts can be created in large quantities for special needs. For more information contact the publisher.

Published by Schiffer Publishing, Ltd.
4880 Lower Valley Road
Atglen, PA 19310
Phone: (610) 593-1777; Fax: (610) 593-2002
E-mail: Info@schifferbooks.com

For the largest selection of fine reference books on this and related subjects, please visit our website at **www.schifferbooks.com.** You may also write for a free catalog.

This book may be purchased from the publisher.
Please try your bookstore first.

We are always looking for people to write books on new and related subjects. If you have an idea for a book, please contact us at proposals@schifferbooks.com
In Europe, Schiffer books are distributed by
Bushwood Books
6 Marksbury Ave.
Kew Gardens
Surrey TW9 4JF England
Phone: 44 (0) 20 8392 8585; Fax: 44 (0) 20 8392 9876
E-mail: info@bushwoodbooks.co.uk
Website: www.bushwoodbooks.co.uk

To all of my friends and family who have helped along the way.

Contents

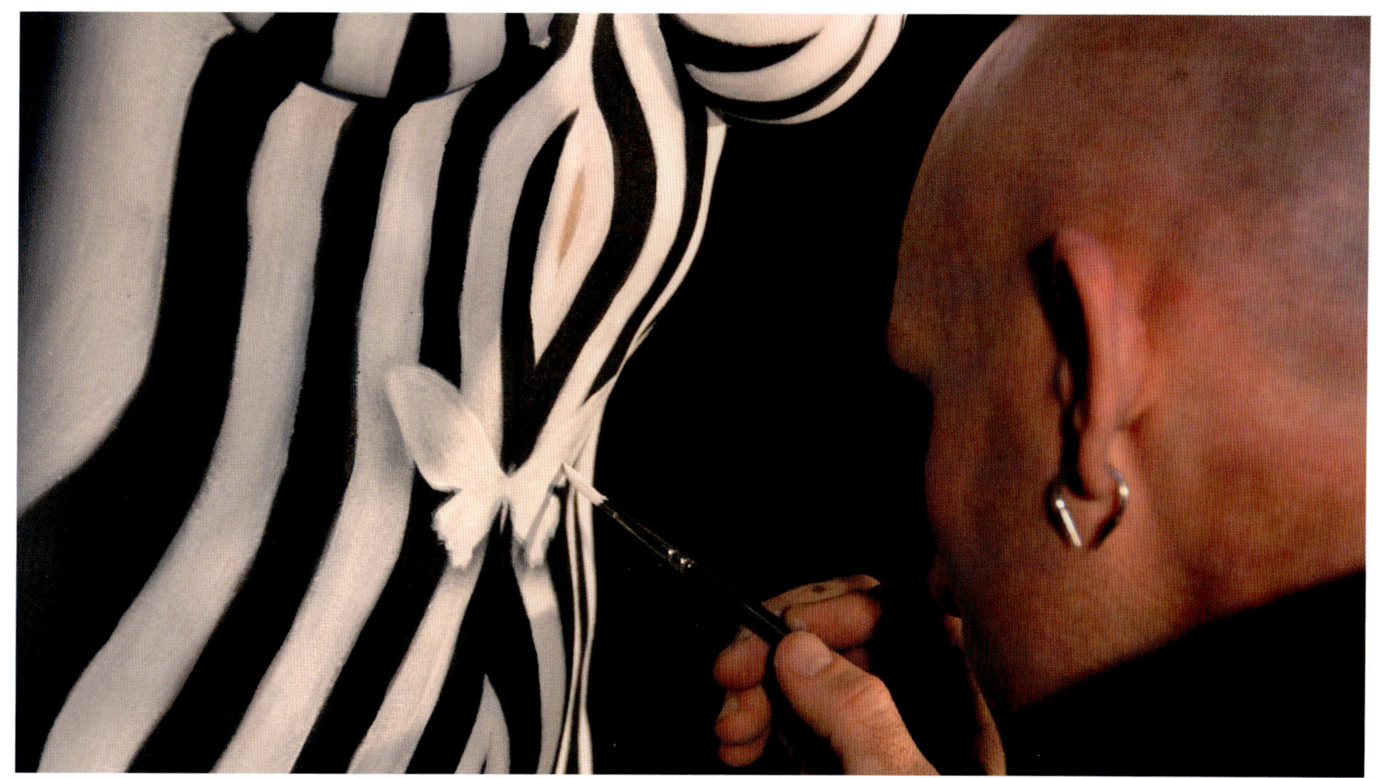

Artist's Statement

It is my intent to continue to explore and expand the limitless boundaries of this most ancient and alluring art form, and to help it find its way into contemporary homes, galleries, and museums within our collective cultures.

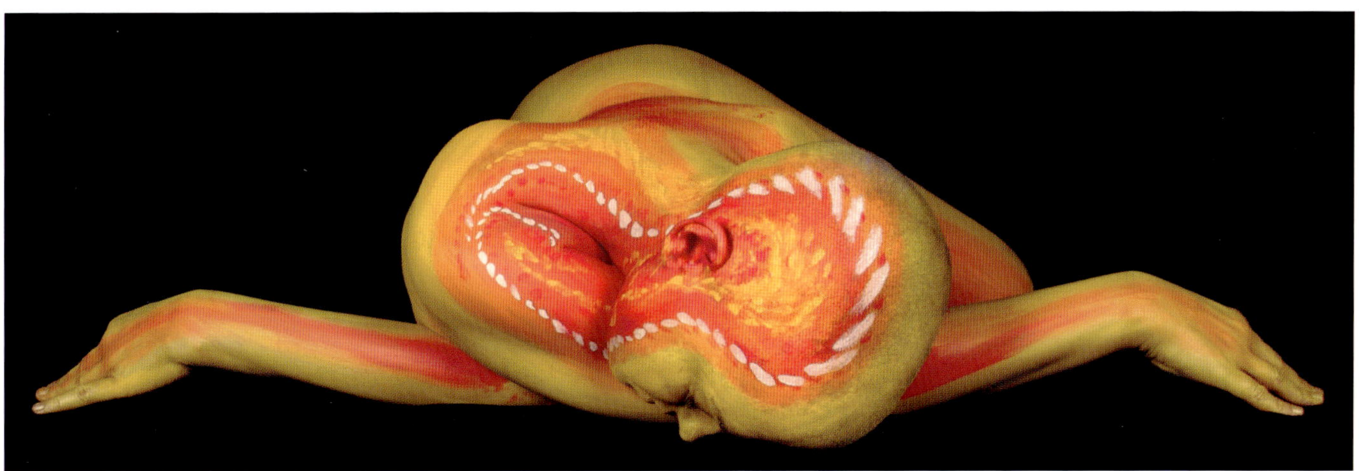

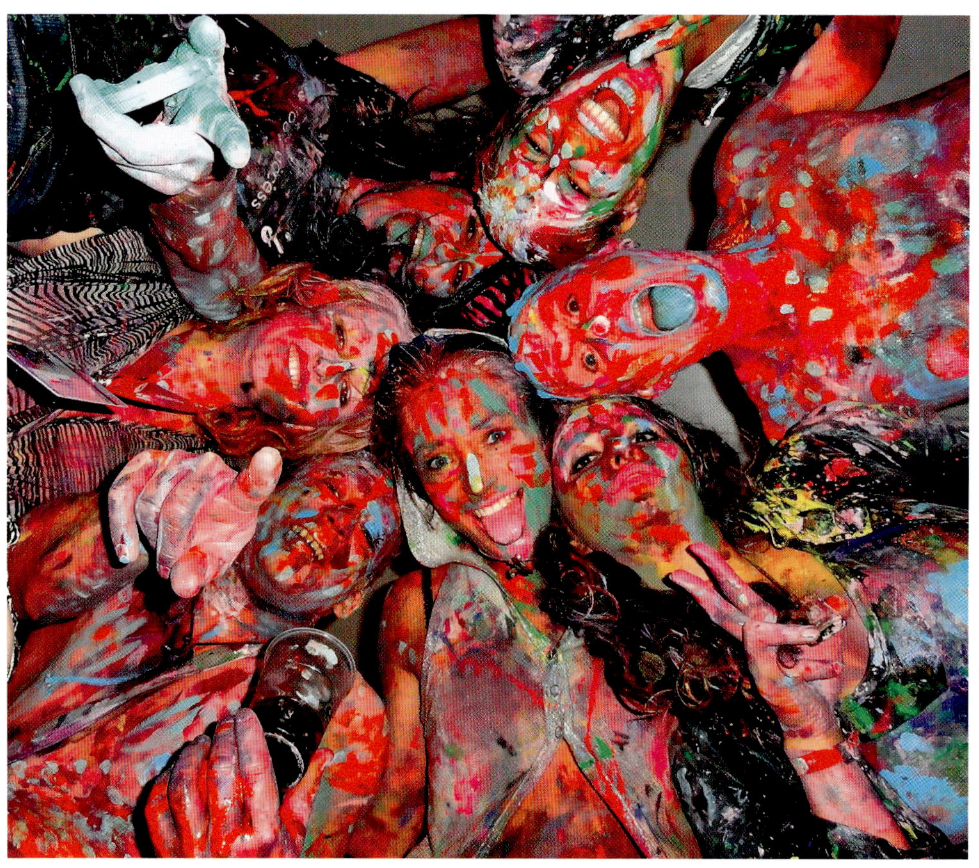

Craig Tracy and Friends, Austria, July 2011

Foreword

The art of bodypainting is the art of communicating life through color, form, thought, and expression. It is the most diverse form of art in our time and the oldest form of art in the history of our beautifully evolving humanity. It is the connection of our desire to understand and express our soul to the physical existence of our body, our solid presence.

Craig Tracy is one of the driving elements in the chemistry of the modern bodypainting movement. To describe him as a person and artist is like photographing a rolling, crashing, and ever changing river. A snapshot of one moment is only a reference point to decades of growing and evolving forces.

Bodypainting has been used in traditional cultures on every continent of this planet for tens of thousands of years. We have used it to connect to our soul as a bridge to the spirit world. We have used it to mark birth and death and as a right of passage into full growth. We have taken the materials of the earth for the health of our minds and bodies, to celebrate our beauty, and install fear in battle. Bodypainting has been a part of human existence in all its forms, as warriors, brides, healers, and child gods.

In the twenty-first century, body art has diversified in technique, style, and direction to the point where it is a part of our daily media, our households, art galleries, and social lives. The greatest evolution of this art form has been its development as a fine art, the results of which you can see for yourselves in the pages to come.

I have worked and lived in the bodypainting industry for eleven years and have taken part in many of its directions, including painting, modeling, and photographing body art. I am the author of two books about the art form: *Bringing Bodypainting to Life,* where I featured Craig as one of the 25 iconic artists of our time, and *Body Art Fashion,* which also featured Craig's work. I was co-organizer of the World Championships for body art over six years and helped develop the World Bodypainting Association as a connecting platform to artists around the world.

I first came into contact with Craig Tracy in 2004, when he entered the World Bodypainting Festival as a competitor, and I was struck by his intense passion and willingness to communicate through words and through art. In the following seven years, Craig and I have formed a deep friendship that has spurred many creative endeavors as we have shared ideas and supported each other to bring them to life.

Craig began his artistic career on receiving an airbrush for his fifteenth birthday. He quickly mastered this technique and worked his skill into an exacting realism over twenty years that was trademark to his bodypainting when I first came into contact with his art. *The Nature Series* displays the peak of this era of his art making with many of his creations, including *Speed* and *Butterfly* becoming iconic images connected to his name.

Knowing him as a World Champion airbrush artist he then surprised me when I saw the *Jazz Series*, a series of body art created entirely with finger painting that captured, through vibrant color, the spirit of his home city, New Orleans. This was the first sign to me of how diverse he would become as an artist and how wide-ranging his creativity could be.

It was around this time that Craig opened the world's first art gallery dedicated to displaying the fine art of bodypainting. Craig Tracy's PAINTEDALIVE Body Painting Gallery was an important step for the artist himself and for the bodypainting community as a whole. It brought bodypainting into the world of art dealership and has been a catalyst to the development of new possibilities to artists working in this form.

In the years to follow, Craig Tracy has created a massive body of work, roughly a third of which is displayed in this book at the time of printing. He has masterpieces of abstract line and form, detailed illusions that reinvent themselves with every viewing, and collaborations with some of the leading artists in the bodypainting field, including Filippo Ioco and Carolyn Roper. He has close friendships with many of the artists who have also been inspiration to him, including the Art Color Ballet from Poland; Bella Volen, who is one of the leading fine art bodypainters; Mike Shane; Birgit Mörtl; and Einat Dan. These friendships have been further support to the diversity of his expression.

Although the variety of his art branches over so many techniques and directions, the connecting line of his work is Craig's eye for the beauty of form. His ability to be inspired by the curve of a hip, the bending arch of a back, or the trailing finger of a falling hand. He takes these parts of what make up our form and transforms them with color, image, and line into expressions of living art that touch the soul.

The works in this book have been some of the ground-breaking creations that have taken the art of bodypainting into a new century. They are a selection from an even greater portfolio of work created in a long and dedicated career. I can only guess at where Craig will take his abilities and expressions in the years to come, and I invite you to follow this journey with many fans and art appreciators around the world.

–Karala Barendregt Wallace
Author, Model, & Producer

The Artist's Process

I never use computer graphics or Photoshop to artistically manipulate my work. I only use the most basic image processing techniques to accurately achieve my final work. The images that I create are not in any way virtual. They are very real surreal moments in time captured and documented photographically. The raw human visceral nature of what I do brings me great satisfaction.

It is one of my artistic goals to not have a definitive style or technique. I prefer the freedom to create without self-imposed or external expectations. I choose to focus on the human body as my surface as it is without doubt the most complex and dynamic substrate in our known universe. Painting on a flat lifeless, soulless surface is generally utilitarian more than inspired, and I have little interest in working with or on such conventional materials.

My inspiration comes in several fashions. Often the shape and curve of the body will inspire me to develop a painting specifically for it. Other times my inspiration comes from feelings or concepts that come to me separately from the body. I'll then choose the appropriate body and pose for that image. Spontaneity also works its way into my work. Several of my paintings were done absolutely or primarily in the moment with little or no advanced thought or preparation. The images that look like I spent plenty of time preparing and developing are usually accurately assessed. I like to keep myself open to inspiration in any way, shape, or form that it can find me.

I do most of my photography myself. When I work with other photographers, I direct the photography and lighting in a very controlled manner. Most of my work is simply flat lit and photographed using whatever professional camera that I have available at the time of the painting. I do not consider myself a photographer and I'm not technically interested in photography at all. I'm interested in creating, not capturing. I believe what is in front of the camera is far more important and interesting then the camera and its operator. My work is not about photography any more than your favorite music or song is about audio recording and engineering. An average photo session with my painted model takes about thirty minutes.

The paints that I use are safe and made specifically for painting on the human body. These body paints generally wash off of the body after one thorough shower. My work on the body needs to be completed in one waking period and my average painting time takes approximately eight hours. If a background is to be created or painted, I will do that work in advance of the bodypainting. My models are primarily volunteers who have contacted me and expressed a desire to become a part of my work. My volunteer models have little to no influence regarding the image being painted. I'm painting my vision, not theirs. I do accept a few private commissions each year where the client and I will work together to develop the concept.

My work is ultimately displayed and sold as signed, limited edition prints on archival photographic paper, fine art paper, and canvas. If you are interested in acquiring my work, please see **www.craigtracy.com** for more details and contact information.

Artist's Biography

Born and raised in New Orleans, Louisiana, Craig Tracy has always been an artist. Craig credits New Orleans, with its authentic and vibrant culture, as a significant factor in what is at the heart of his passion, creativity, and bliss. His family's photo album is filled with images that captured moments of the family members ritually painting each other's faces for Mardi Gras. Mardi Gras is perhaps the largest costumed celebration or carnival in the world where individuality and self-adornment are considered standard practice. "There was never any question regarding my being or becoming a professional artist. It was always just obvious and understood."

As a child, Craig's loving parents nurtured his creative development. They also gave him the gift of freedom to mature as an absolute individual. His parents were living in a special time, in a place filled with radical changes. Categorized best as working-class hippies, their nonconformist principles were instilled firmly in the young artist. It's safe to say that "Flower Power" and "Power To The People" are vastly responsible for his unique perspective on art and life. Coincidentally, it was that same hippie movement that reignited the soon-to-be interest in and practice of bodypainting in the Western world.

Craig's early years were filled with drawings and paintings of idealized love and beauty. He continued to expand his artistic horizons well into his teen years, and at fifteen, he received his first airbrush as a gift from his parents. Airbrushing would become the technique that would dominate his next twenty years of painting.

One year later, at sixteen, in his junior year of high school, Craig was working nights and weekends as an airbrush artist in a local shopping mall. There he primarily painted custom t-shirts and other personalized gift items. It was an important time for the young artist as he quickly learned how to paint almost any image on a vast multitude of surfaces. "Anything, on anything, was what those days were like. I'd often paint fifty to eighty hours a week and in doing so, I learned some very important and useful skills," states the artist.

A graduate with honors from The Art Institute of Fort Lauderdale, Craig was a professional freelance illustrator by the age of twenty. This period of work dealt primarily with airbrush illustration for advertising agencies and editorial publishing houses. Craig hated being an illustrator. "I was so disappointed by just how mind-numbingly boring and lonely it all was. The isolation created a cabin fever vibe and the fact that I was painting mostly commercial and industrial images seemed empty to me. I had no real interest or connection to the work and it seemed to suck the passion and energy right out of me." Six years later he retired from illustration altogether to venture back into painting murals, t-shirt designs, and just about anything and everything possible.

It was this regained freedom to paint for both himself and other individuals on a limitless variety of surfaces again that led him to his inclusion of faces, and then full bodies. "It really clicked from the very first time that I painted a face, it was strangely powerful. I later realized that I had quite literally fallen in love with bodypainting."

It did, however, take Craig years to properly process and respect such an uncharted and ancient art form. "People often don't take things seriously because they have no example to follow, rock and roll or rap music, for instance. It was hard to take these two seriously at first, but we see how that all turned out. I personally didn't take bodypainting seriously for five or six years. One day I finally asked myself 'Why, why do I like painting on people so much?' This led me to...'Well, what if I take this passionate interest seriously?'" With that question, and a quick Google search, a whole new world unfolded right before the artist, one he felt a strong calling to pursue and conquer professionally.

Craig researched with a renewed passion that surprised even him. He also started collecting bodypainted images from other artists that he respected and admired. "I wanted this work to surround me in my daily life. I found tremendous inspiration from having these images hanging in my home, beautifully framed and displayed in the majority of my living space. If I were to expect that others would purchase my images then I should have the respect to collect this beautiful work as well." His personal collection of bodypainting works from other artists continues to grow and delight all of his waking hours.

Collecting images was soon followed by his first serious creation of images. His first series of bodypaintings, *The Nature Series*, is a collection of fifteen unique images that were very well received. Certain images from his nature series have become iconic, as they are visually, emotionally, and creatively relevant. The artist's belief in the concept that not everything has been done, and that we the living have room to grow and explore are fundamental principals that are clear and present in these first works. Shortly thereafter he ventured to Europe to meet and share with fellow bodypainting artists. The World Bodypainting Festival (WBPF), held annually in southern Austria with more than 180 artists from forty different nations, brought them all together. In 2005, Craig participated in the festival painting alongside his very good friend and artist, Jeral Tidwell, as a creative bodypainting team. They were awarded a first place honor. Craig has since been a judge at the festival several times and he credits the WBPF as being one of his life's greatest passions. He attends the event every year.

Considered a cornerstone in bodypainting's progressive movement, Craig Tracy now bodypaints exclusively, while he also owns and operates the first art gallery in the world dedicated to fine art bodypainted images. The gallery allows even the most seasoned art collectors and novices alike to see and experience first hand what bodypainting is ultimately capable of expressing.

PAINTED ALIVE

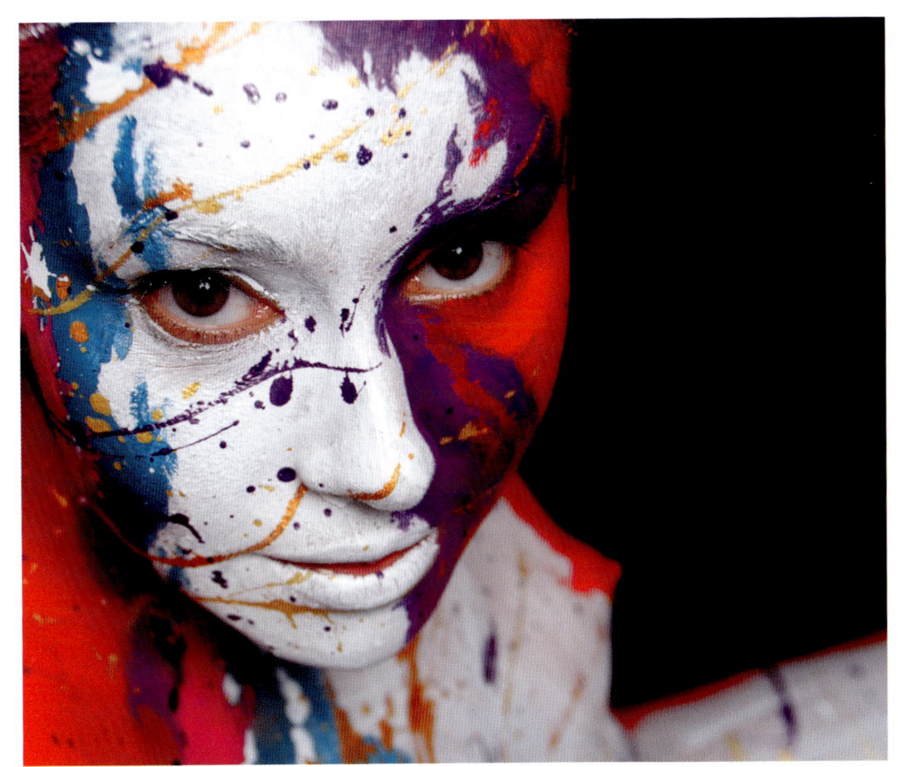

Olympian

If a human is able to excel in a specific defined physical activity, they often have the opportunity to become recognized and distinguished as exceptional. The highest plateau for many of these exceptional individuals is to be invited into the Olympic arena. They are then and will forever be Olympians. It was my privilege to work with one such Olympian here, within this piece. She is and will forever be exceptional.

Model: Heather
Photographer: Craig Tracy

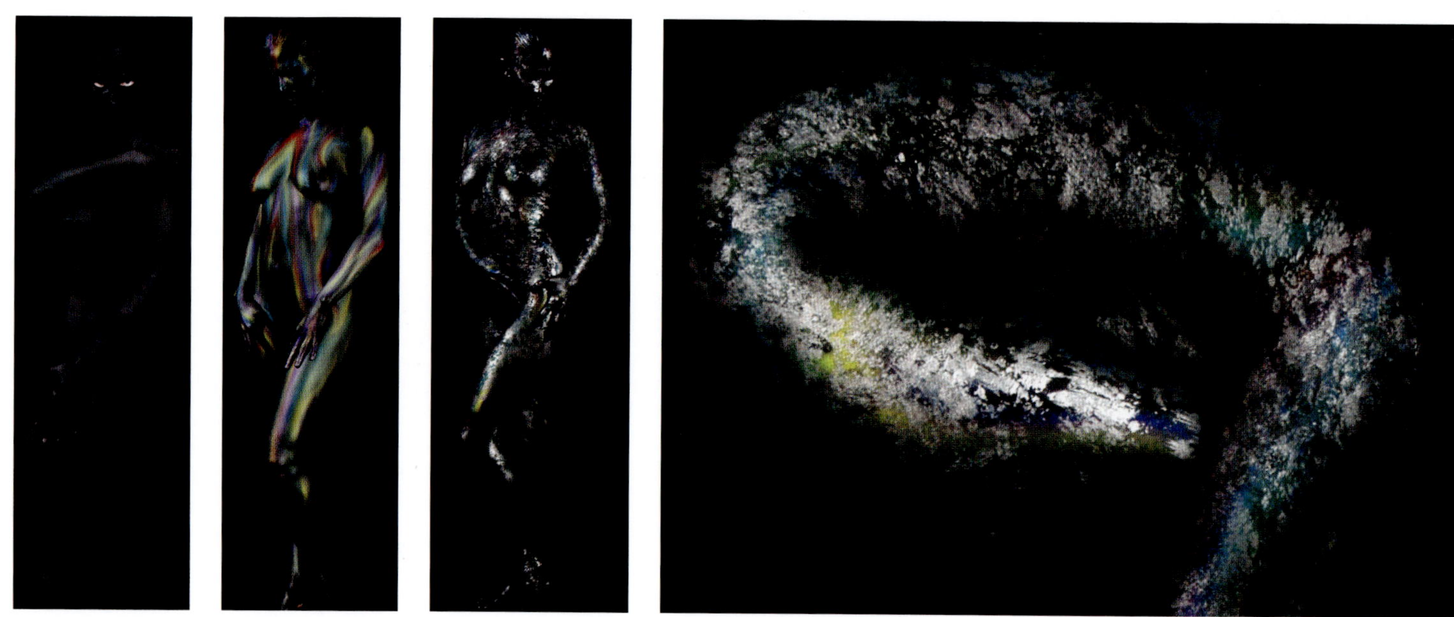

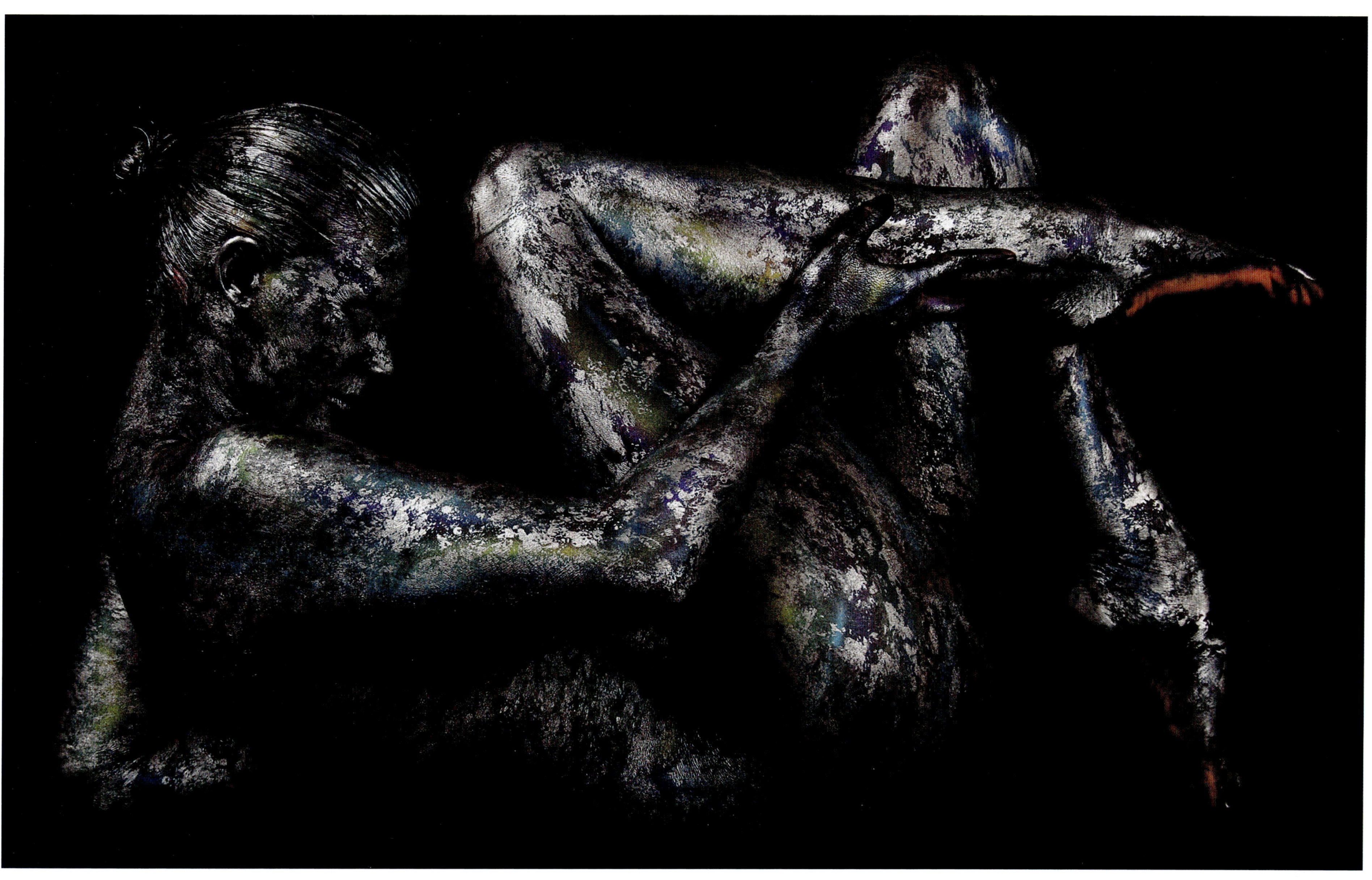

Quondam

Quondam is a reference from the past. Two very subtle images can be found inside of the eagle itself. Both a Native American profile and the head-to-head buffalo were inspirations I visualized while intensely searching the original composition for something more. With this image, as well as several of my others, I've learned to not become overly concerned with blending the model seamlessly into the background. I instead strive for a balance between the two that pleases the eye.

Model: Missi
Photographer: Chris Mathews

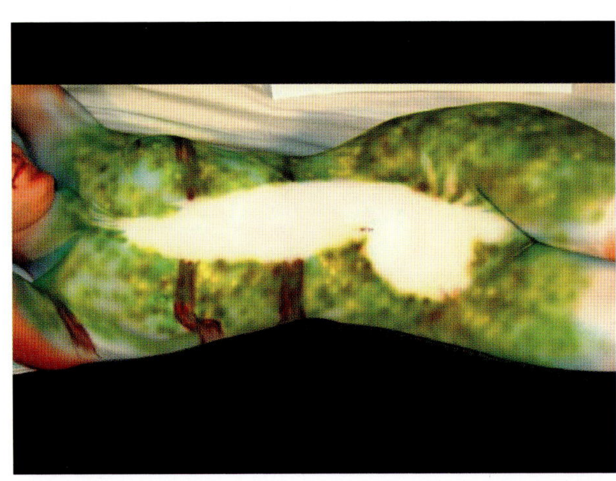 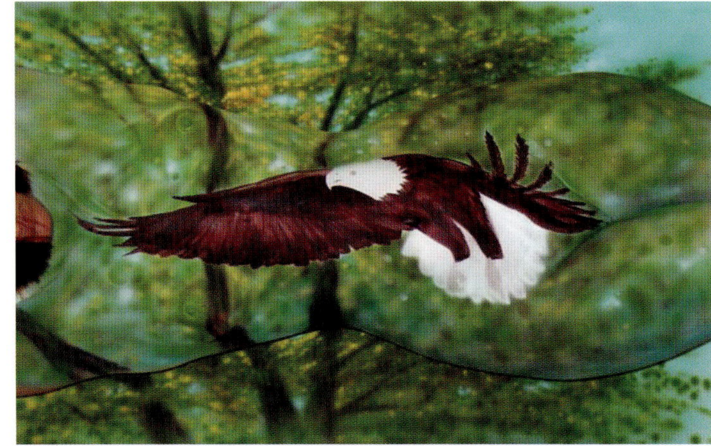 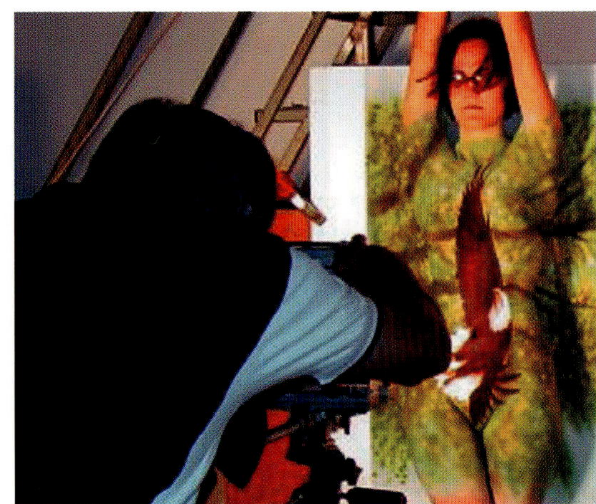

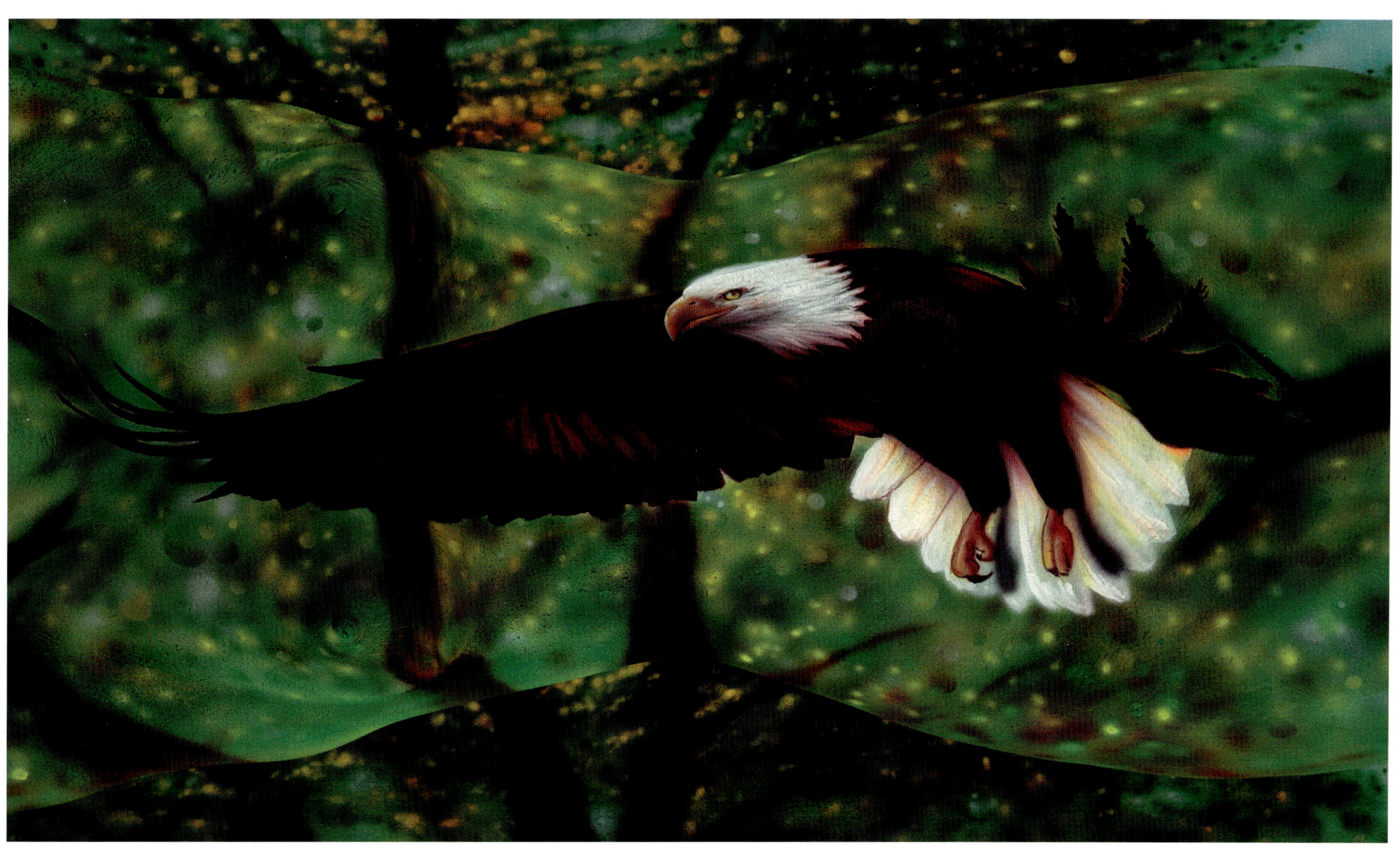

Poydras Rouge

I do love working with nature. I love the opportunity to collaborate with that which I have little or no control over. I was inspired to include one of my creations here in what was already a beautiful landscape. The truly unique circumstance involved in this painting is not at all visible. This image was captured in the center of downtown urban New Orleans. Everything surrounding this image is concrete, man-made, and steel. High-rise buildings, traffic, and typical city life are just outside of the cropped image. A security guard actually tried to make us leave the property while I was photographing the image. Luckily, I had security of my own intercept and dissuade her long enough to finish my work.

Model: Cat
Photographer: Craig Tracy

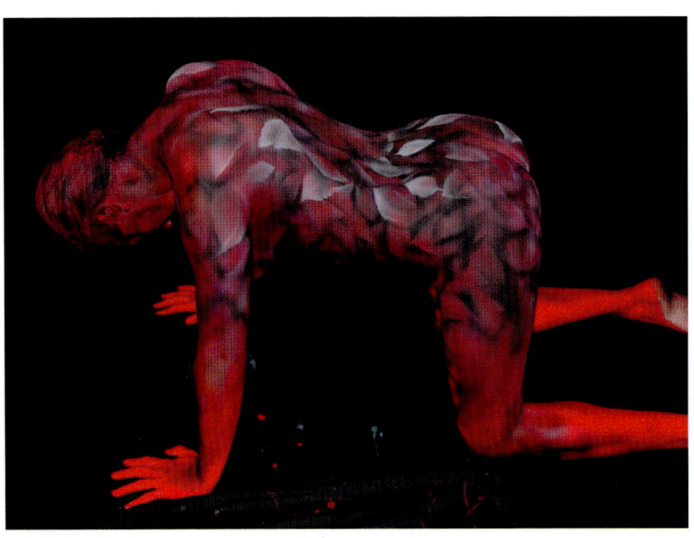
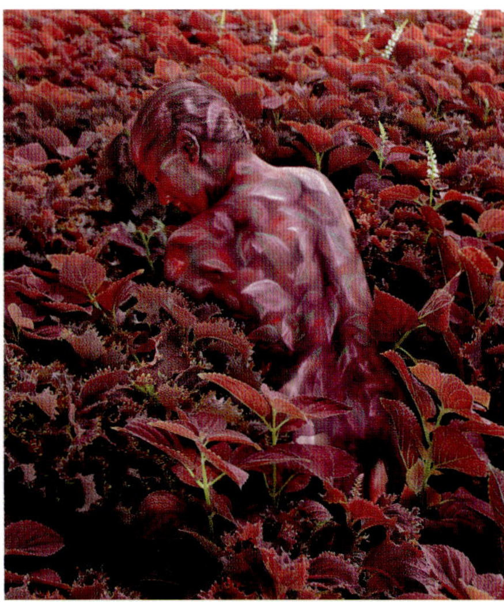
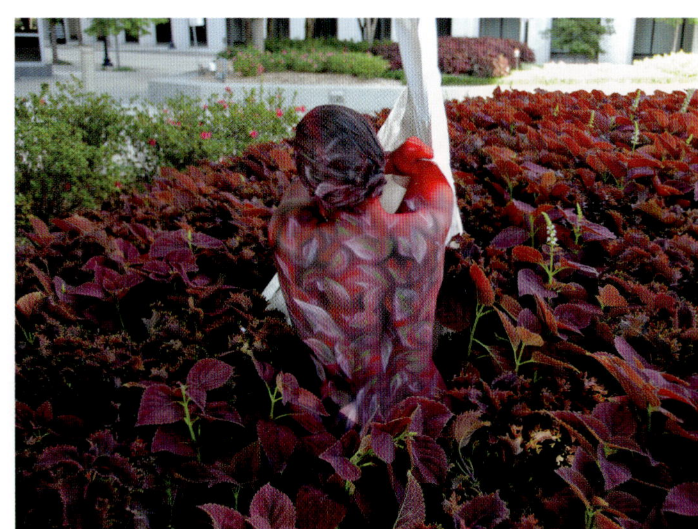

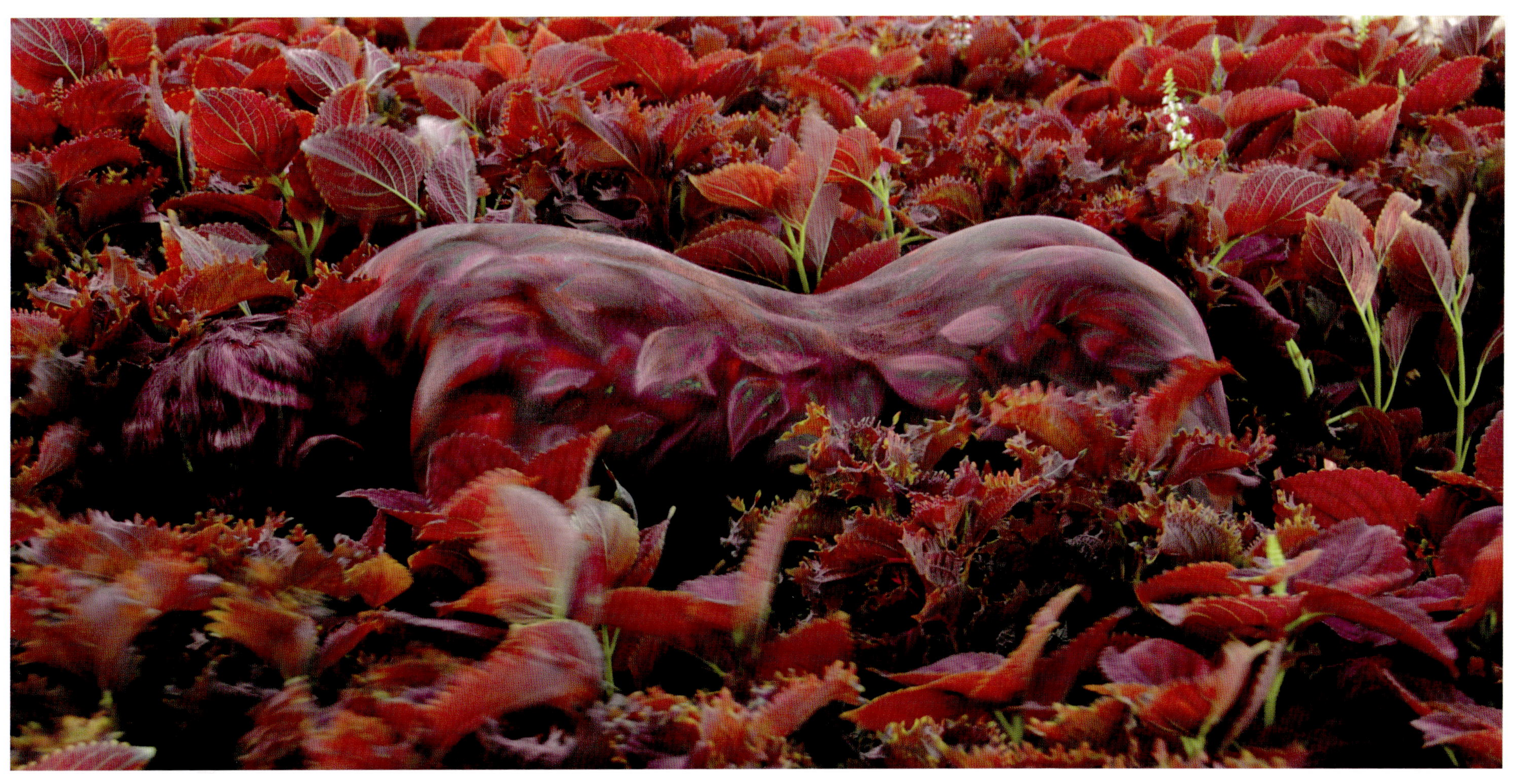

Golden

Each time I work with a newborn I'm humbled and reminded of just how fortunate I am to be a bodypainting artist. Babies are so very precious, and working with and on them makes for a very exceptional experience. I do everything I can to prepare for their comfort and for the comfort of the mother. I keep the studio extra warm and I ask that the mother bring her new baby to my studio both tired and hungry. The goal is to have the baby sleeping long enough for me to paint and do the photography. This goal is not always realized, but luckily I've had some success. Patience was the key here as our tiny model answered the call of nature and was breast-fed no less then six times while in my studio. The baby's toes are my favorite element here, adorable in all of their golden majesty.

Model: Leslie & Mason
Photographer: Craig Tracy

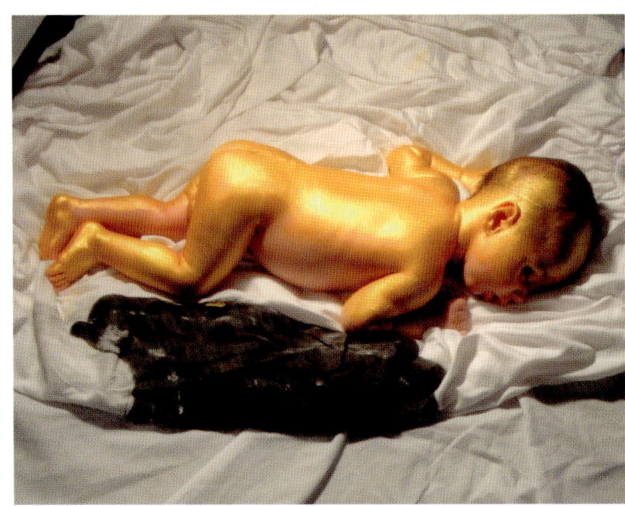
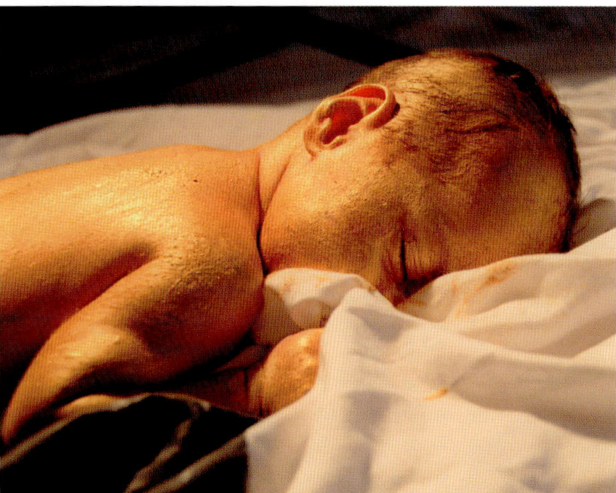
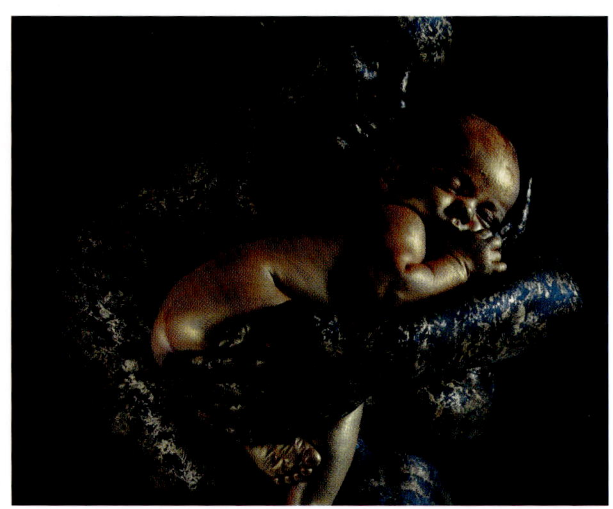

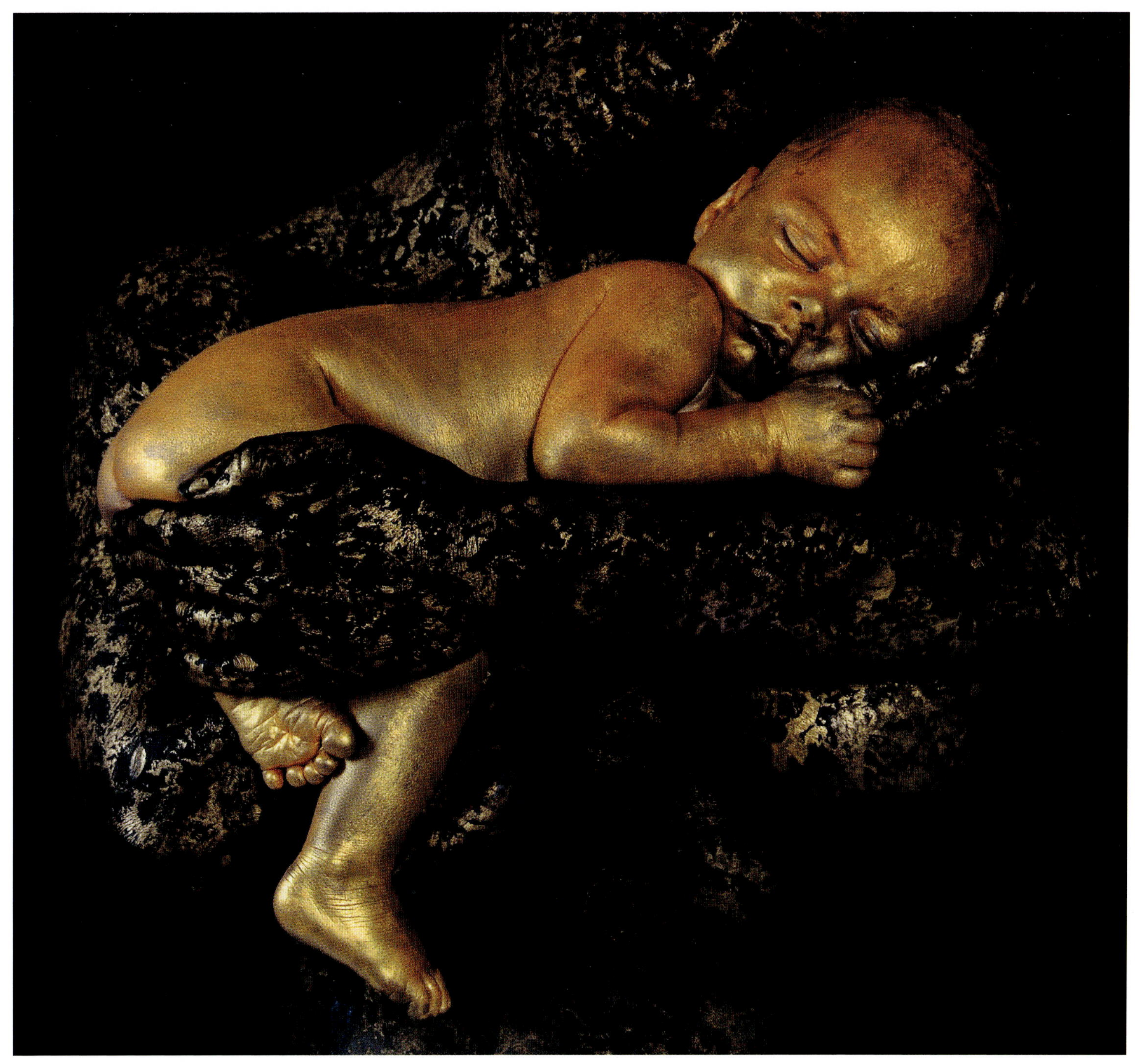

Seven Angel

Unique in many ways, *Seven Angel* plays with its viewer and offers several surprises. Here we have seven vastly unique models working together to create one harmonious image. I've learned from past experience to not worry or attempt seamless perfection technically with my work. Much of the pleasure in viewing a bodypainting is found in seeing the diverse and alluring contours of the human body. I try to balance and interplay the body of the model or models with the subject being painted, or the often abstract design work being created and presented. This image seemed to design itself and I genuinely felt more like a guide to its creation than its creator. Nothing is more difficult to paint than a human likeness on the three dimensional human body. I offer my attempt here with humble appreciation to the team that helped me create it.

Models: Teri, Lauren, Cat, Kim, Zeola, Luisa, & Sarah
Photographer: Craig Tracy

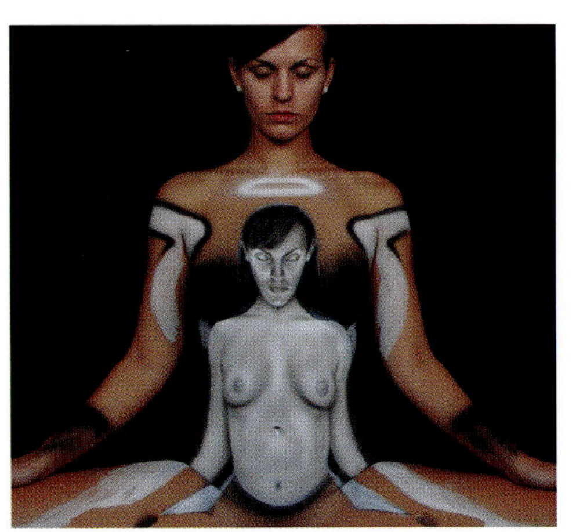
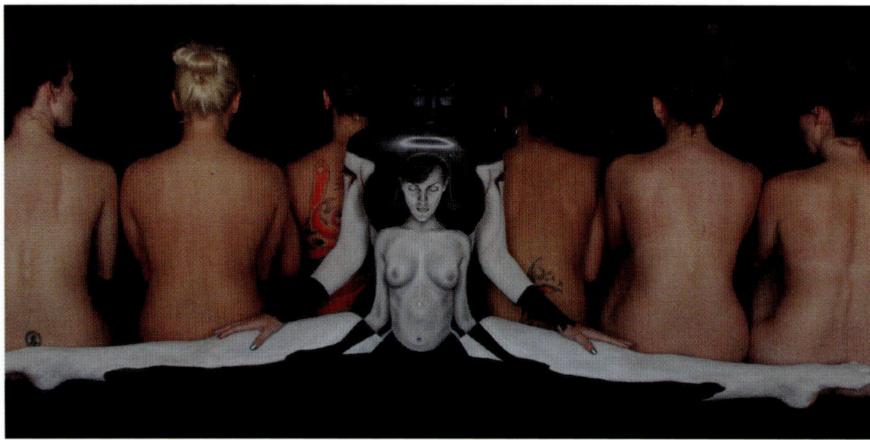
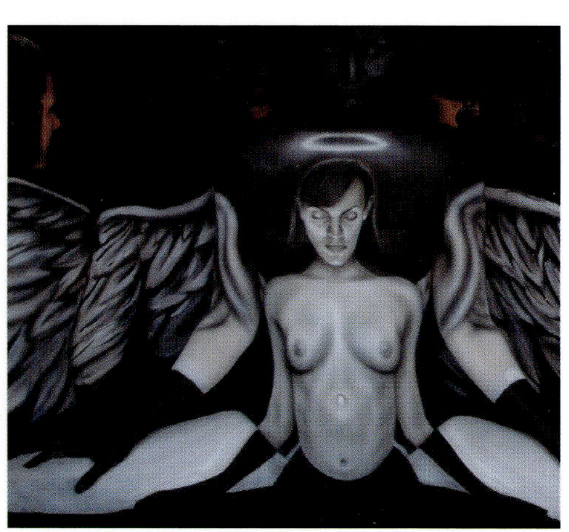

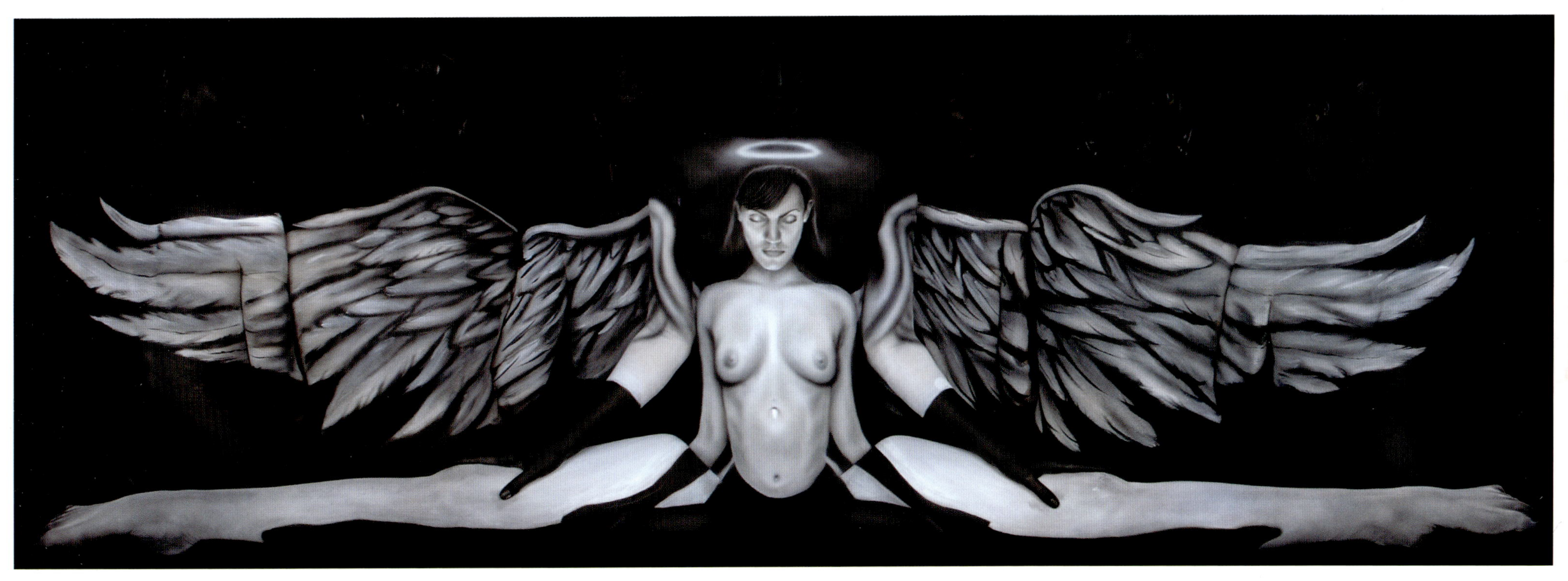

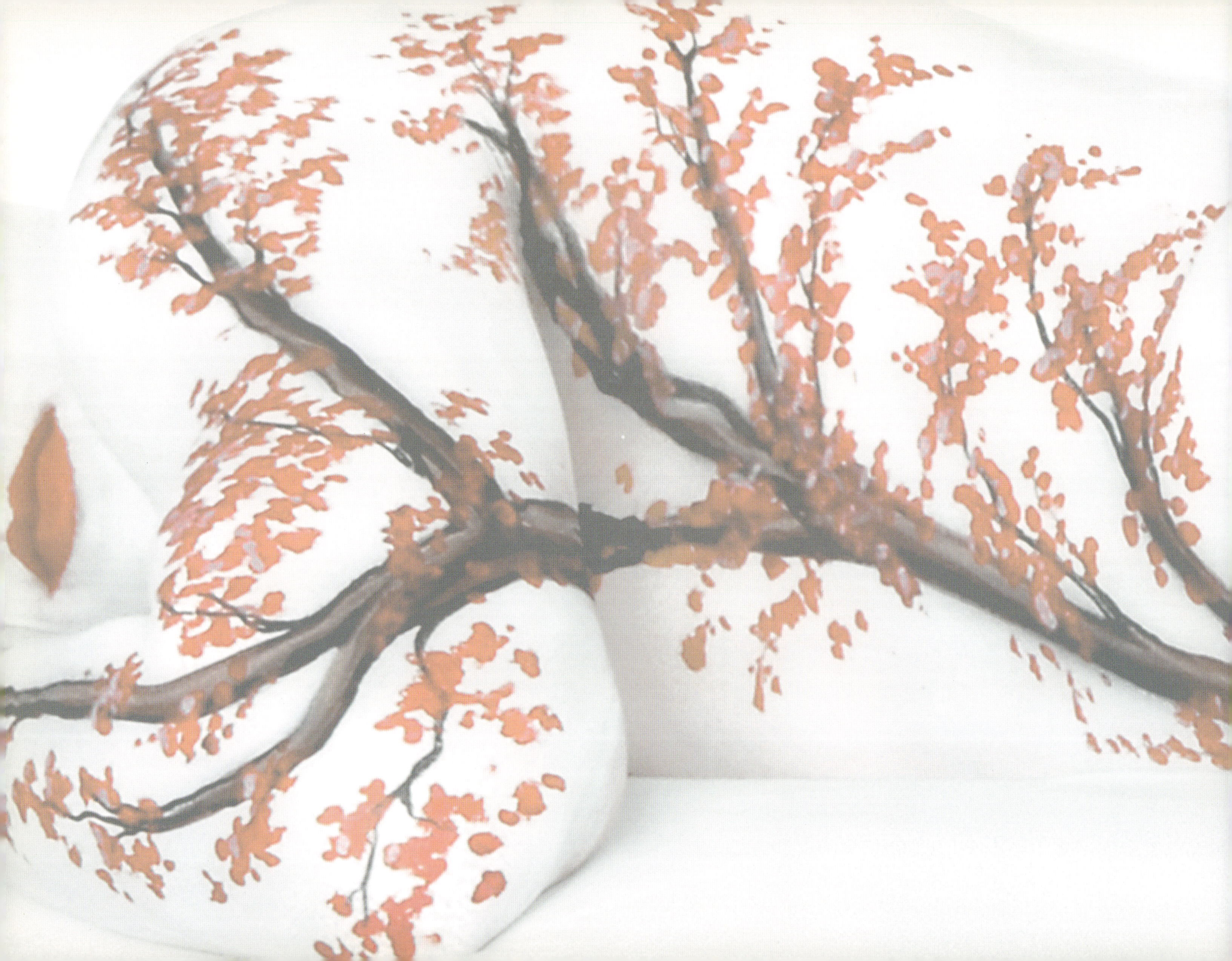

Promise

With seven different connection points, *Promise* challenges the viewer's eye just as it challenged me in its creation. I rarely work with an all white background but in the few times that I have, I've found tremendous power in its visual and emotional communication. An alluring, deceptive, complex simplicity exists here that is often found in my work. Feminine accents also contribute to her beauty with the seemingly disconnected elements of the lips and toenails being painted. Trees are perhaps my single most repeated subject matter and I'm hopeful this will never change.

Model: Alex
Photographer: Craig Tracy

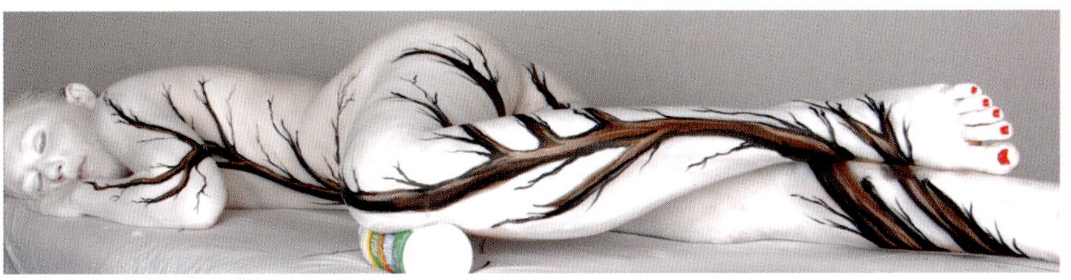

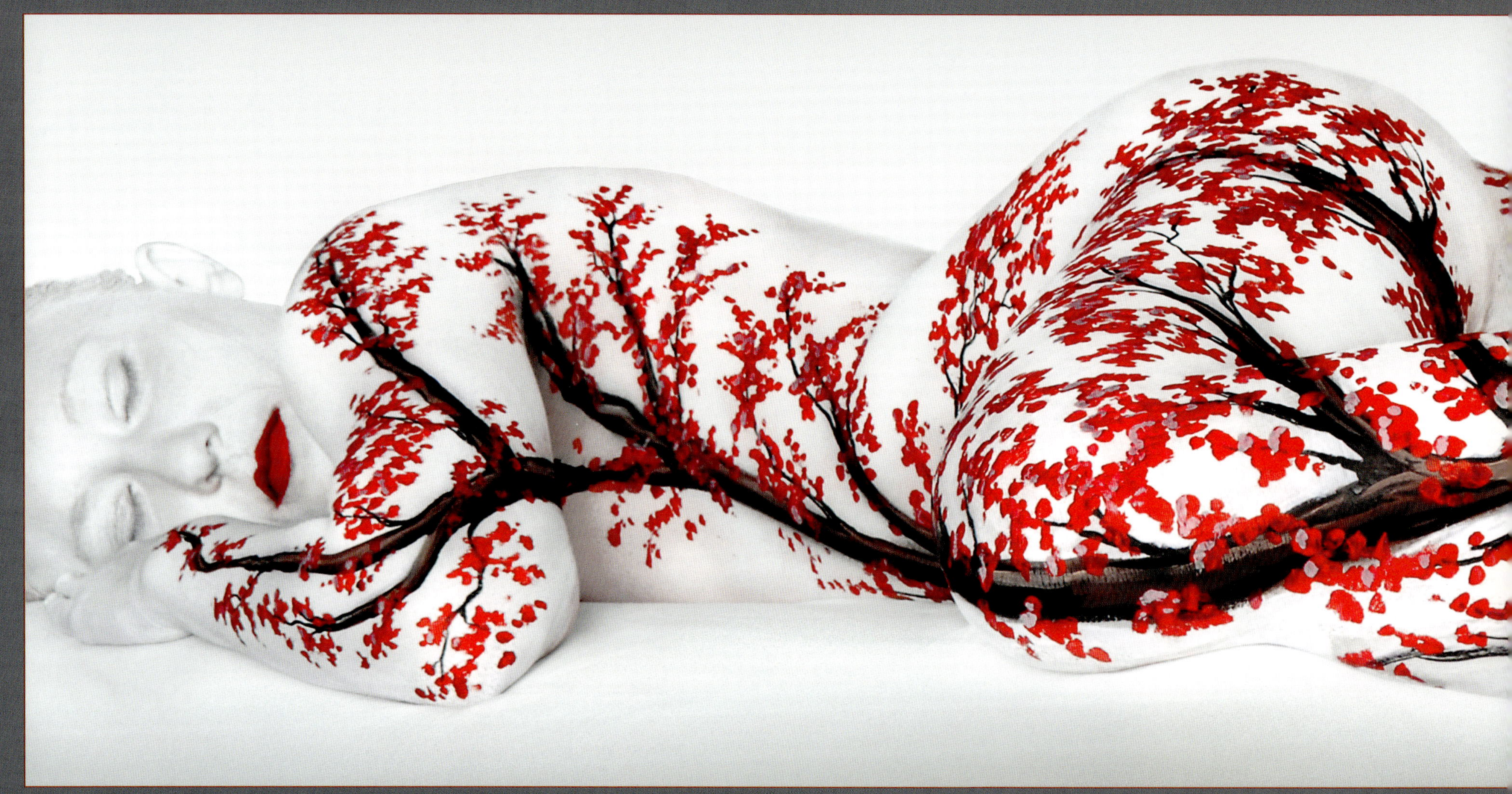

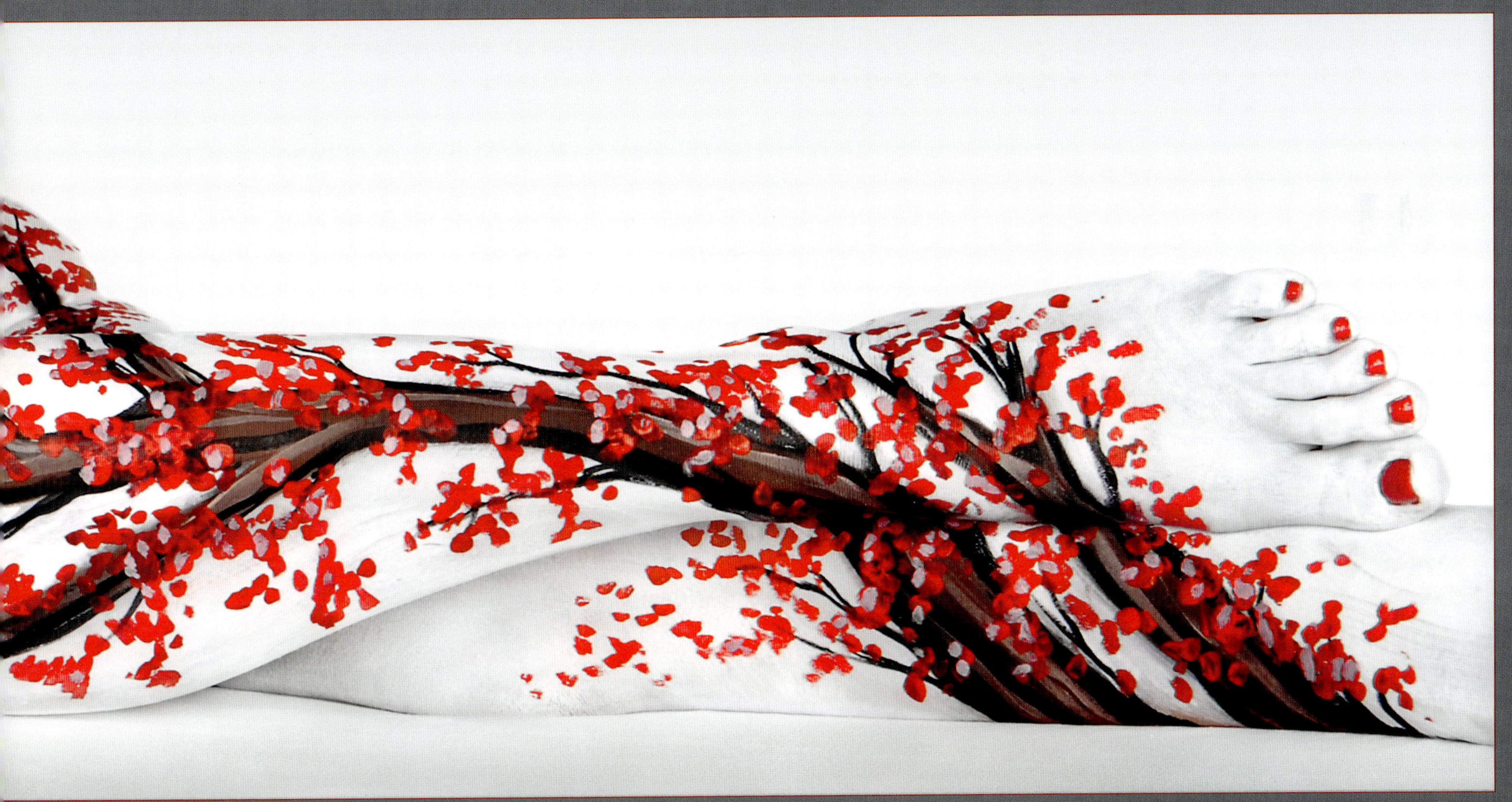

Bleu

This series of images was created from one bodypainting and photographed in many different positions. I consider this a spontaneous piece but there was some minor preparation and forethought involved. The concept was for the model to look as though she were painted conventionally, on a flat surface. I love the results achieved here and hope to explore this sort of project a bit more. My model was a dream to work with.

Model: Maria
Photographer: Craig Tracy

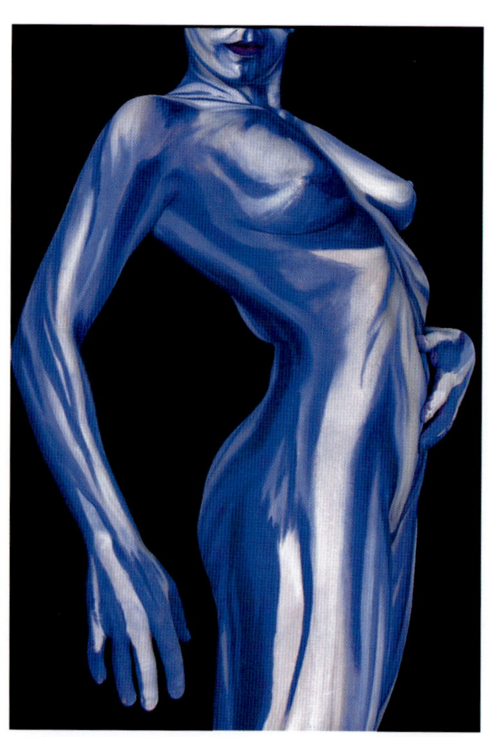
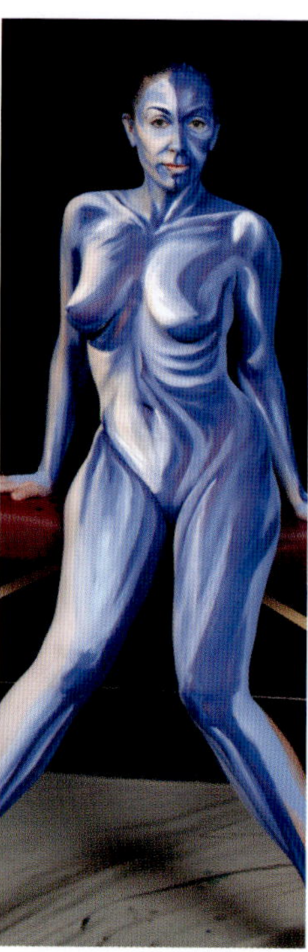
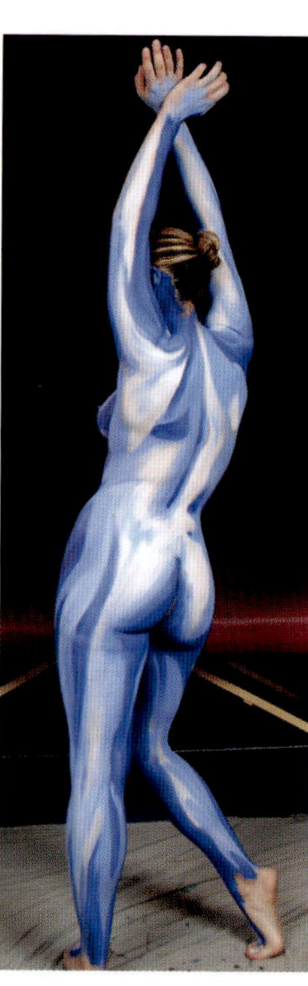
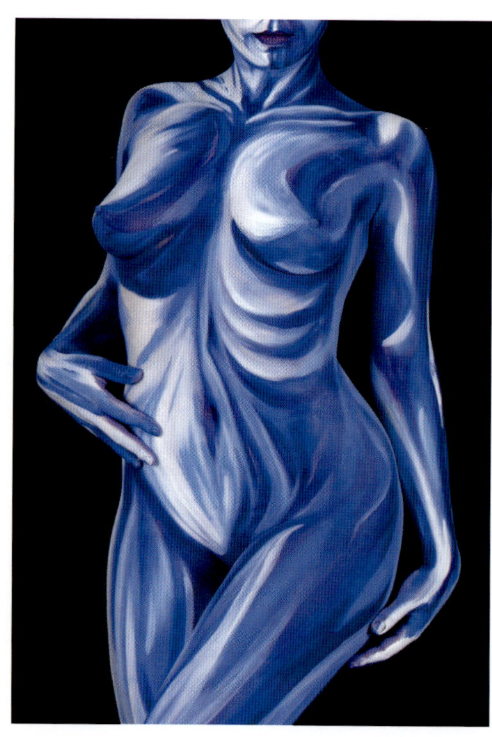

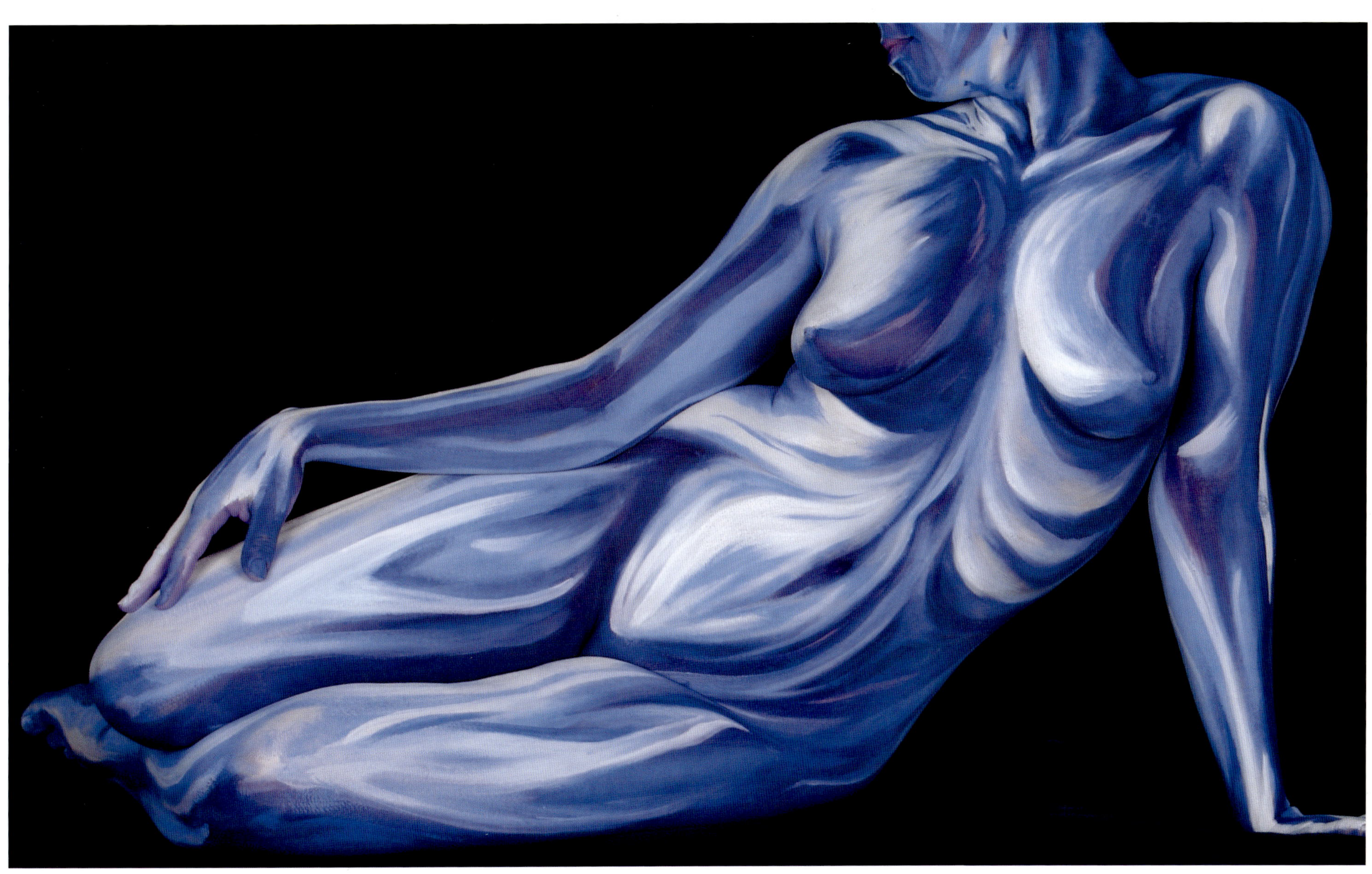

Koi

Koi began as a commission. Katie, the client/model, mentioned koi as a possible subject matter and I developed it from there. I first photographed her in multiple poses as I usually do in search for a definitive and optimal pose to then work with. It was after choosing the pose that everything started to fall into place. The yin-yang design quite organically developed as I started to figure out how to handle the negative space that was so abundant in the top half of the composition. Her body separates the two halves in what appears to be an ideal fashion. Several technical and mathematical issues needed to be worked out for success and I credit my photographer Max, with helping to guide me through the bottom half of the circle pattern. (See the photo in the process area where Max is viewing the image through a roll of tape.) This was a brilliant idea of his that really helped keep things balanced. Katie was a delight and pleasure to work with as well.

Model: Katie
Photographer: Max Trombly

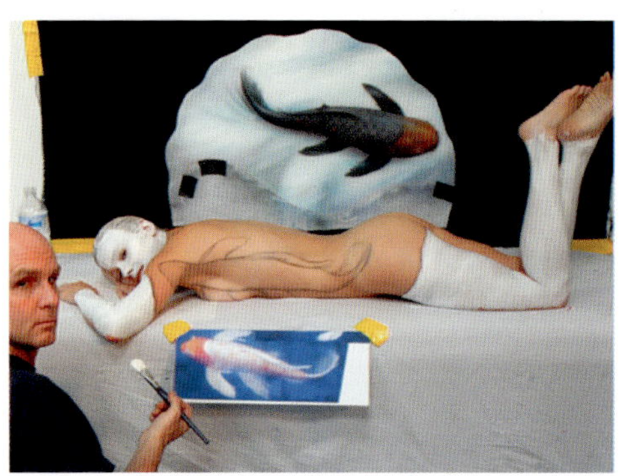
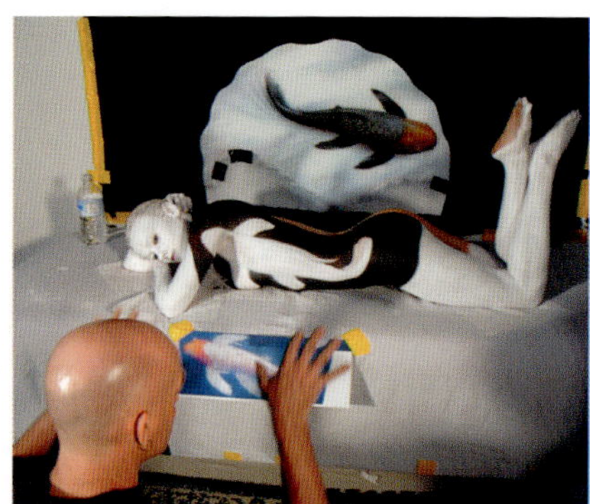
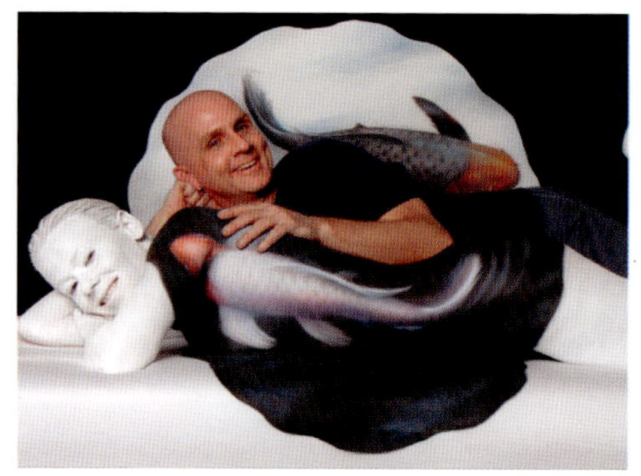
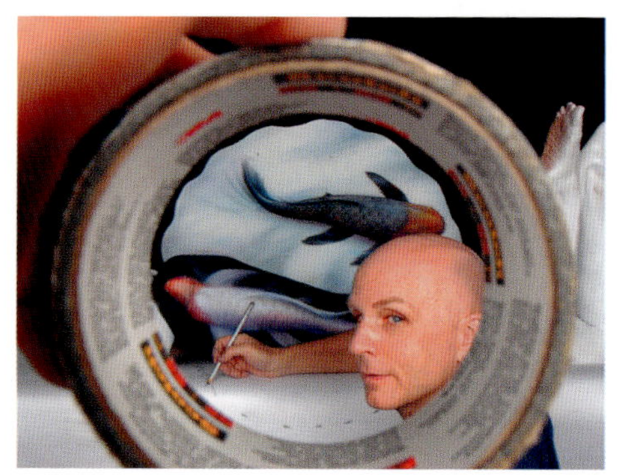

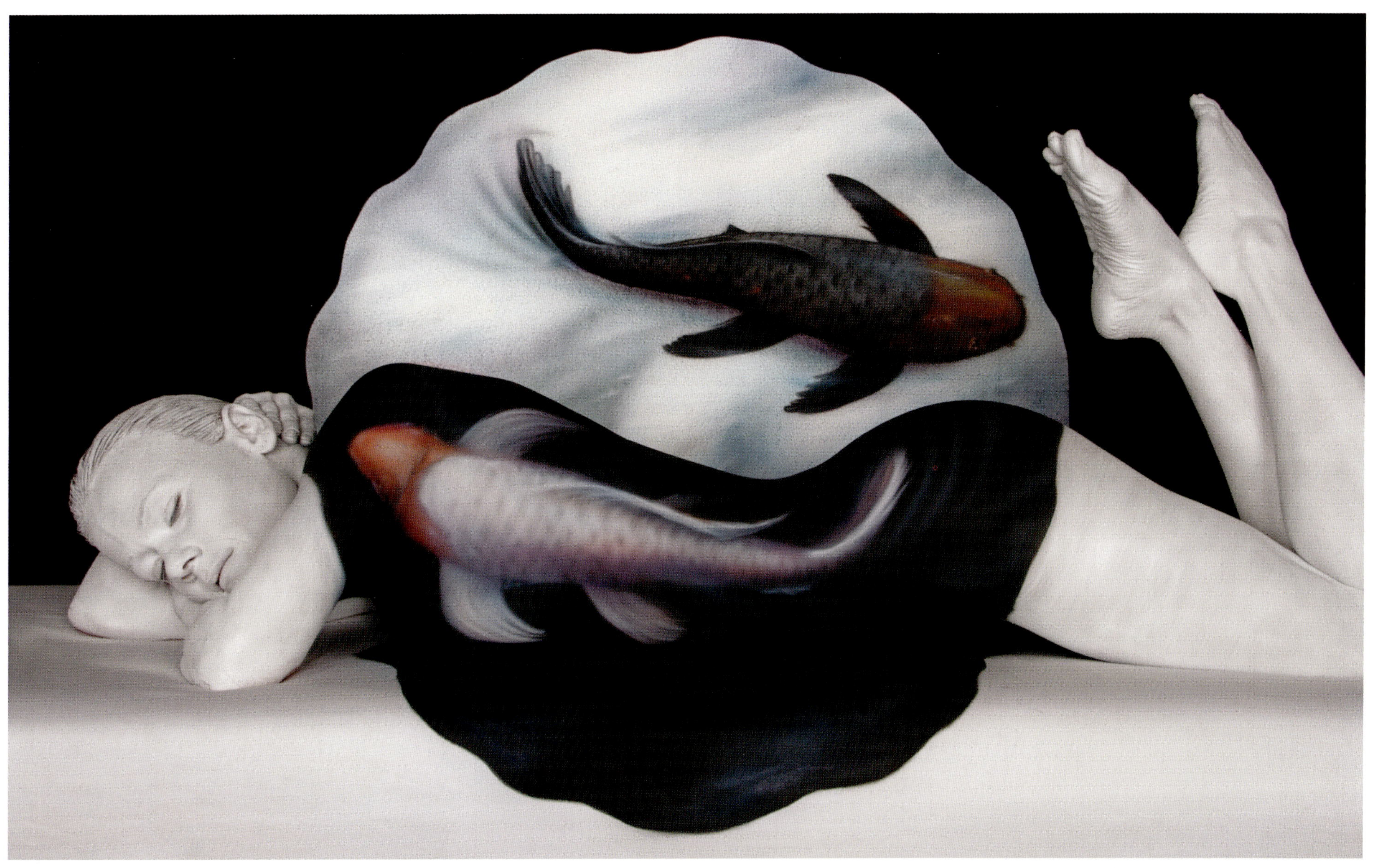

K-Squared

This image was inspired heavily by my model and how lovely she was to work with. I designed this image just one day after meeting her. As I knew that she might move in the near future, I wasted no time in getting busy. The pose was first chosen and then from there the design was created. The hand touching the leg was my starting point and from there the design just grew.

Model: Kelley
Photographer: Craig Morse

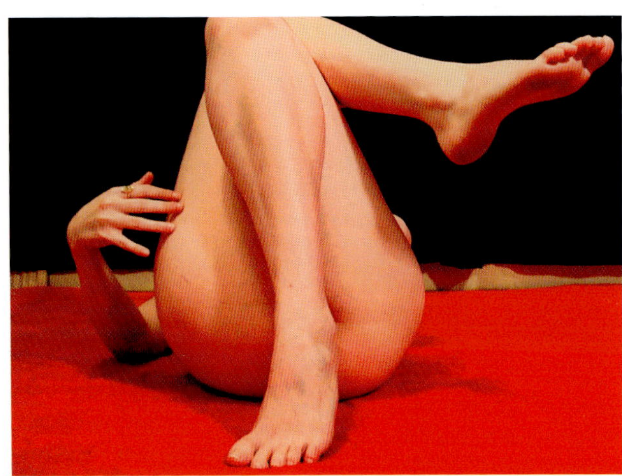
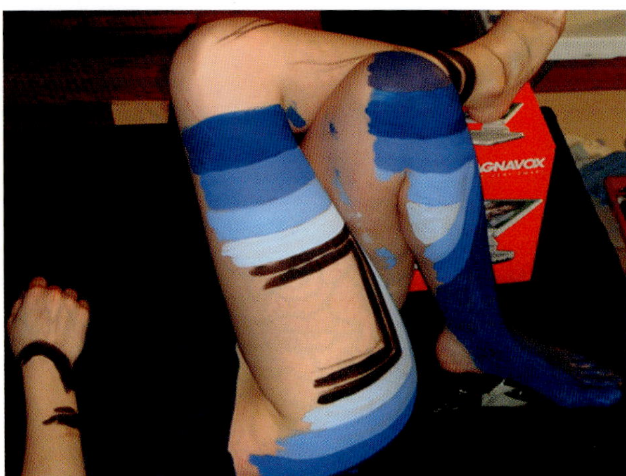
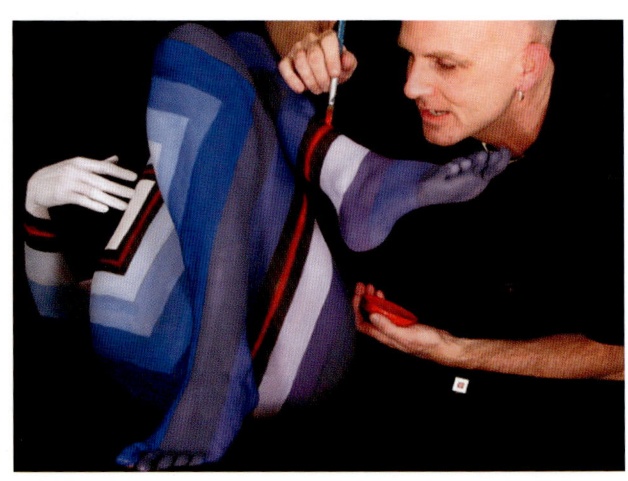

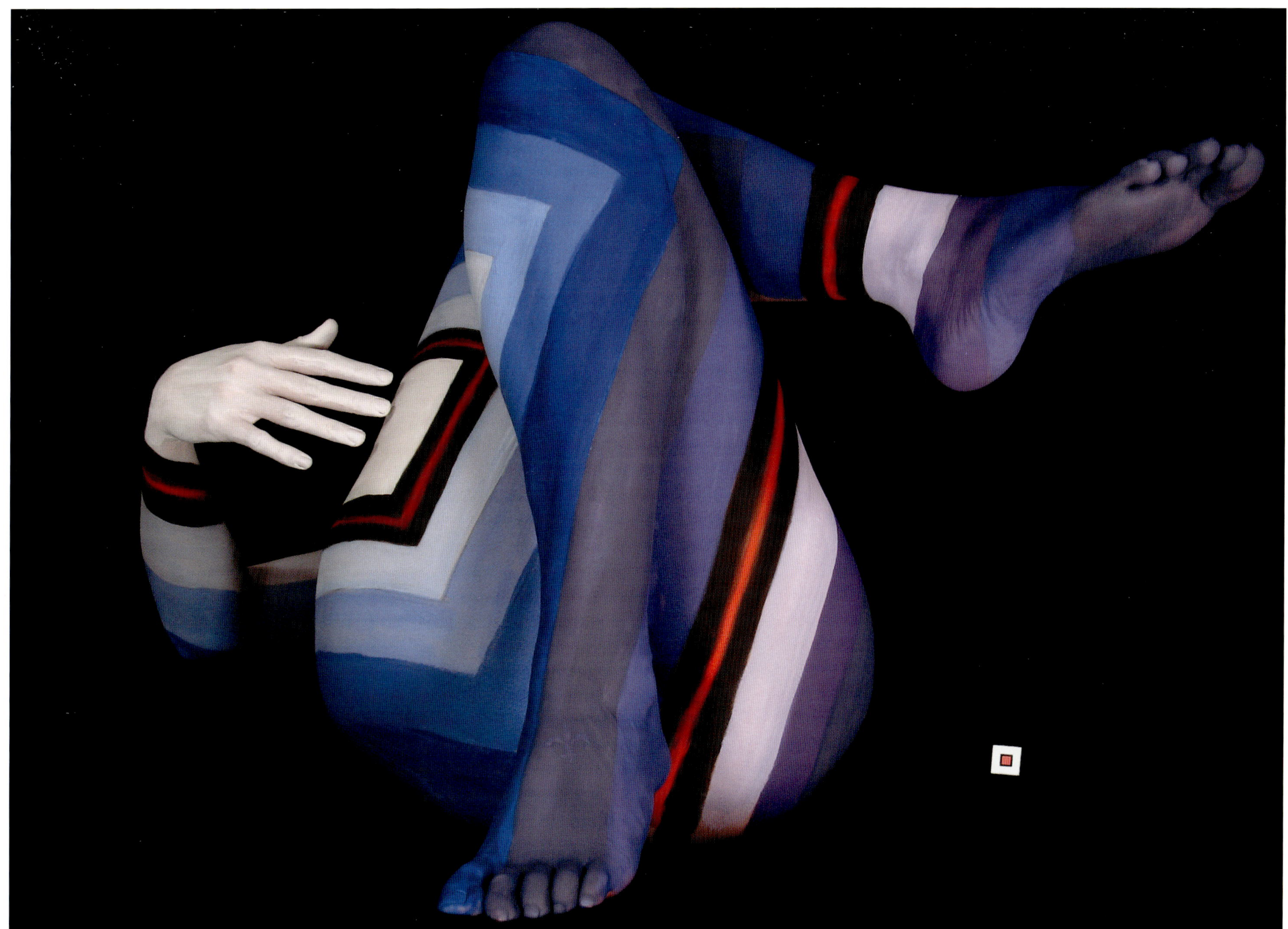

Twogether

The uniquely spelled *Twogether* is a literal reference of the two trees reaching so intently to finally be united. A very mysterious landscape of desire, stress, and comfort, where contrast abounds as foreground and background, model and pose work together, yet at odds, to complete a harmonious tranquility. The intended four-panel version of *Twogether* has the creative benefit of being joined together by a single piece of custom-designed and cut wood. This connection allows for both a utility and aesthetic addition. As for the cropped version, my intent is to focus heavily on the substance that is offered, and minimize the black, negative space that is also eliminated in the four-panel composition.

Model: Katie
Photographer: Robin Walker

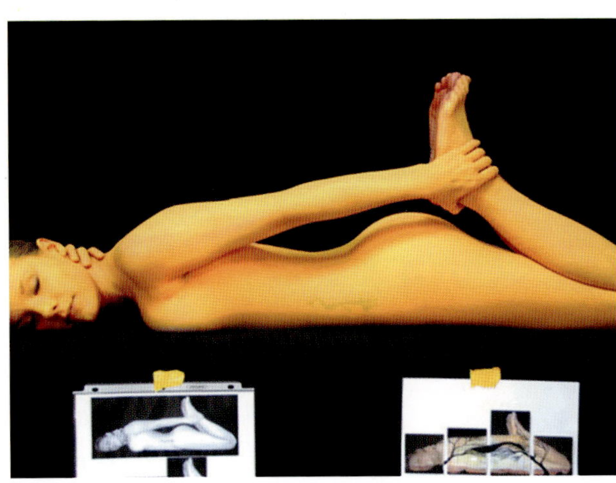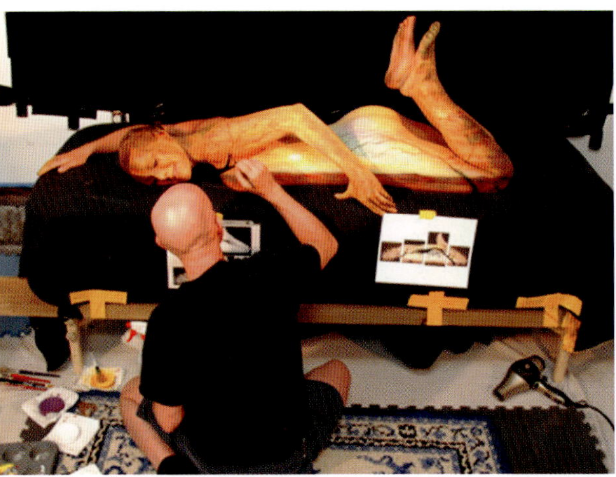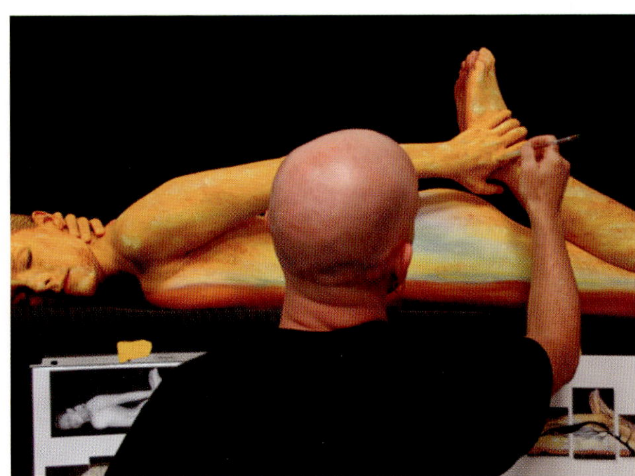

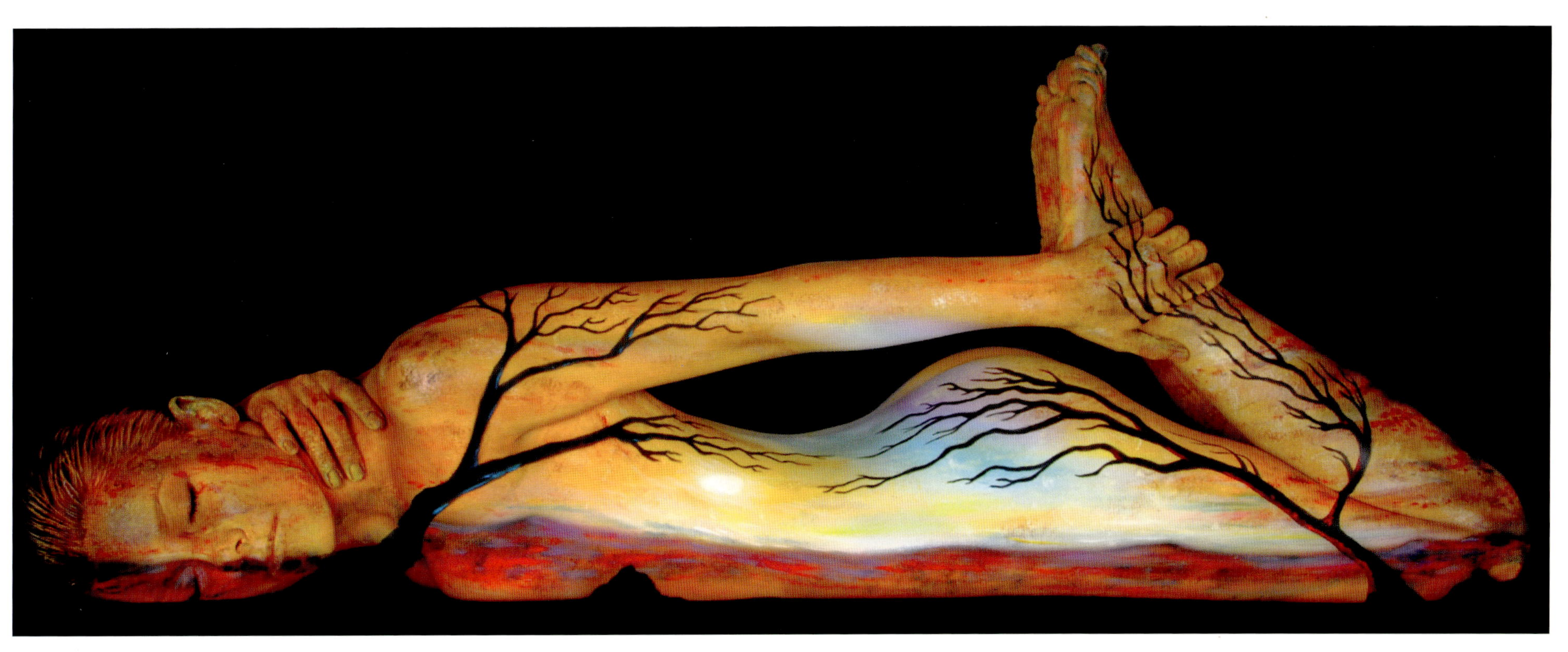

Fiya

I so enjoy this image. It was exceptionally challenging to develop and create. It stands alone in many ways and seeing it live in the studio was my pleasure, as if I hadn't created it myself. My model in this image offered me so many options because of her natural flexibility and shape. Her hair was special as well, in its length, volume, and color. *Fiya* is my only image to date that utilizes motion. Her hair, in its natural color, is being blown by four very powerful fans, one of which is hand-held just off camera, and used to control the hair's movement. The other three fans were required to simply lift her hair and direct it in roughly the desired direction. A total of four photographic lights were simultaneously used to light both the model and the backdrop, where normally I only require two lights. The combination of size, shape, contrast, motion, and design culminates here to offer an image that joyfully defies most convention and categorical description.

Model: Erin
Photographer: Libbie Allen

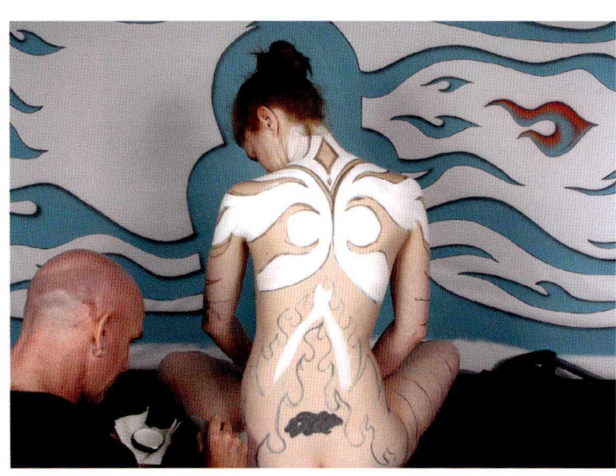
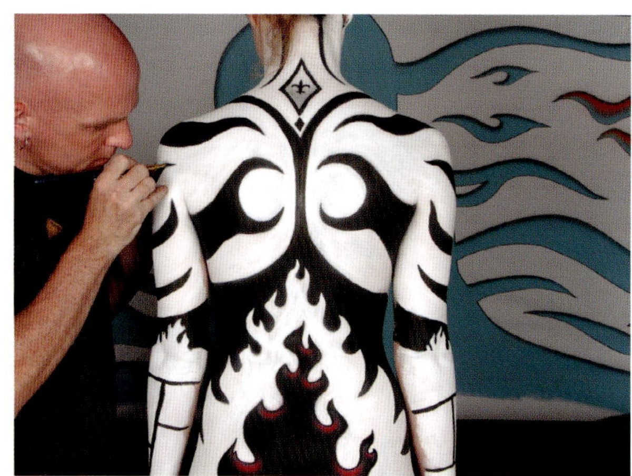
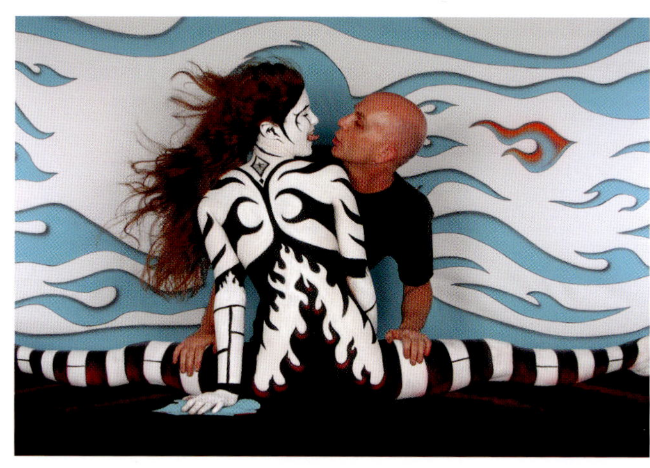

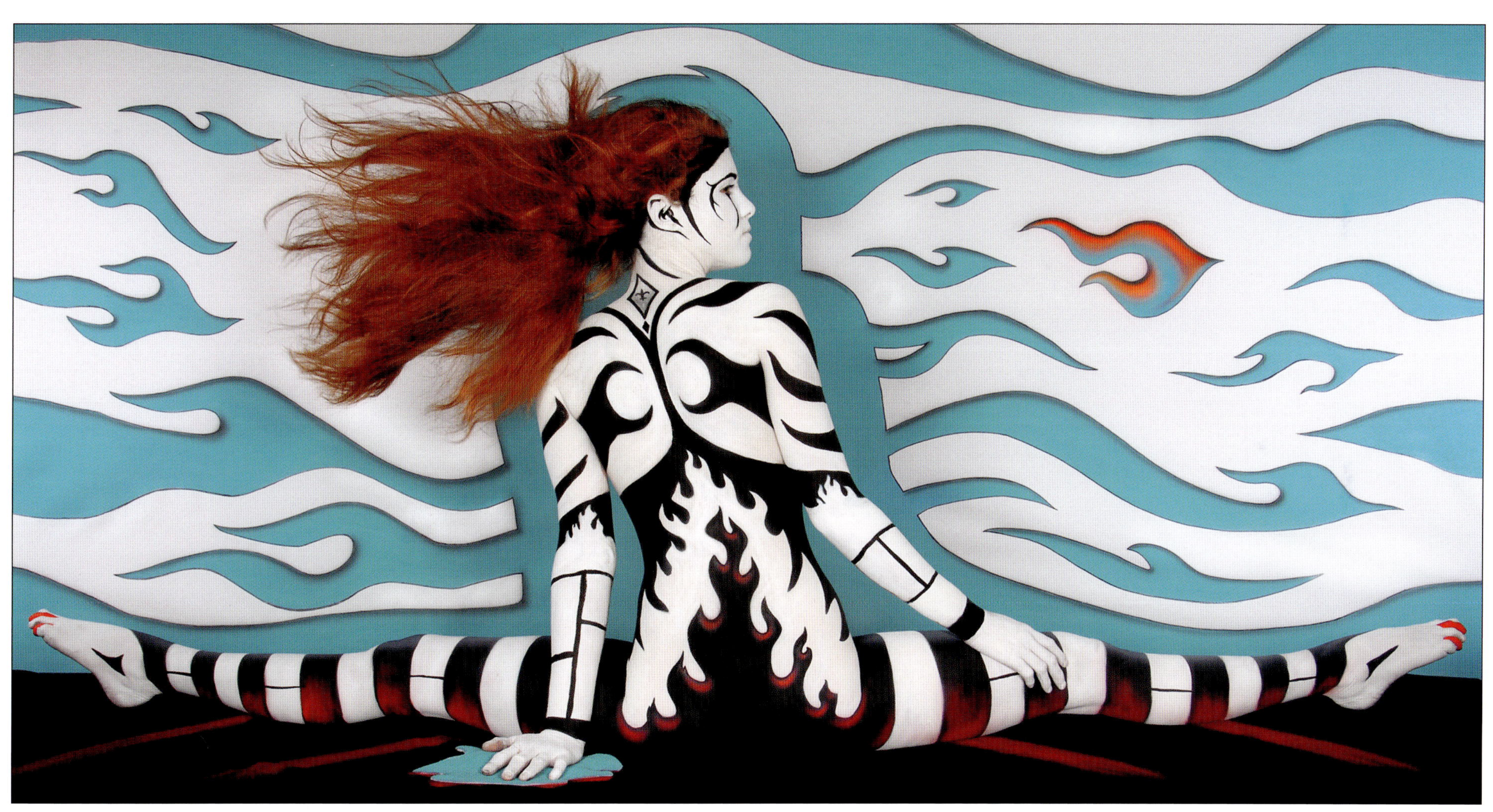

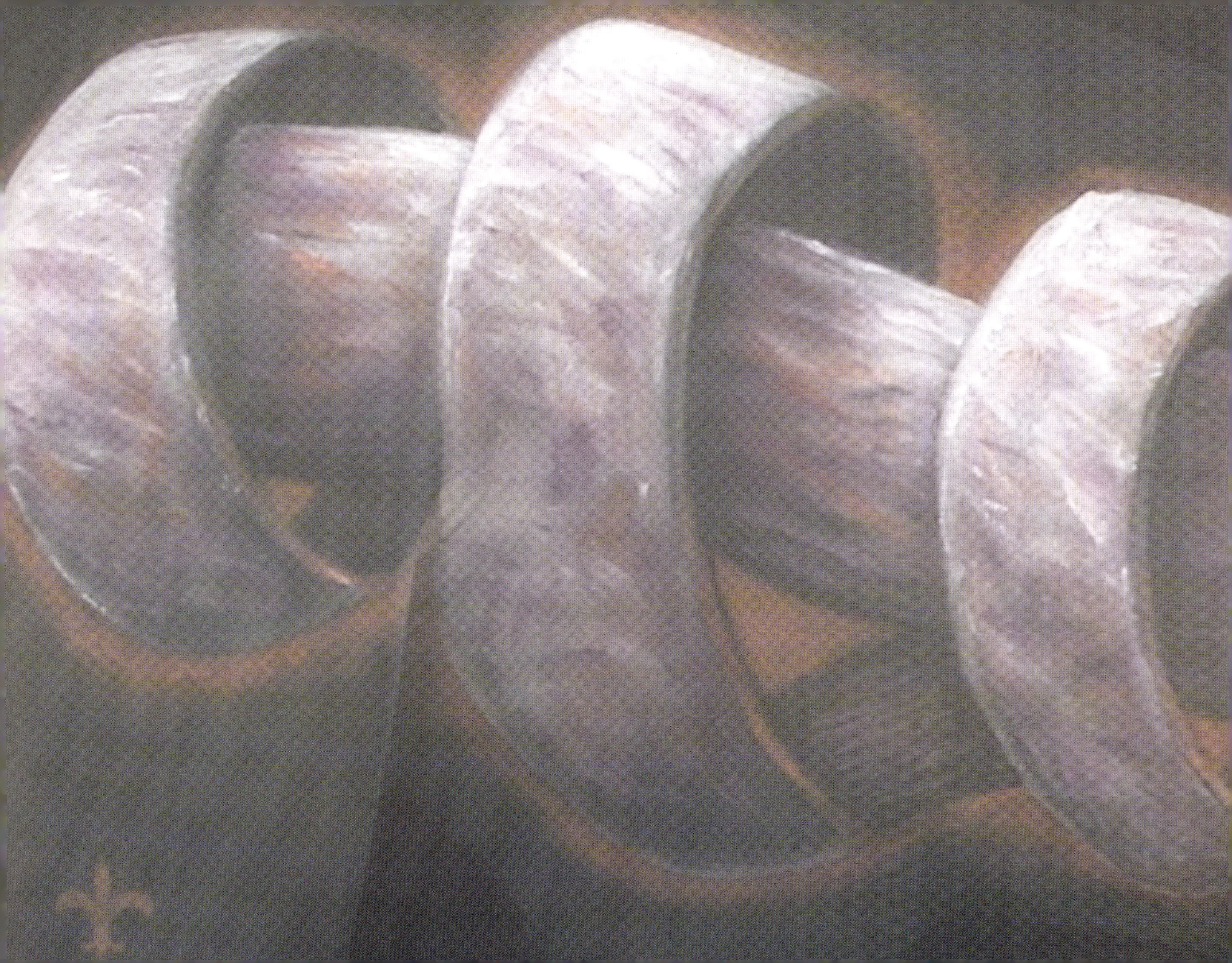

Coil

Inspired by both the image of an industrial piece of rusted metal and the exquisite curves of my model's body, *Coil* transcends conventional thoughts and visions. An organic fusion of both the real and unreal exist seamlessly in this vastly surreal image. This painting intrigued me far in advance of its completion. The sketch alone made me excited and pleased that it would soon become both a realization and a part of my life, forever.

Model: Kim
Photographer: Libbie Allen

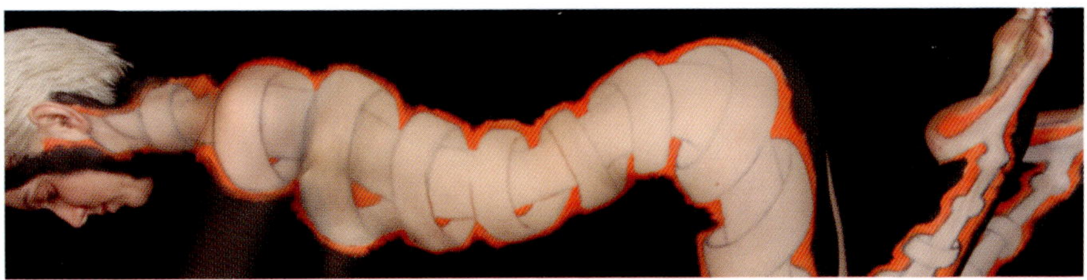

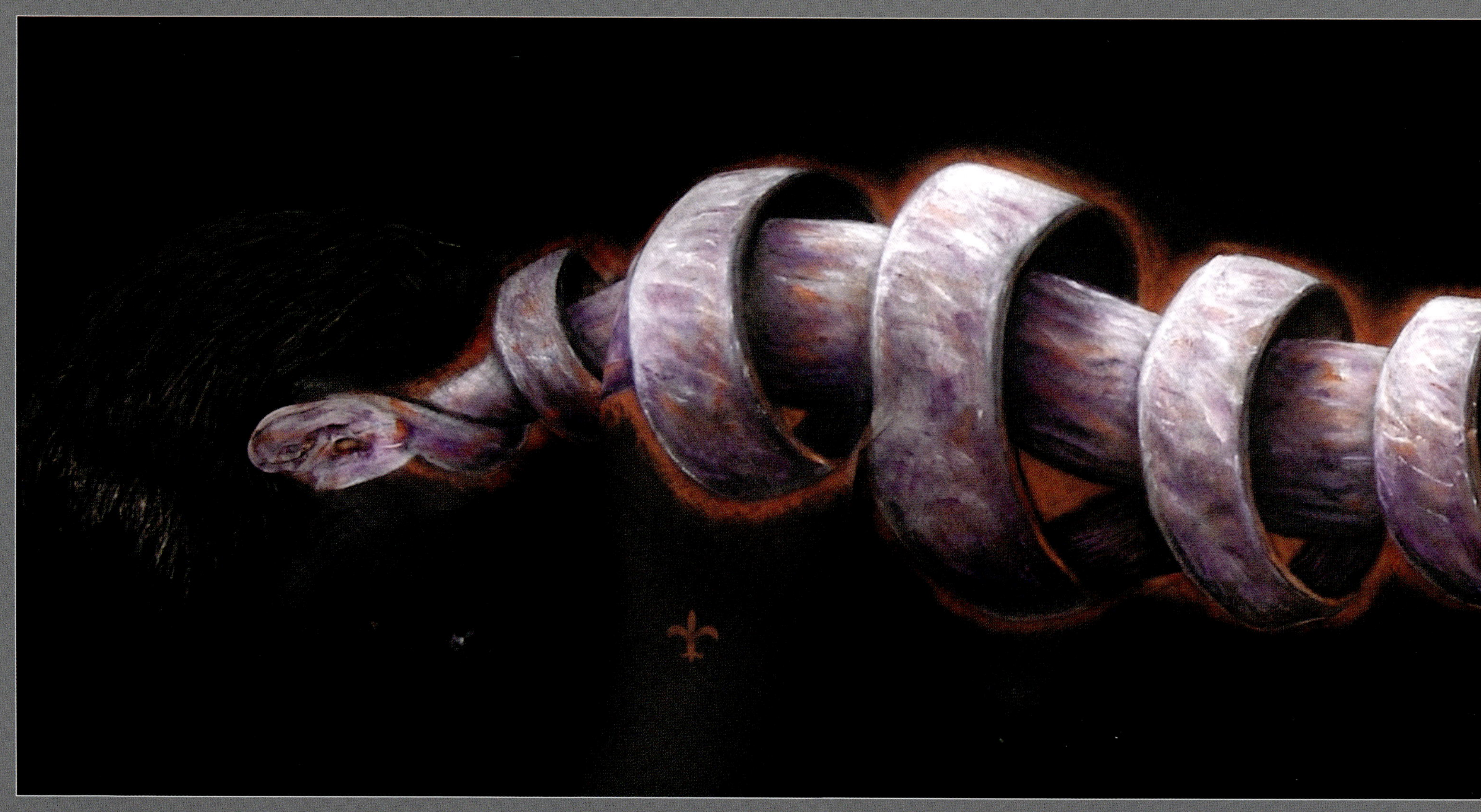

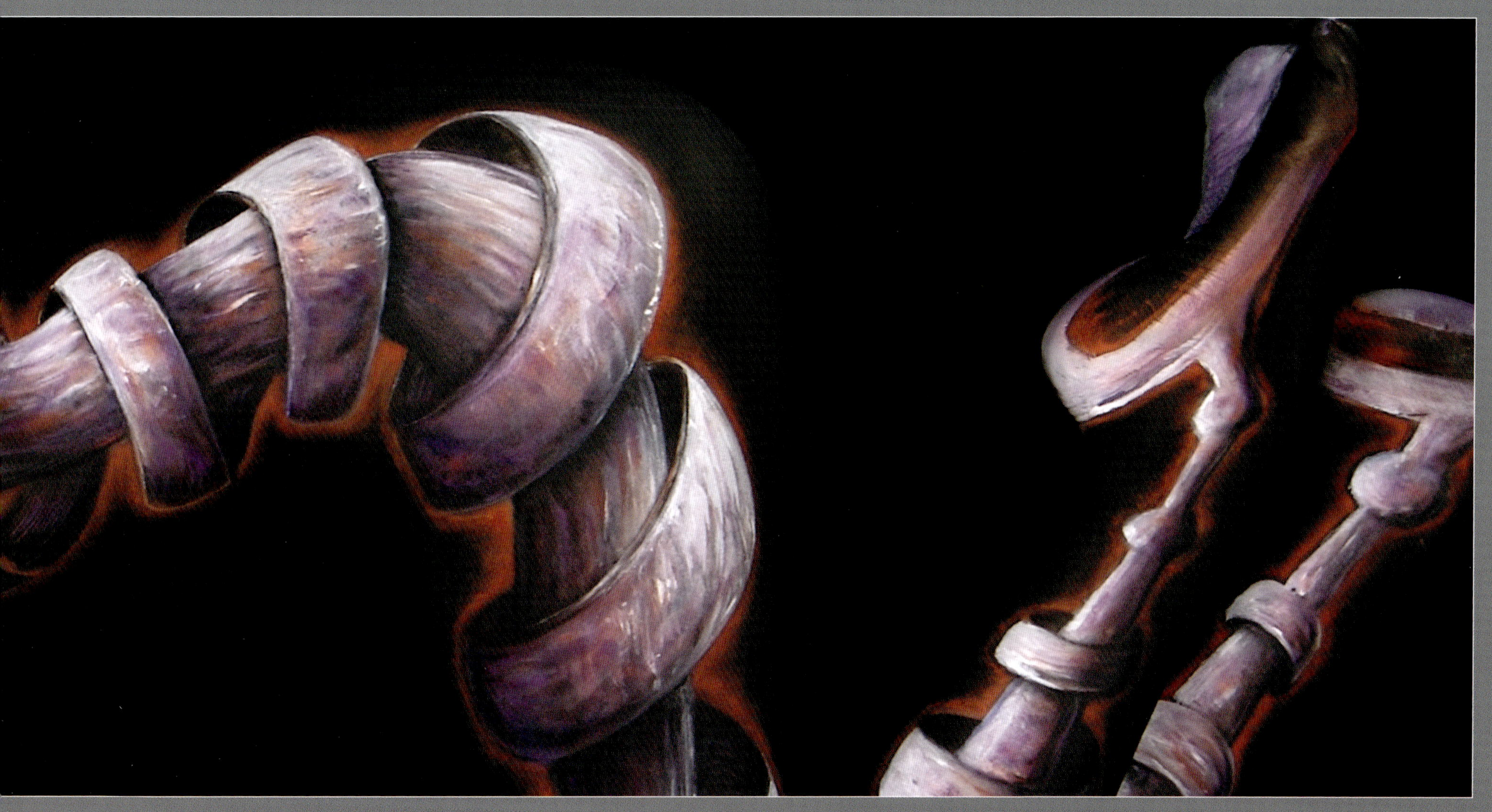

Goddess

I met the model four years before I ever painted her. She would visit my gallery about twice a year and talk with me about my work and the chance that she might one day be painted. As I'm horrible with remembering names, I always remembered her as the girl with the beautiful hair. Her hair however was not my initial inspiration. It was an oil painting that I had seen in Shanghai, China, a year earlier. The painting depicted a close-up of a female face painted ghostly white, eyes closed and only her lips were wet with the brightest crimson. This inspiration grew to become the image seen today. Lace was also used subtly in the background and its pattern mimicked in the white-on-white painting on her chest.

Model: Alex
Photographer: Craig Tracy

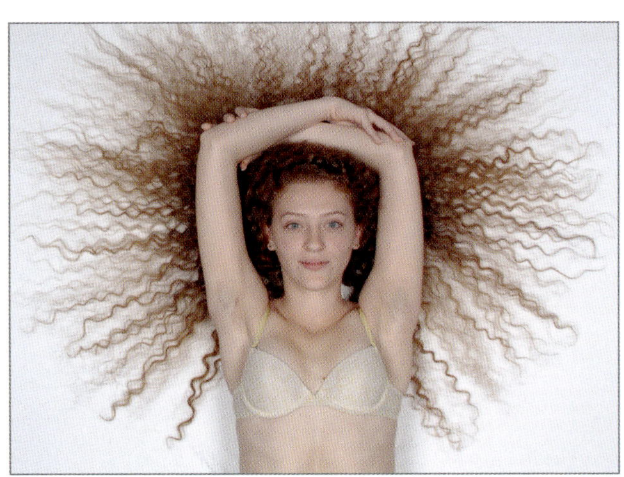
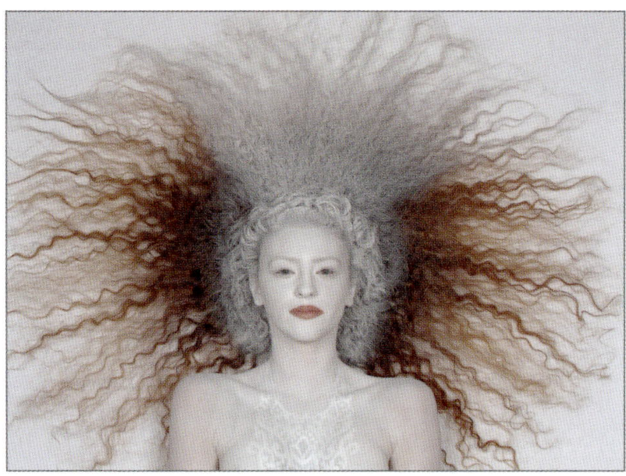
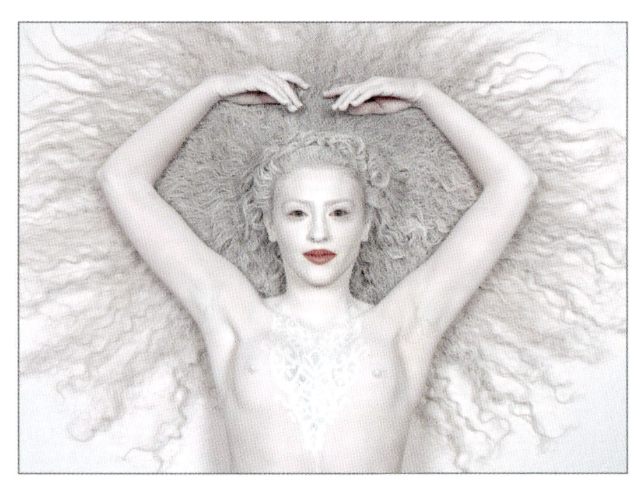

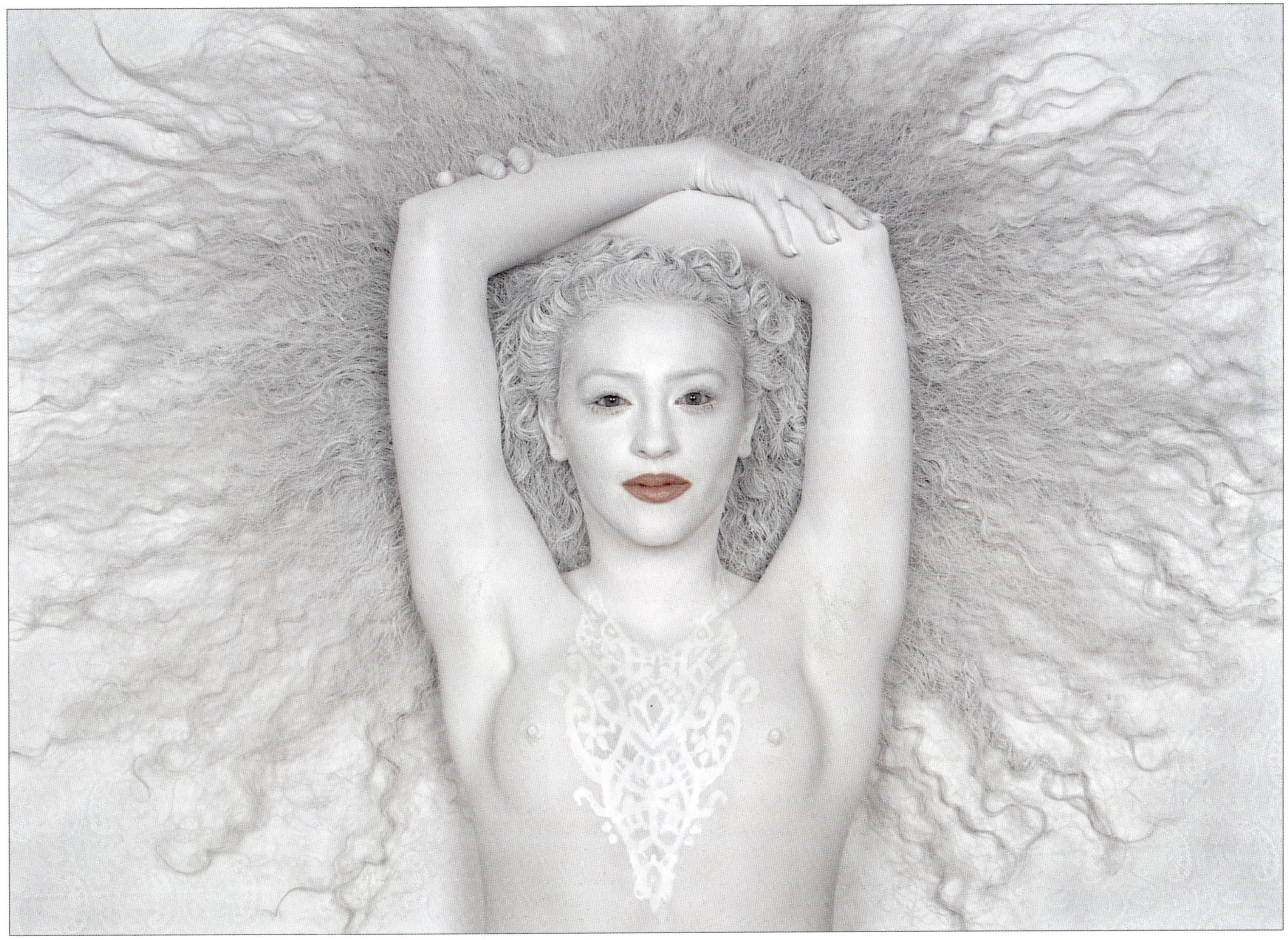

The Keeper

This piece was created live in Lake Tahoe, Nevada, one snowy night inside an art gallery that represents my work. *The Keeper* was a pleasant surprise in that I really took some chances and dealt with some time and creative limitations. When I'm not in my studio, just about anything is possible. Each location that I paint in is different and each model that I work with while traveling has the potential to make or break the feeling and expression of the painting that I'm trying to create. All of the elements were, fortunately, perfect for me to paint one very special image. The feelings that are communicated here with *The Keeper* are just as I had hoped they might be. She is soft and mysterious. She is dark and strangely light. She is *The Keeper* and we simply bear witness to her and what she allows us to see.

Model: Jamie
Photographer: Craig Tracy

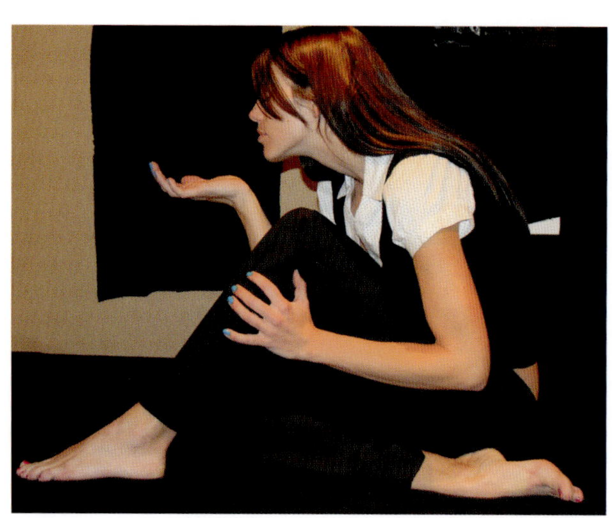
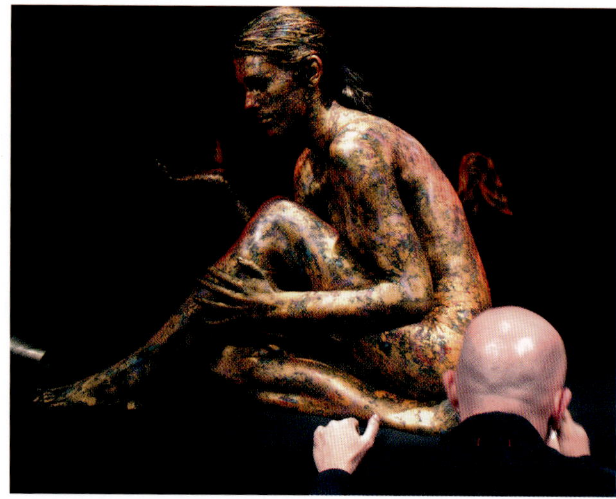
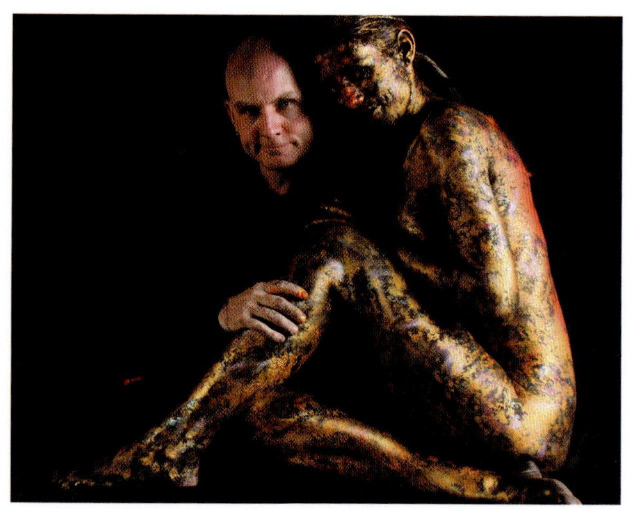

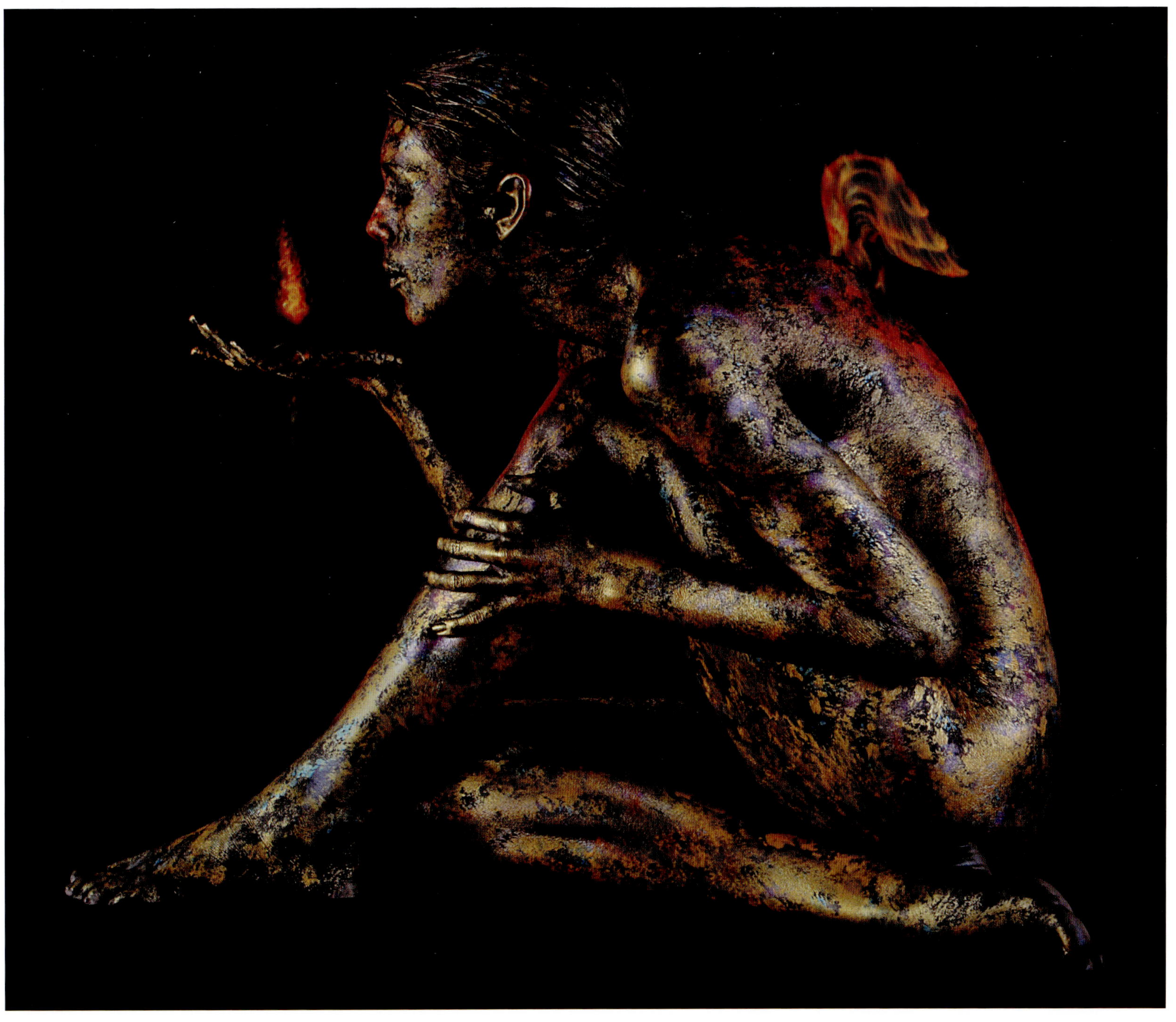

Sunshine

This is my very first "cute" bodypainting. It was my second time ever working with a newborn and mother, and it was also the very first time that I didn't use a photographer for the photography. The baby was five weeks old and the mom here is a very talented bodypainter herself. The baby was sleeping while this was painted and photographed. Working with newborns is such a challenge and treat.

Models: Stephanie & Presley
Photographer: Craig Tracy

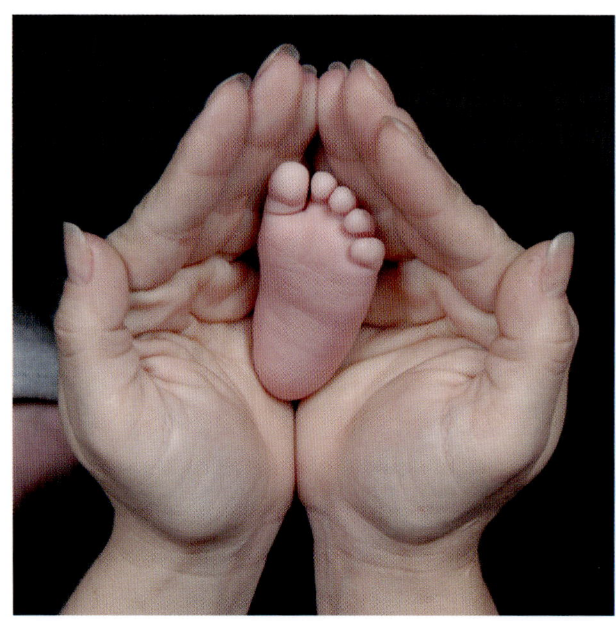 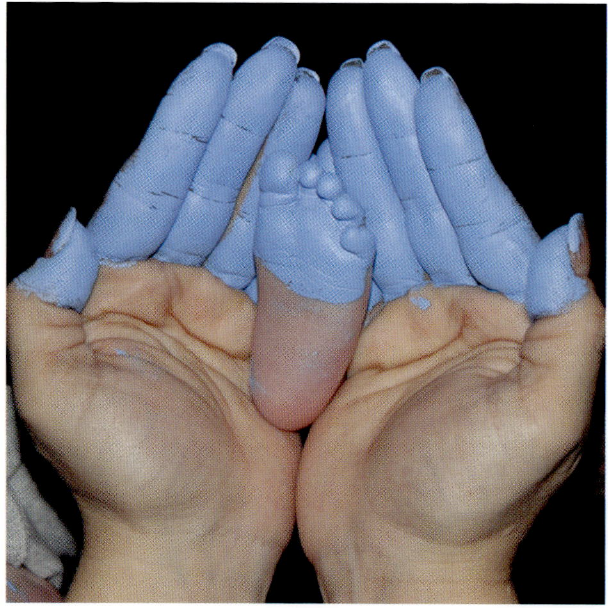 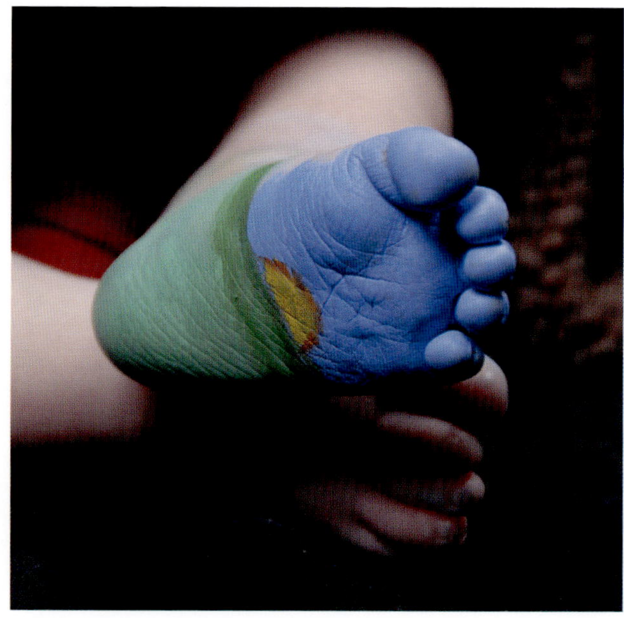

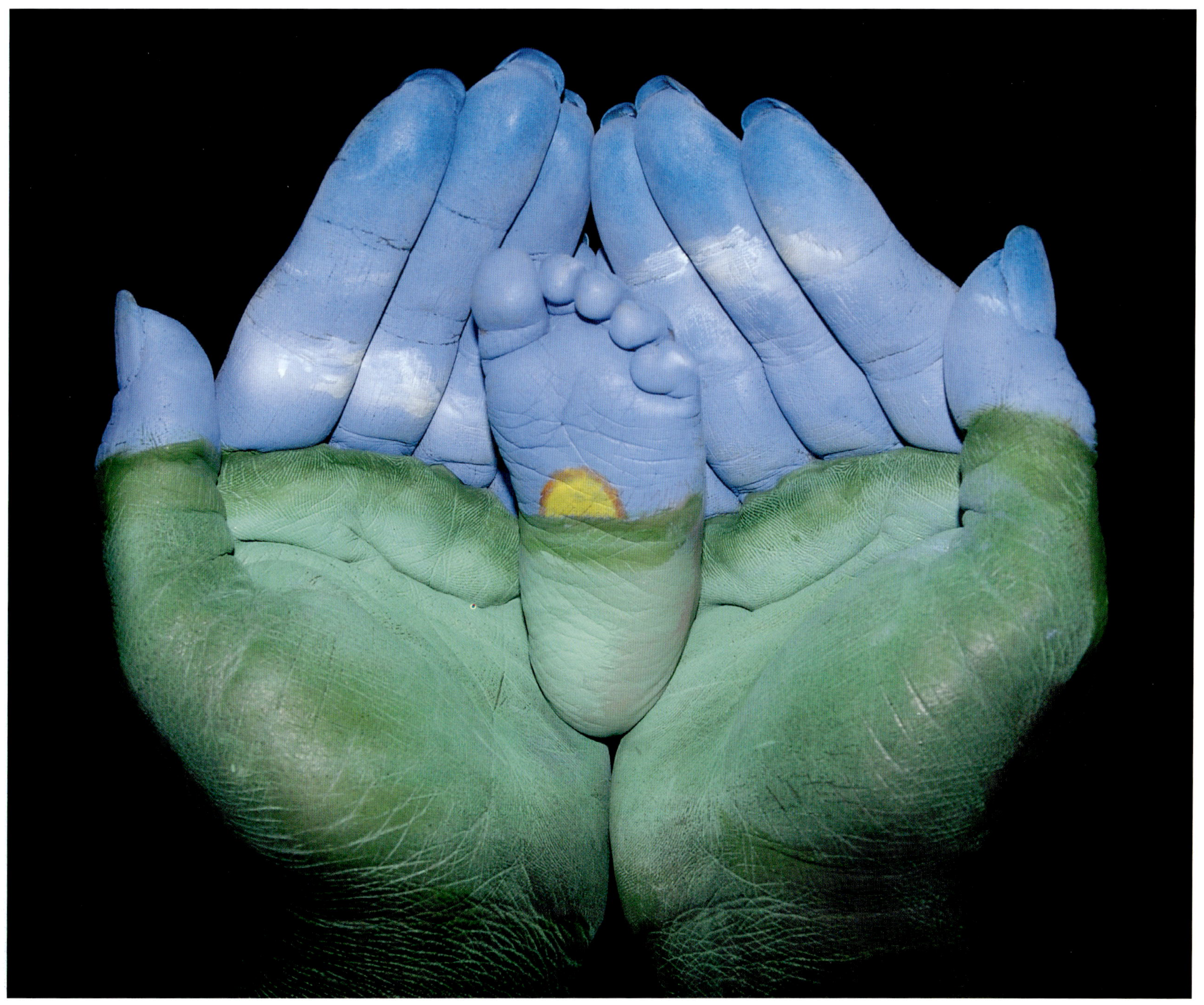

Elise

Elise, the model, offered me many pose possibilities and I chose the one that delighted and challenged me most. Her natural feminine curves and qualities communicated a very strong primal response in this pose. I wanted to alter and reverse that natural response to her unpainted body by use of design and color. This is what I do when I paint on skin. I alter the natural perception of the unpainted body. I distract, confuse, and creatively take you where I'd like you to be. With *Elise*, I want you to be both attracted and confused, for with each curve of her body you are more deeply committed to understand and enjoy her natural glorious simplicity.

Model: Elise
Photographer: Craig Tracy

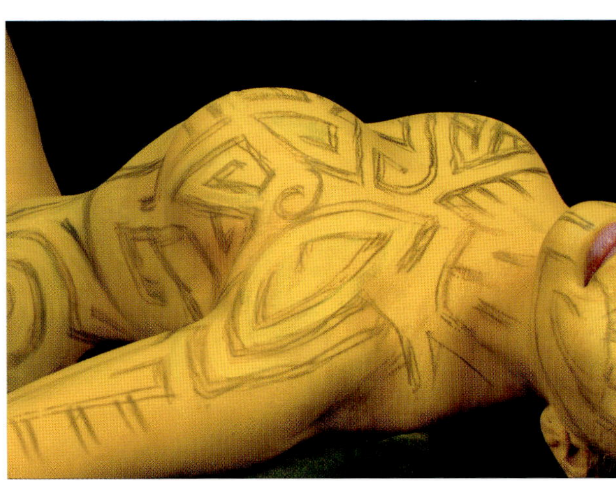
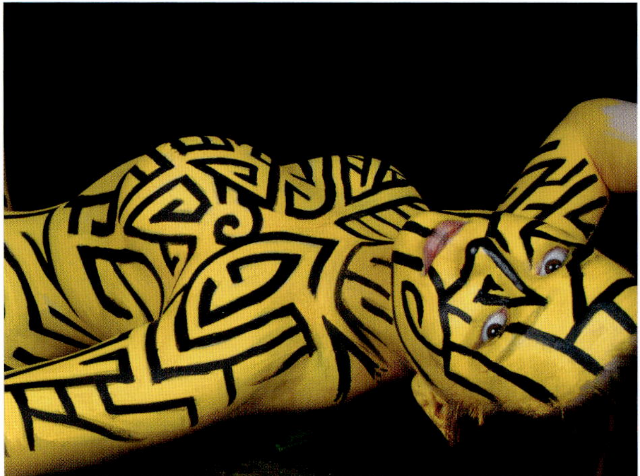
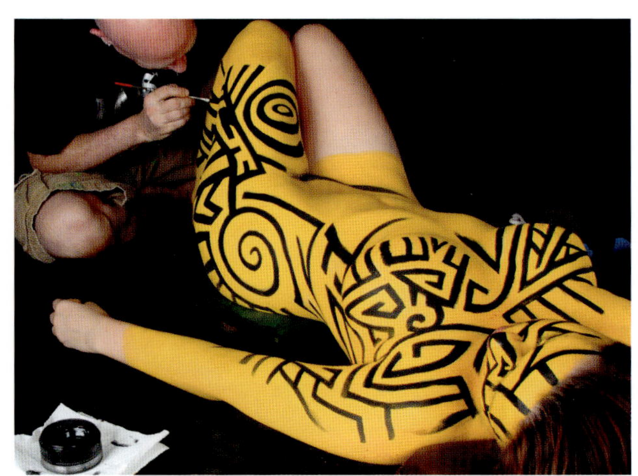

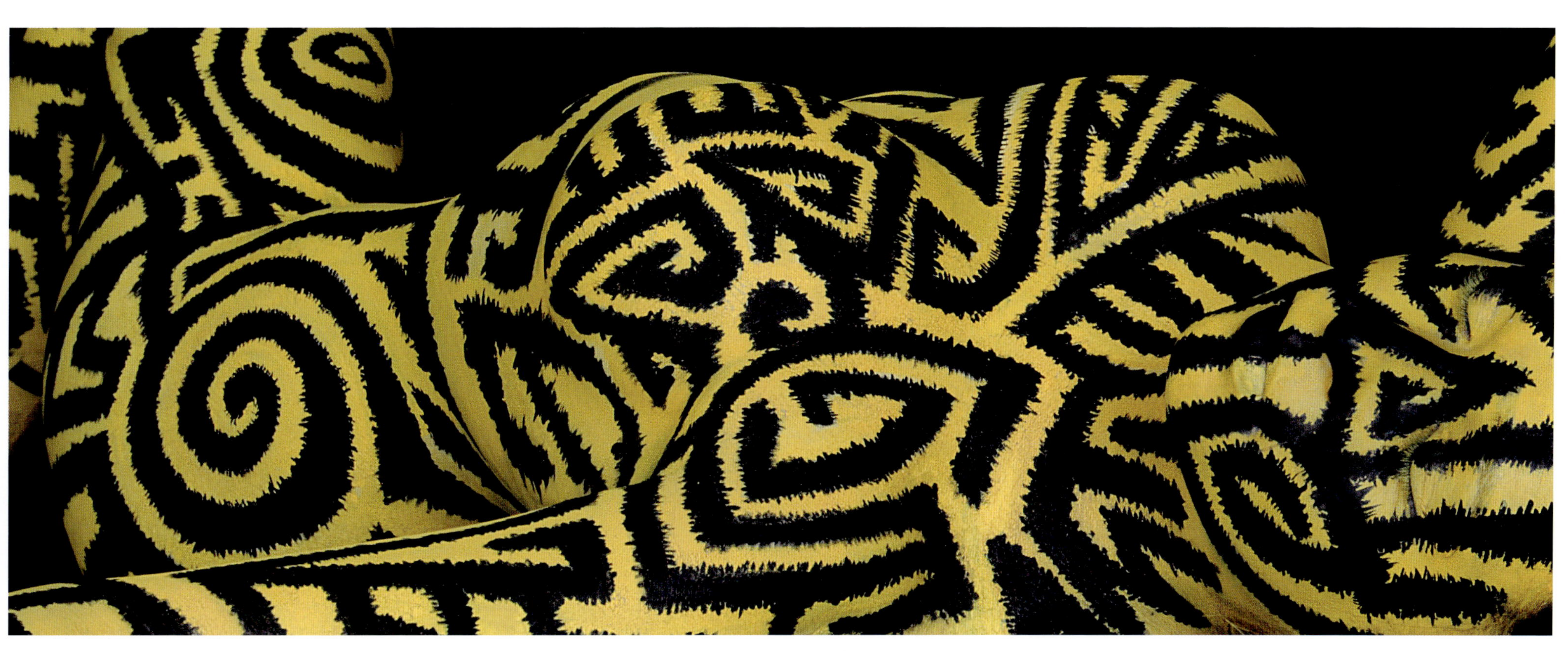

Immaculate

Some unions are "set in stone." This is my first ever painting involving a couple. This particular couple is very real and they are married as well. Several technical issues needed to be resolved, as the background is also the foreground along the bottom of the image. I hand painted and airbrushed the backdrop as the process photos should clearly indicate. I chose to allow plenty of disconnecting lines so as to afford the bodies more visibility and to be less integrated with the surrounding design. I've learned that sometimes perfection and absolute accuracy are a bit dehumanizing.

Models: Samantha & Josh
Photographer: Libbie Allen

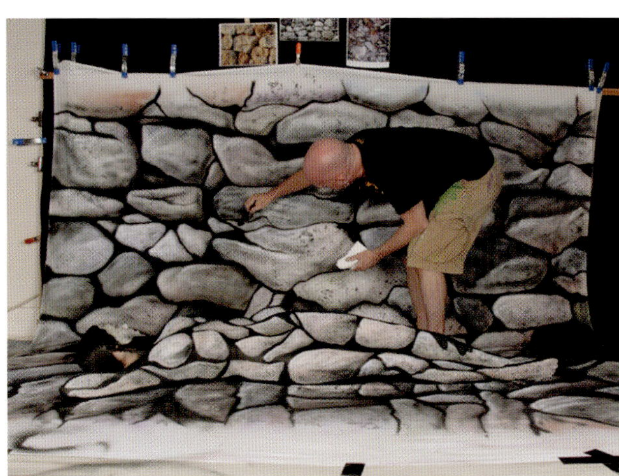
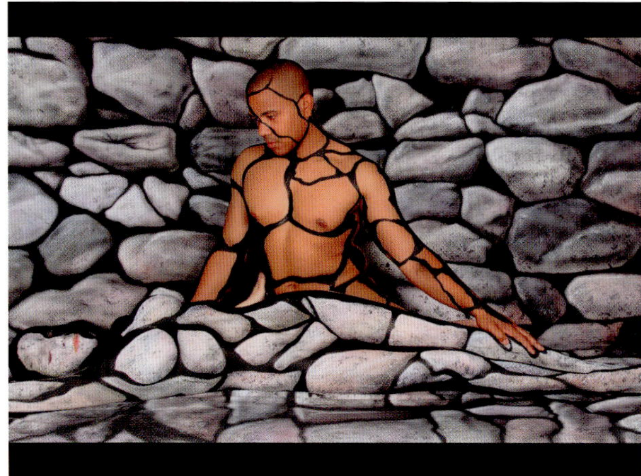
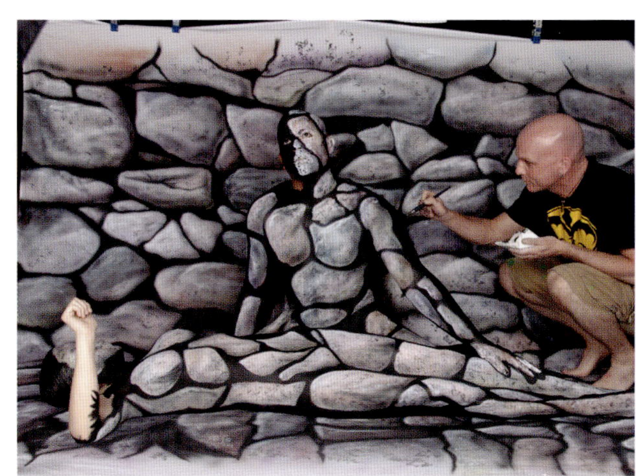

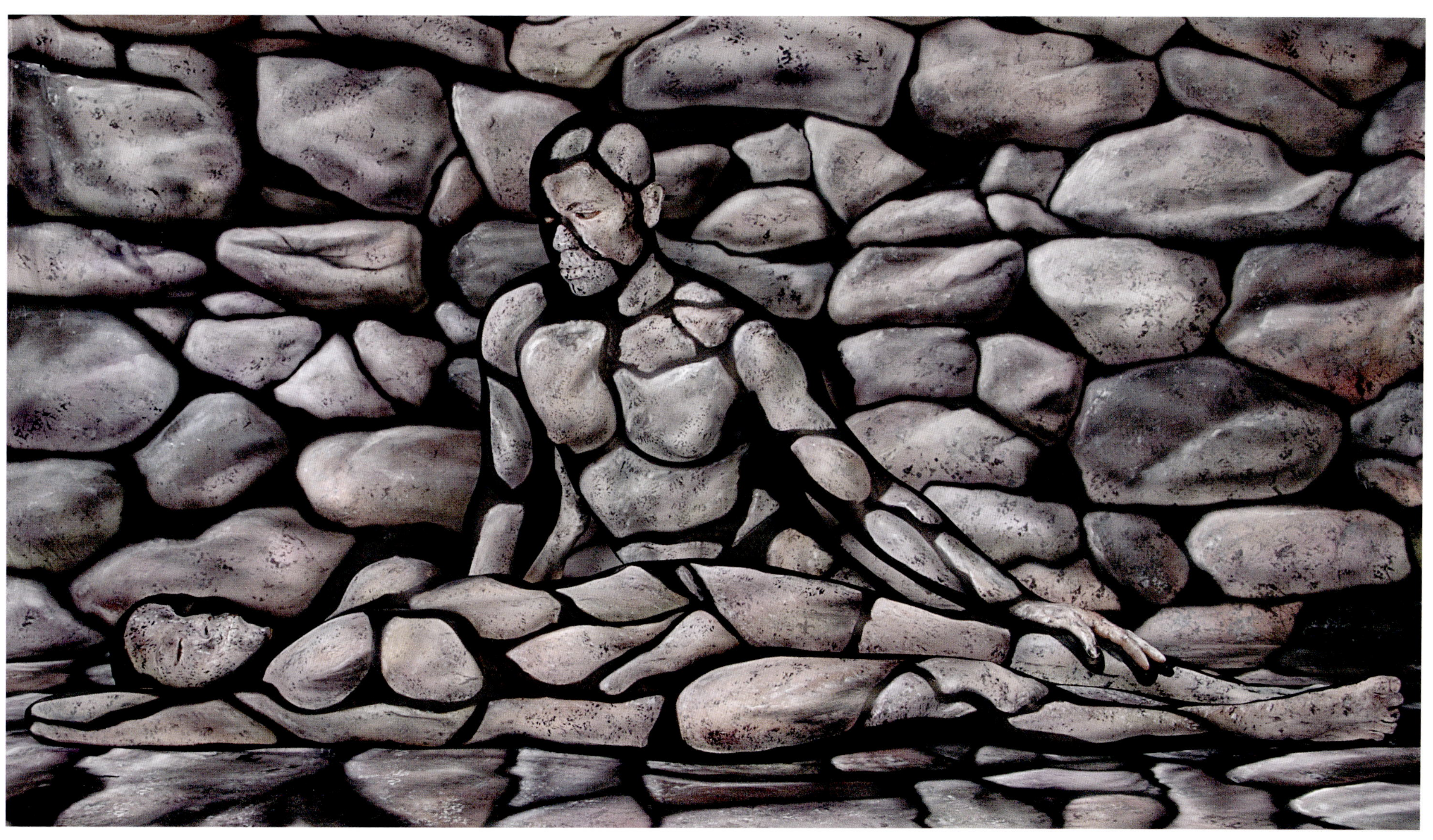

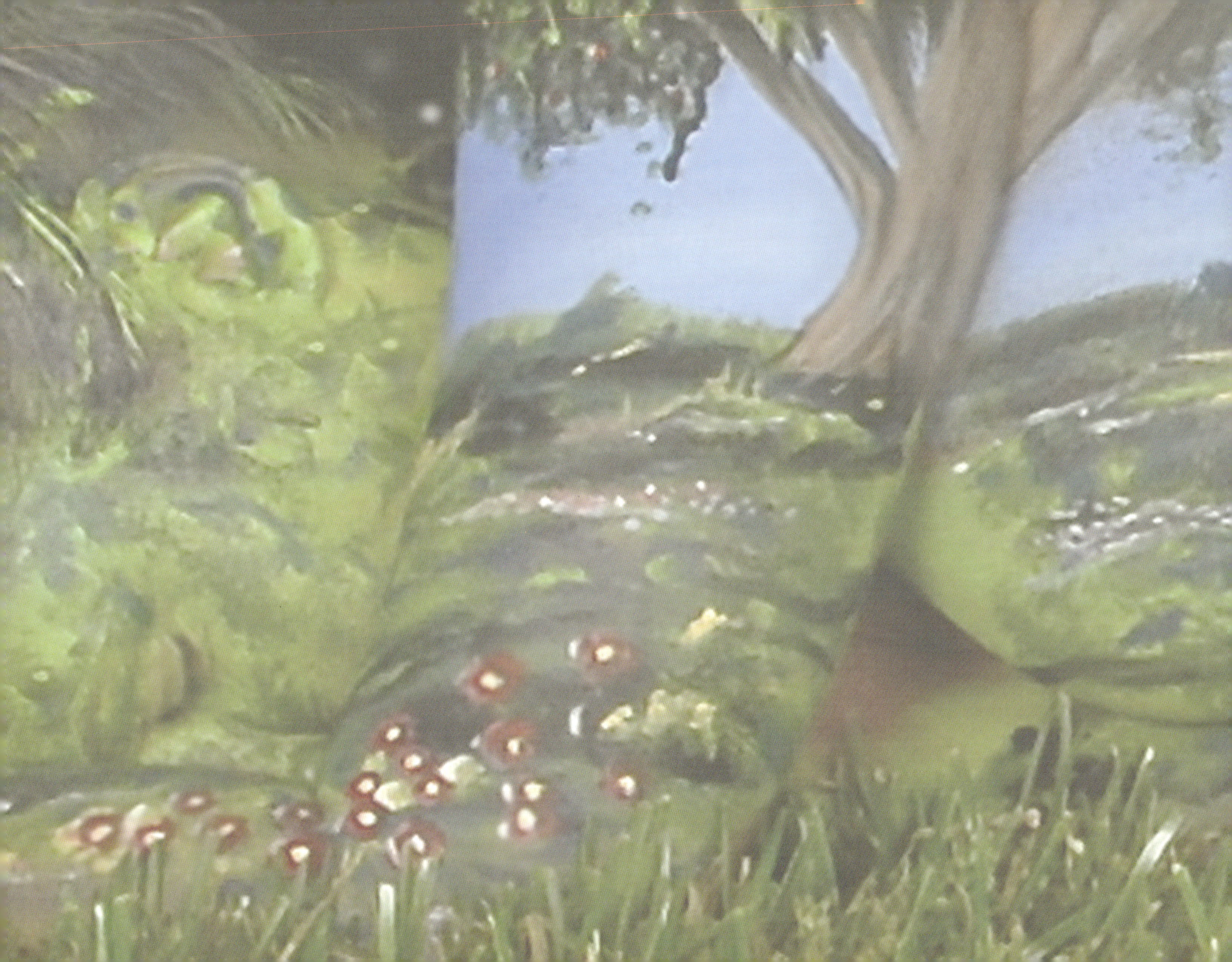

Genesis

Encompassing and harmonizing contradictions: day and night, serpent and dove, the real and the surreal. This very personal image speaks of both a mythic past and an awaking transformation that is still in process. Our journey in this Eden is shared and reflected, giving peace and promise to those willing to live freely without the repressive weight of our ancestor's unrelenting sins. Beauty is mostly found alongside freedom. Freedom is too often realized through effort and struggle.

Model: Bobbie
Photographer: Craig Tracy

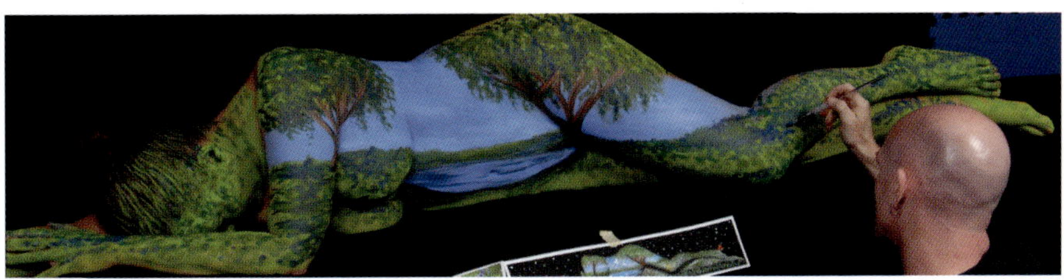

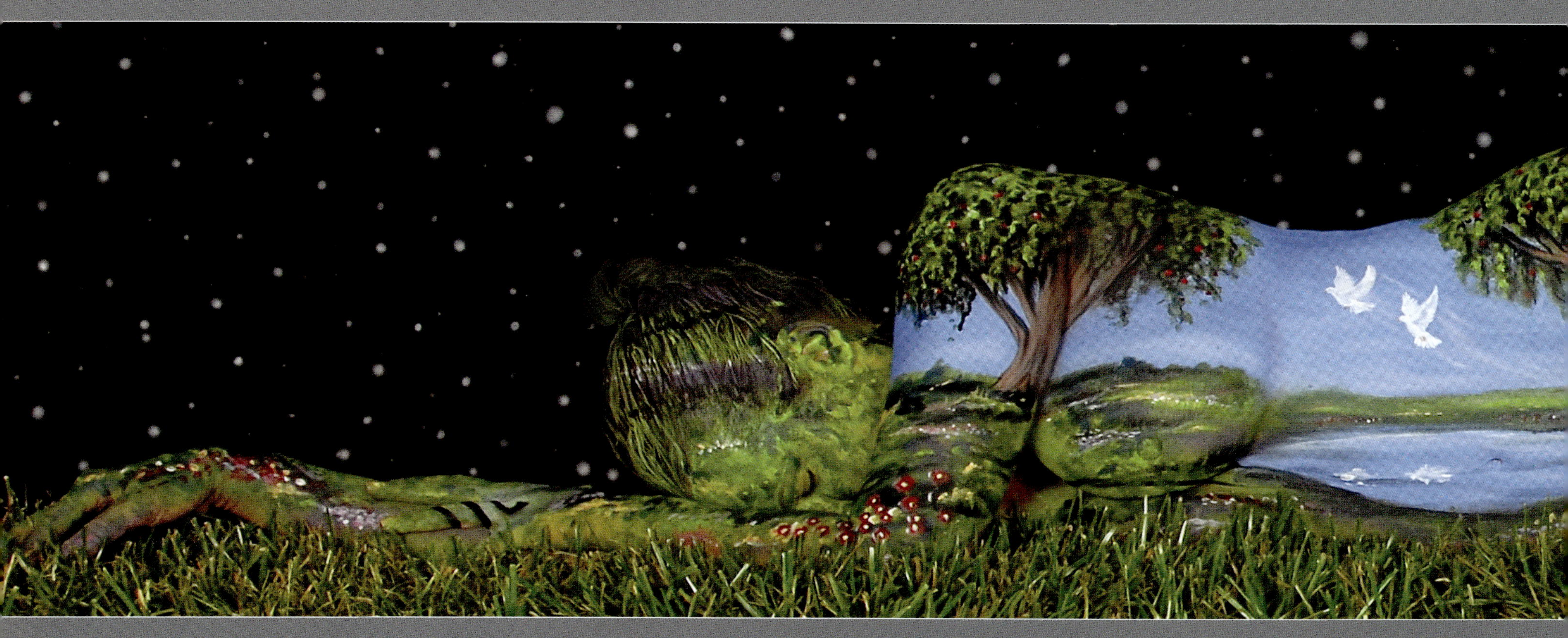

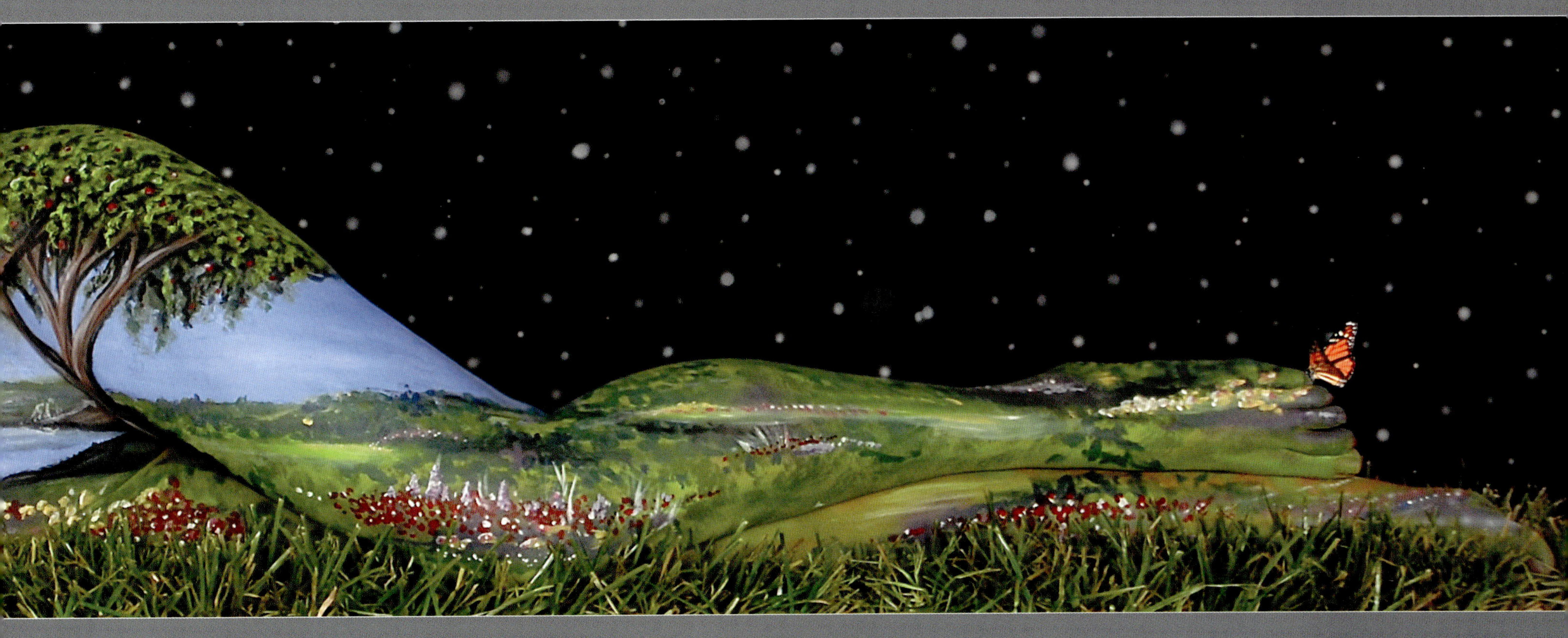

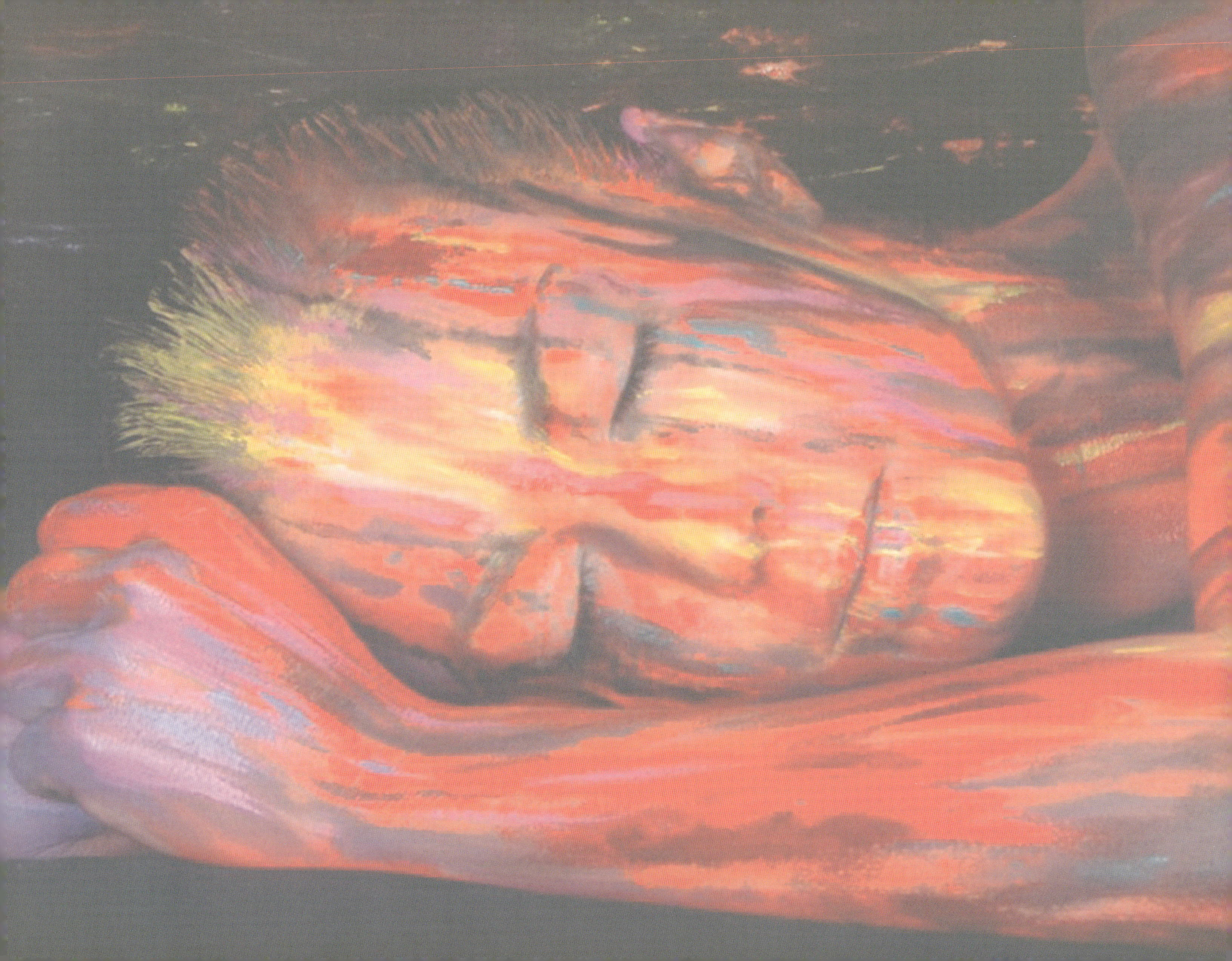

Dream

Sometimes when designing a bodypainting I just say, "no." I say no to all of the complicated, clever, and complexly challenging thoughts that swim around inside of my head. Sometimes I just say "yes"—yes to beauty, pleasure, and simplicity. This image challenged me only in that I needed to "let go" in order to make it happen. I chose to relax and enjoy the exceptional beauty of my model and the simplicity of color and the way I decided to add it to her body. Dreams do come true.

Model: Kristyn
Photographer: Robin Walker

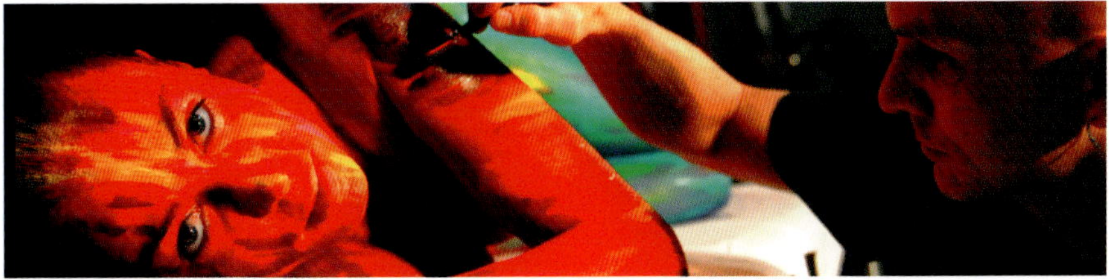

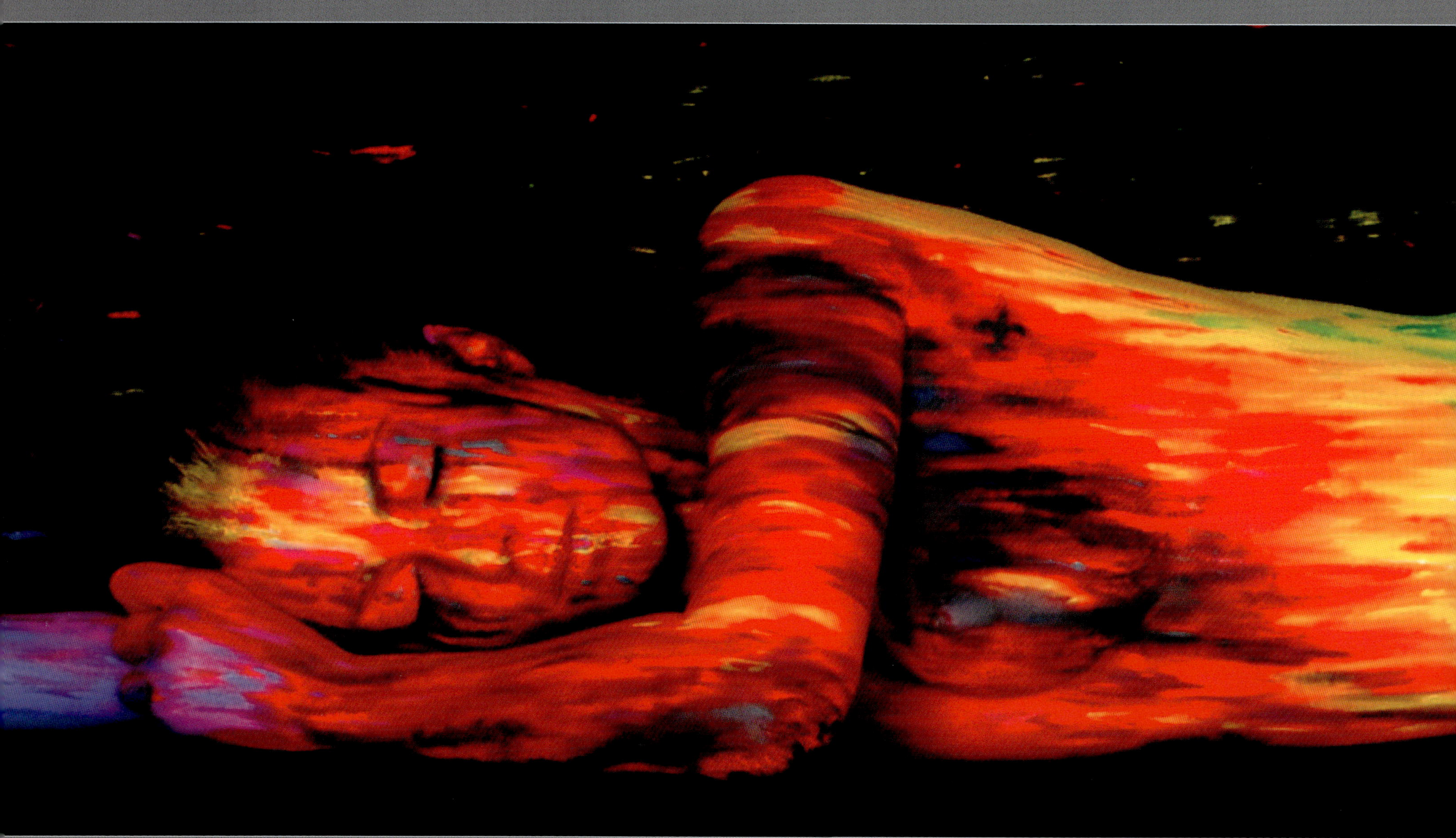

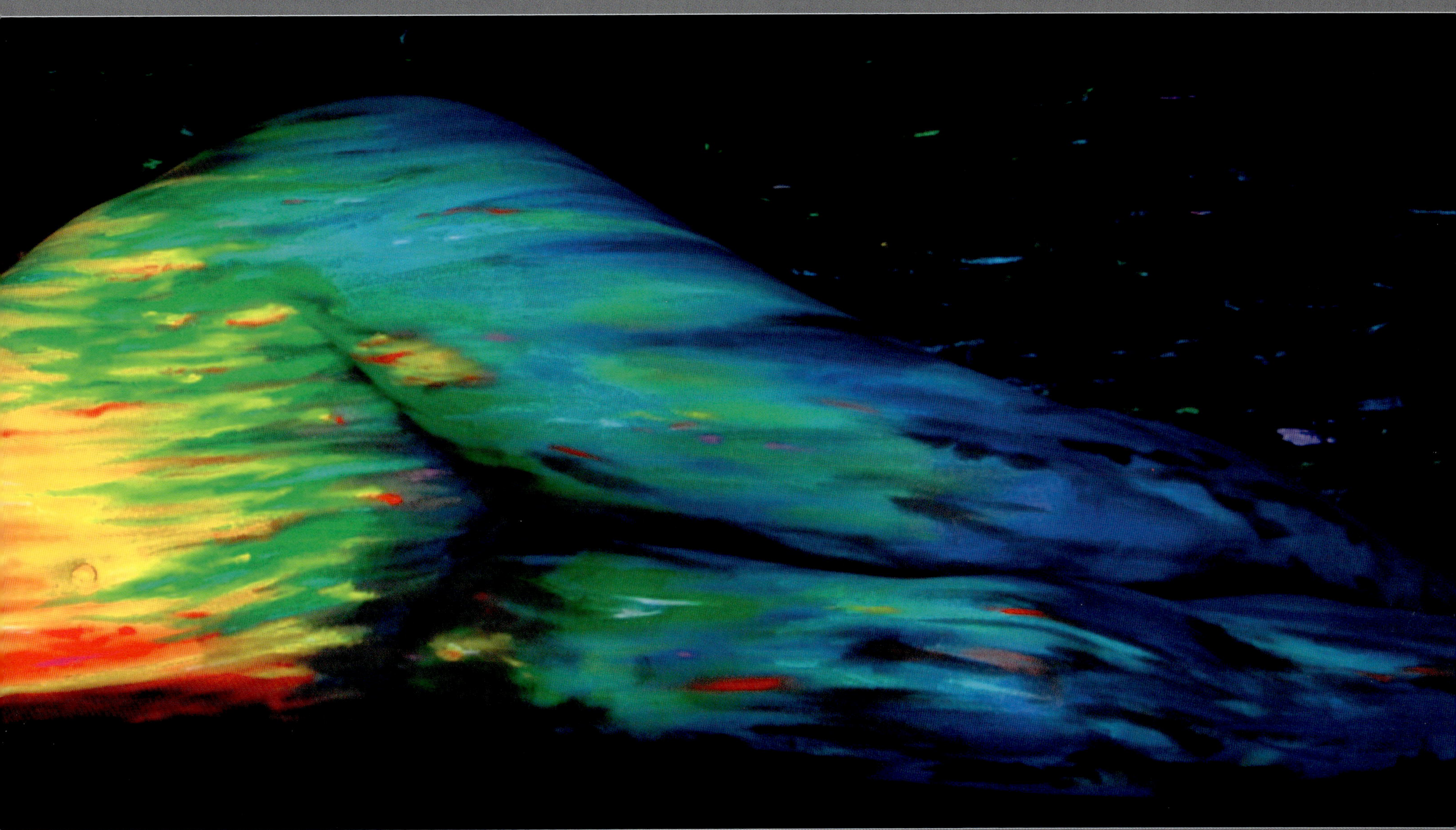

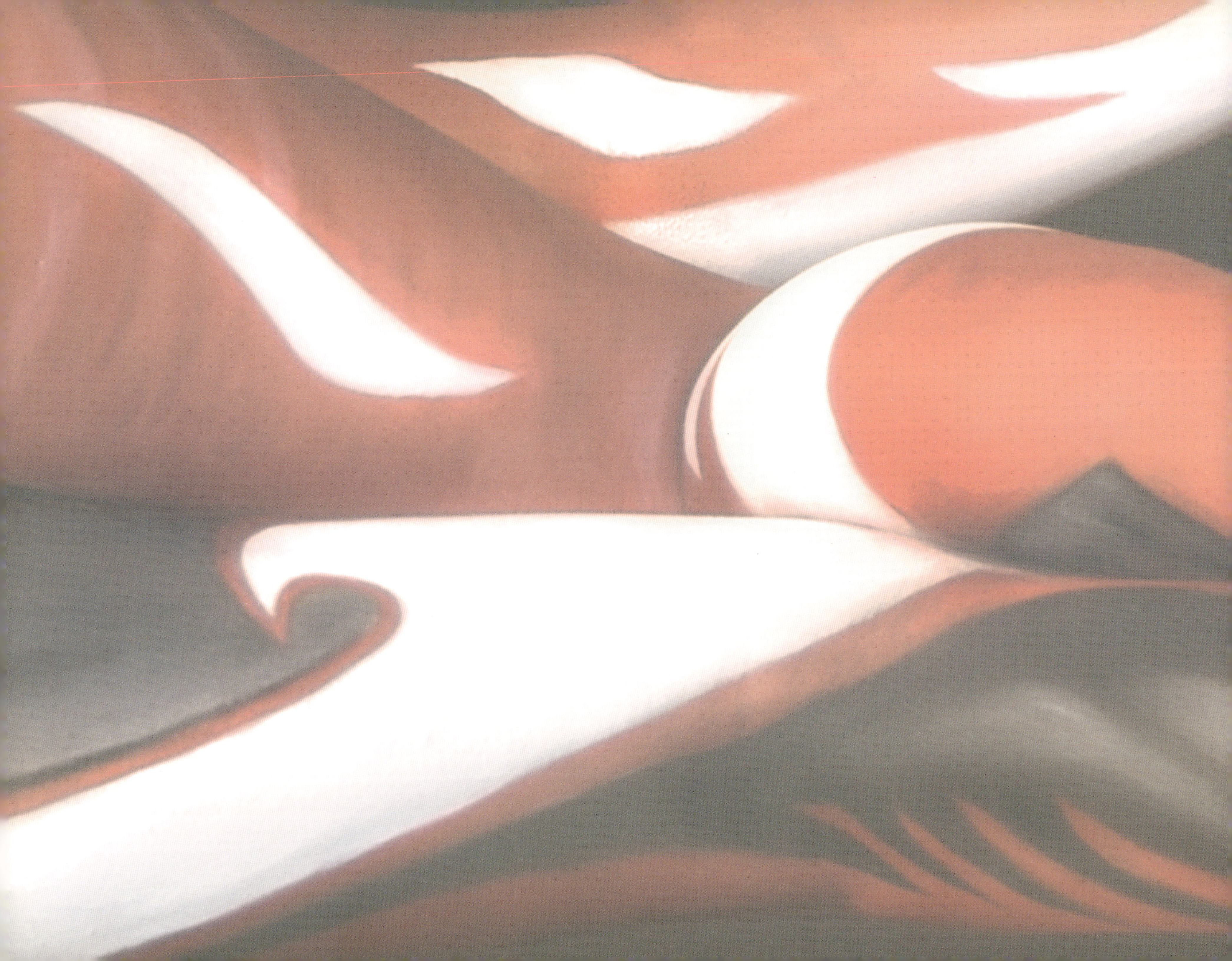

Feather Wind

The design of this piece was effortless, and filled with delight! All elements in the universe were aligned regarding *Feather Wind* and I'm really pleased with its inclusion in my life. My model was exceptional and we enjoyed the process of its creation. The image here speaks of the sun and its responsibility and influence on the wind. The balance, flow, design, color, contrast, and vibe of *Feather Wind* all make this artist smile.

Model: Hannah
Photographer: Libbie Allen

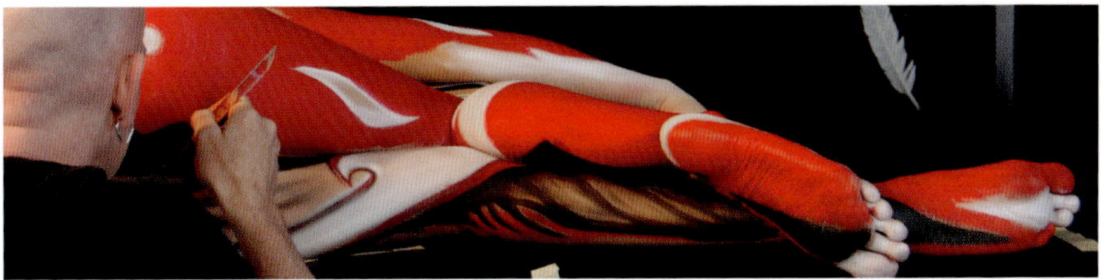

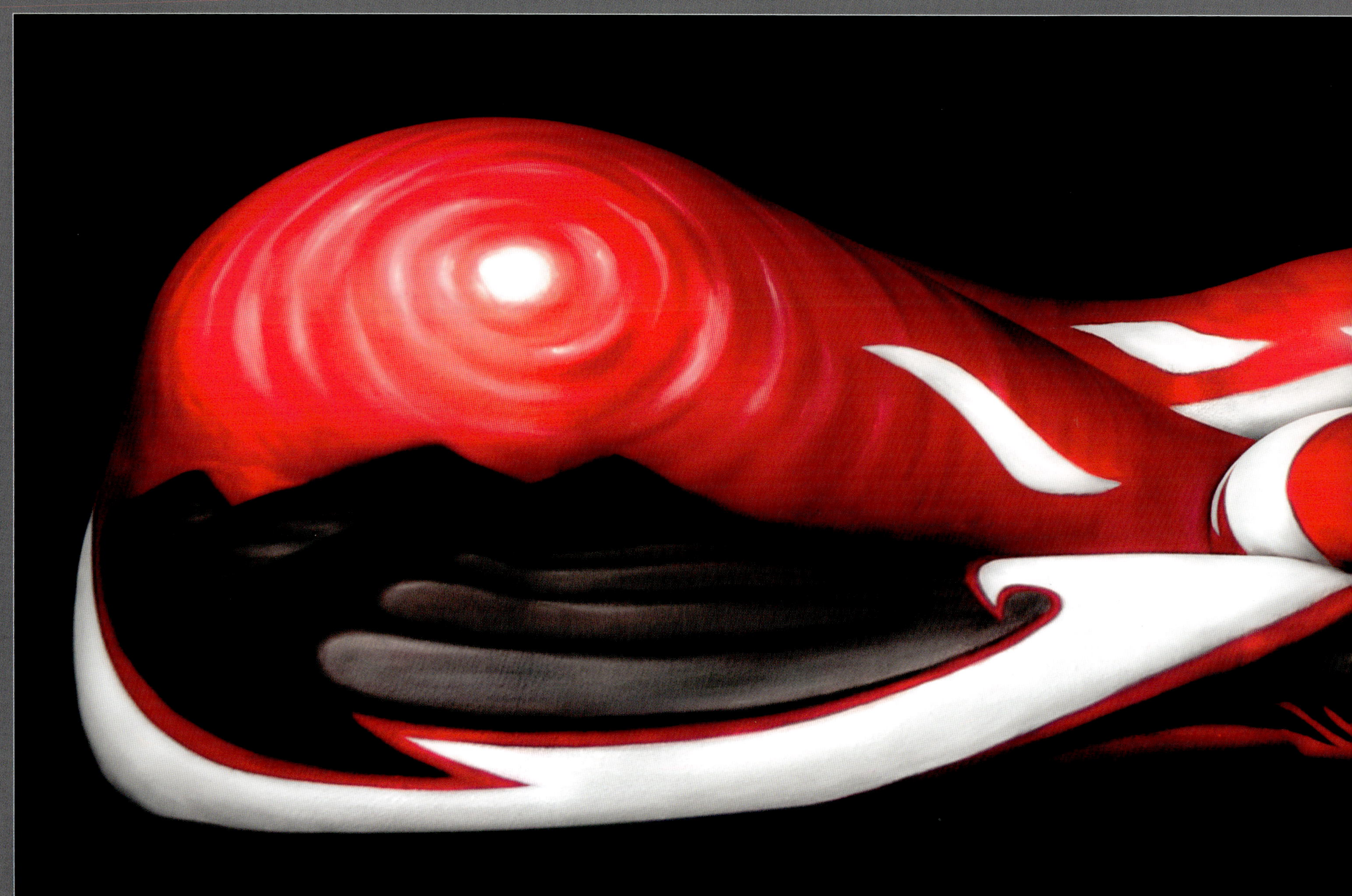

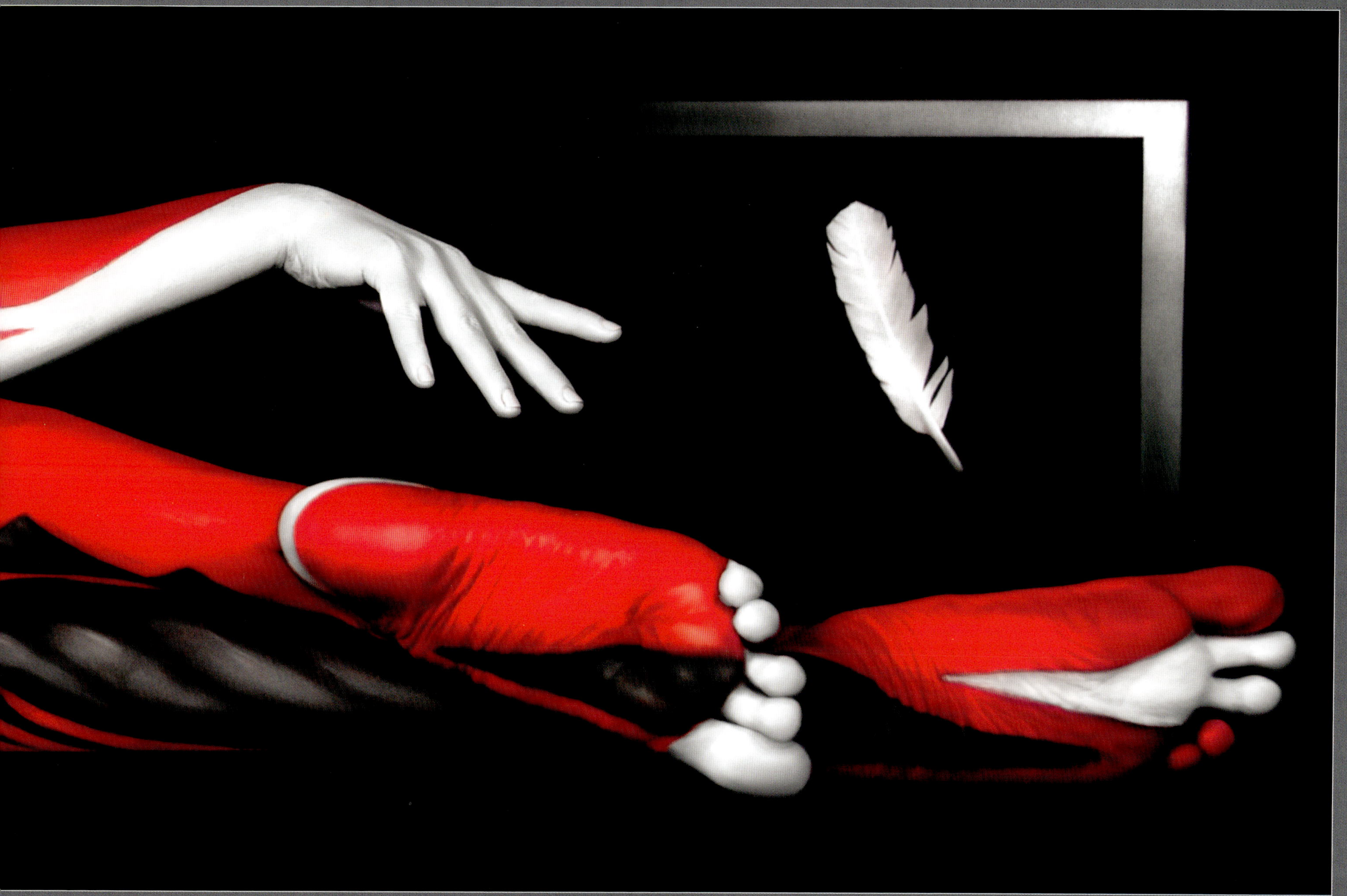

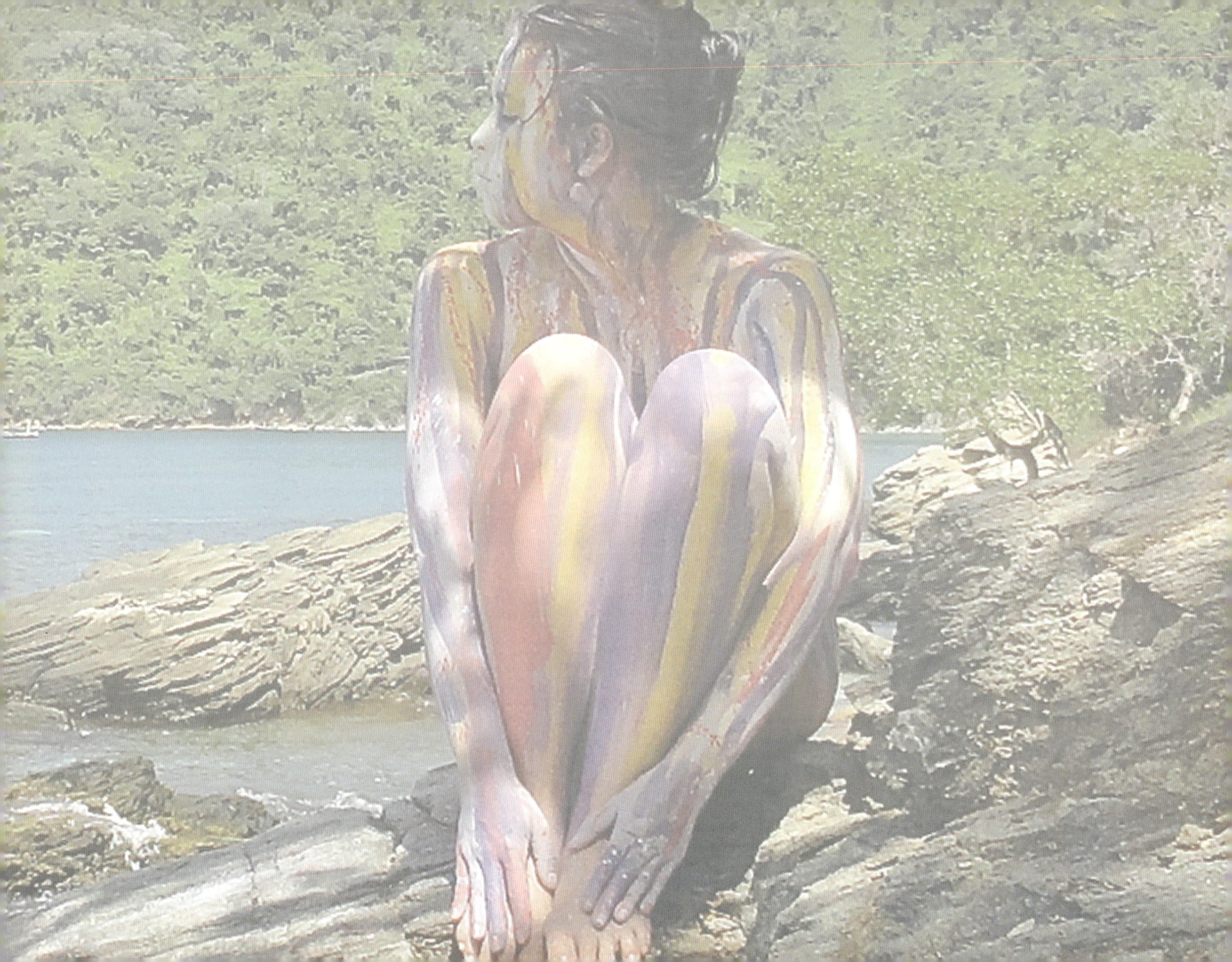

Last Day

This was my last full day spent in Venezuela in 2010. It was a relaxed, pleasure-filled day at the beach, whereas the days before were in an urban environment filled with activity and responsibilities. I knew that I wanted to paint something just for myself while on this trip to South America. I packed some bodypaint colors and one paintbrush in my beach bag. My model here is my guide and interpreter. She was, fortunately, the perfect model on the perfect beach on that perfect last day.

Model: Kriss
Photographer: Craig Tracy

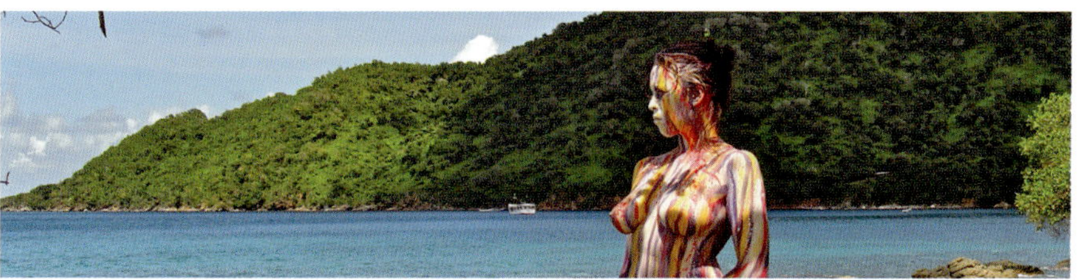

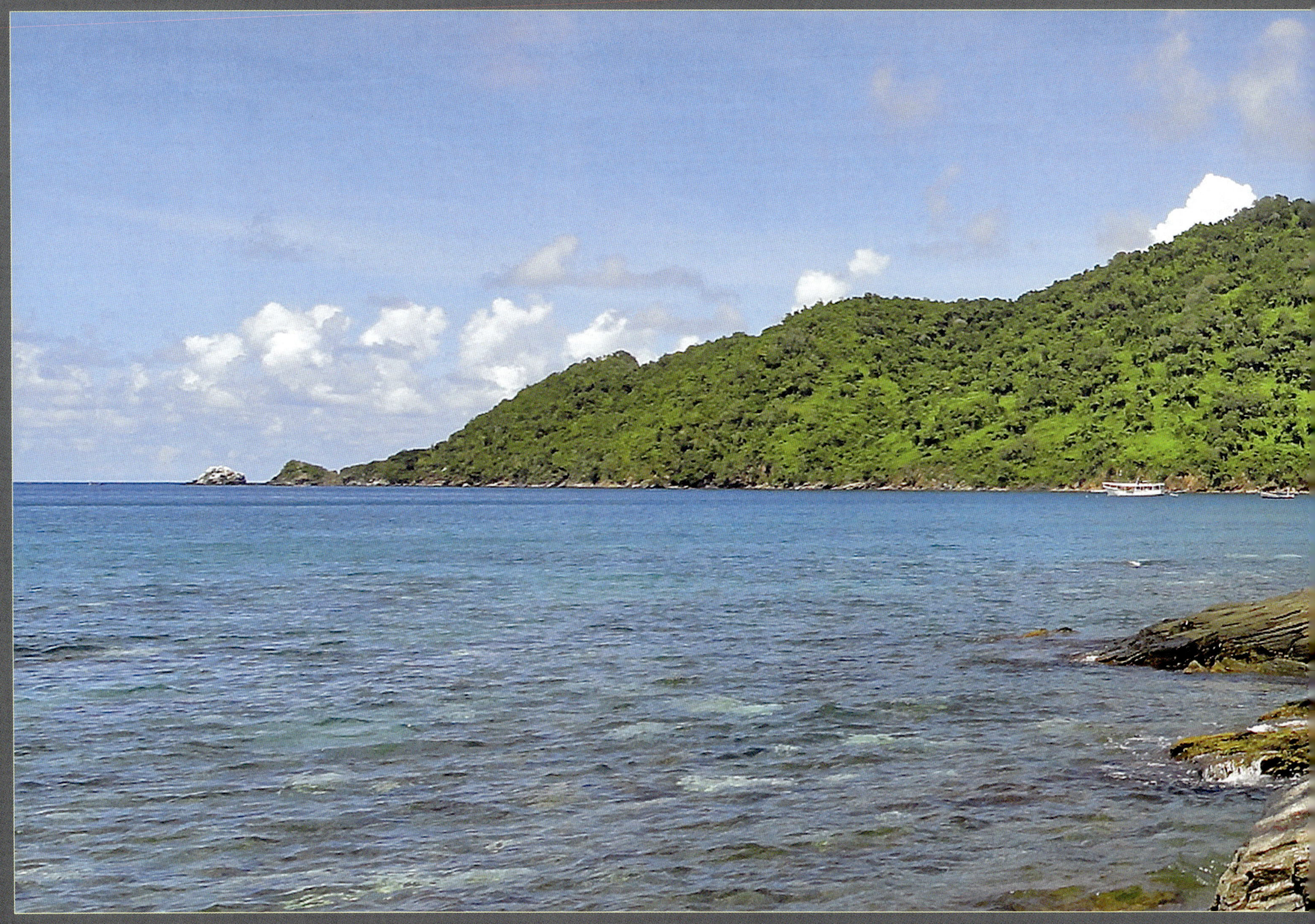

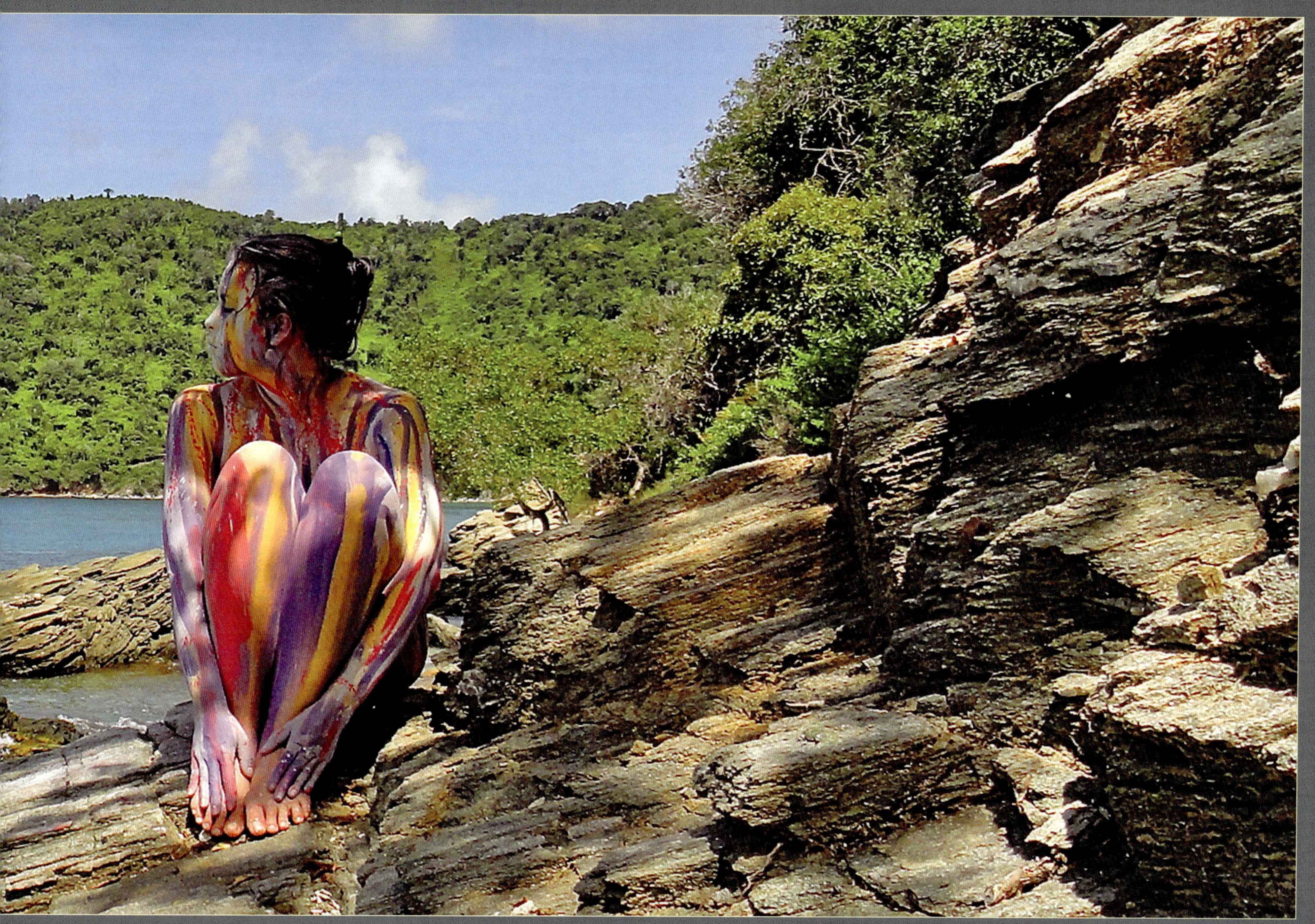

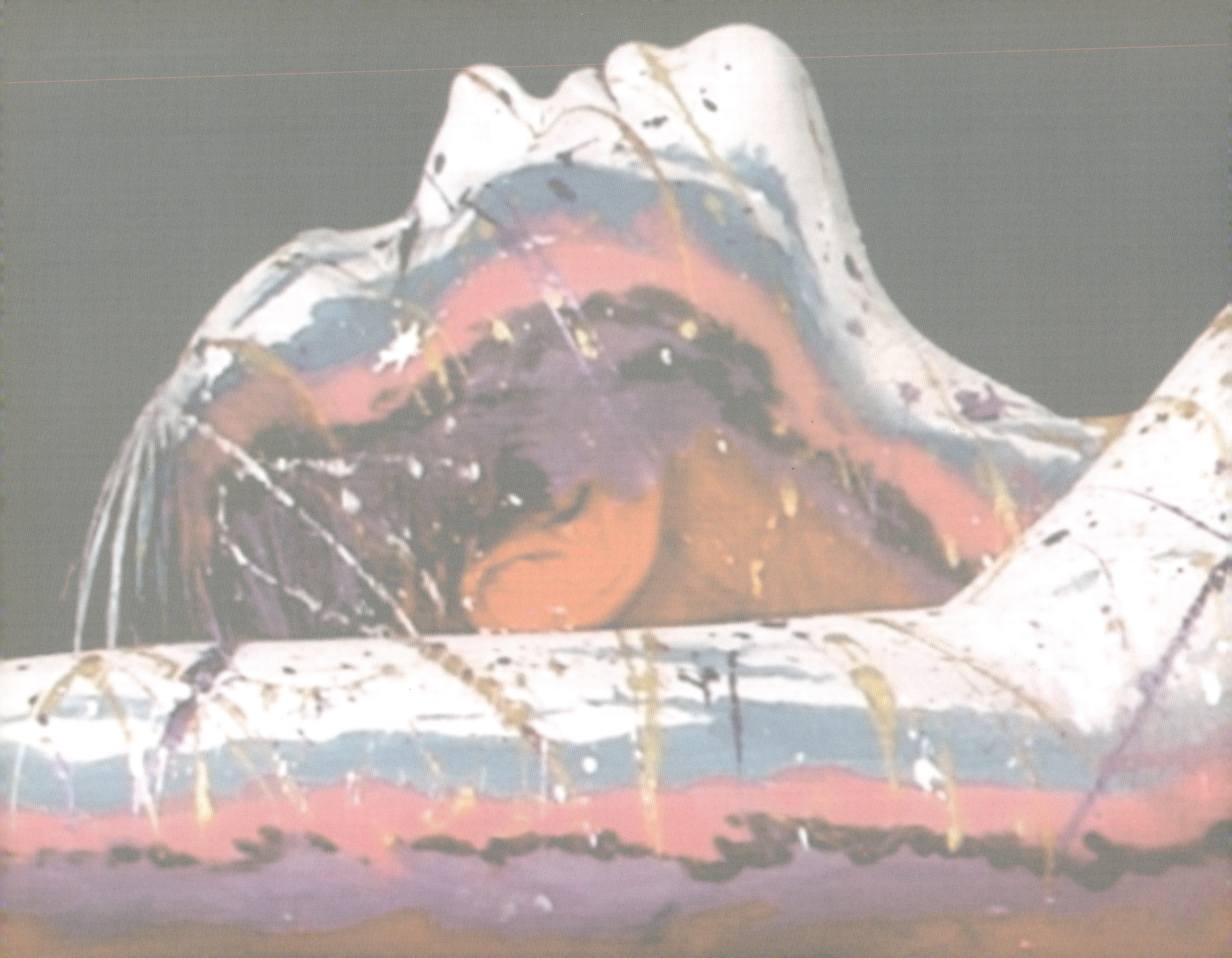

Spontaneity

Like a lighting strike on a clear day, I really didn't see this painting coming. I had never worked this spontaneously before and yet, here it is and I love it! The model asked me if I could paint her, but she would need to be painted within hours, as she would soon leave New Orleans. At first I said no as I usually do, but then I had a change of heart. I decided that I would make "something" happen. *Spontaneity* is that something. I now allow a few magic paintings to happen each year.

Model: Ann
Photographer: Max Trombly

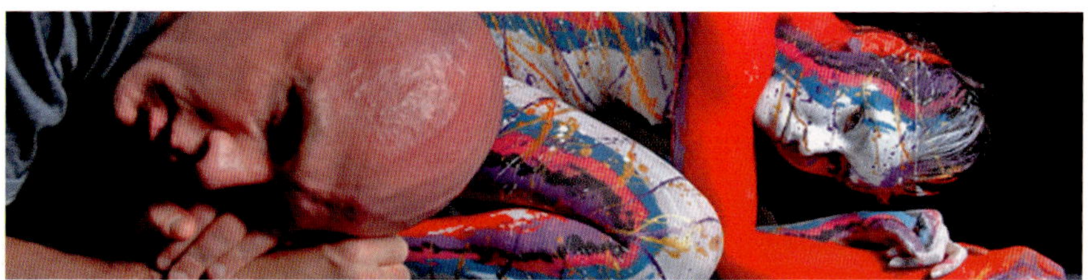

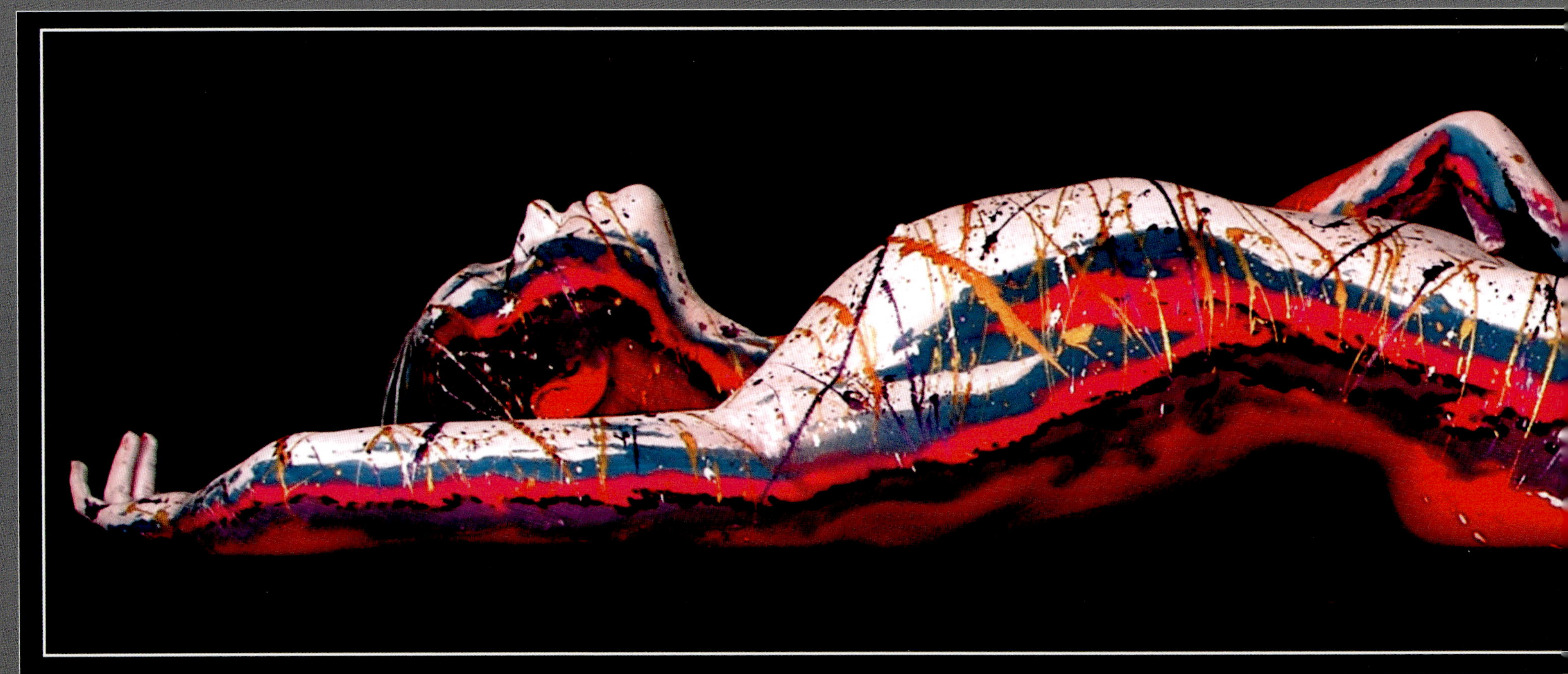

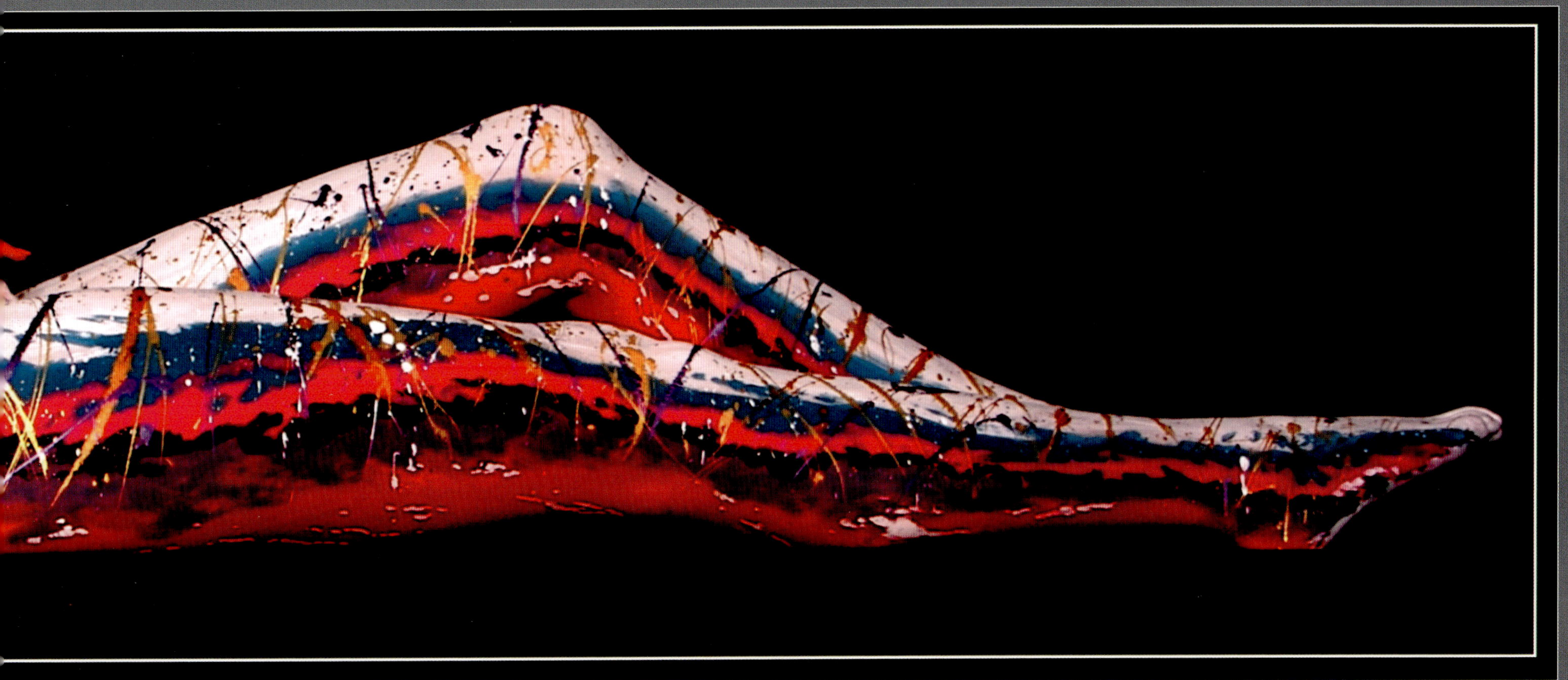

Perfect 10

I often make the joke that working with newborns is difficult because they don't seem to speak English or appreciate my artistic vision. All of the struggle and challenges feel worthwhile once the final image is captured in my camera. When asked how I manage to paint and capture such images, the answer is always: sleep. The only time babies seem to stop moving and squirming is when they sleep. Getting babies to sleep and stay asleep is an art all in itself.

Models: Nelson Family
Photographer: Craig Tracy

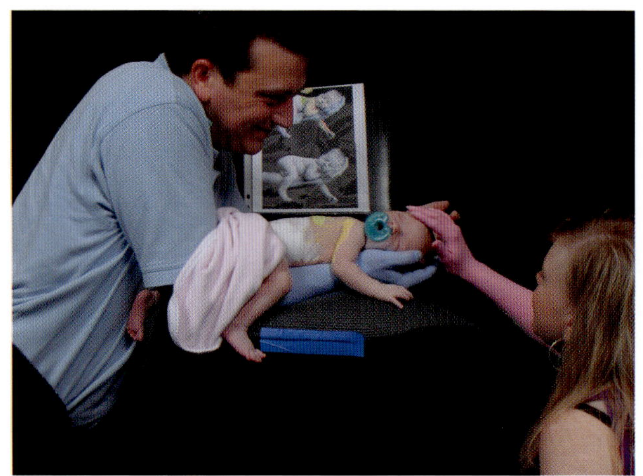
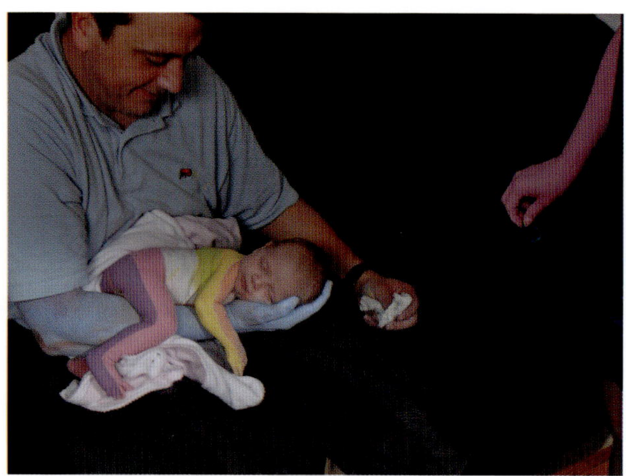
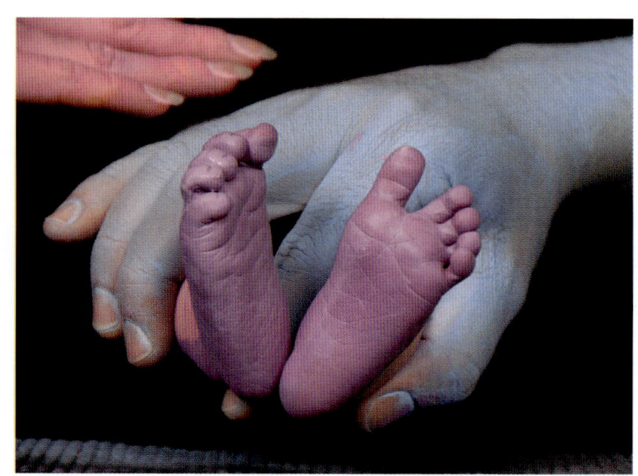

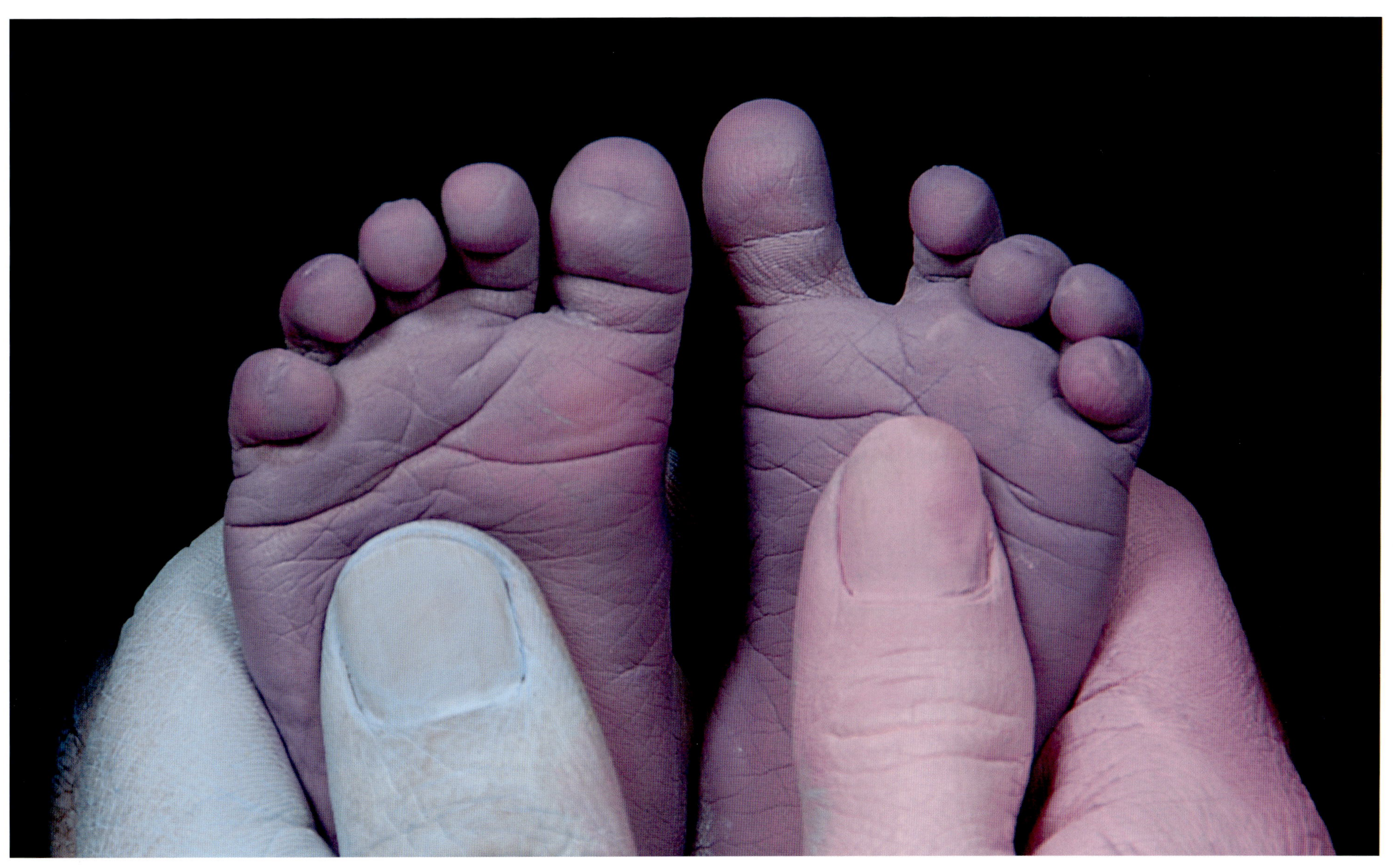

Purr

Purr was painted live in an art gallery in front of whomever cared to visit with us that particular night. This is not my normal way of creating. I'm usually in my studio away from visitors and distractions. Painting live offers many unique challenges and opportunities. I try with each such event to enjoy the process and allow the unexpected to present itself. This image communicates in a way that I was not expecting. It seems to have a primal inexplicable effect on many that view her. I'm delighted by how this image has been received and again I've been reminded that not having control of everything makes life much more interesting and pleasurable. Big cats are my favorite animals, and *Purr* toys with both the feline and feminine that captivate me so.

Model: Anna
Photographer: Craig Tracy

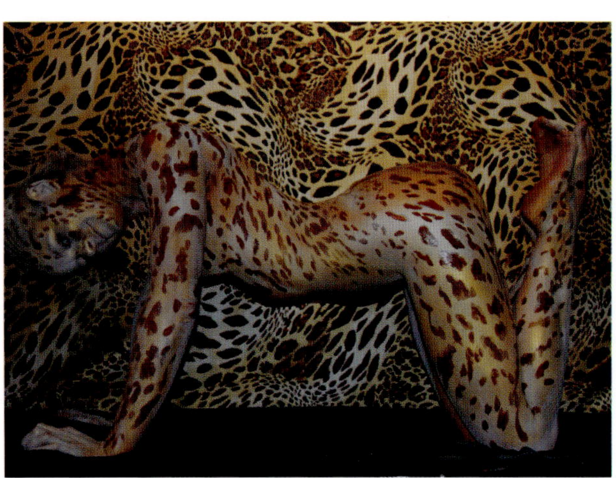
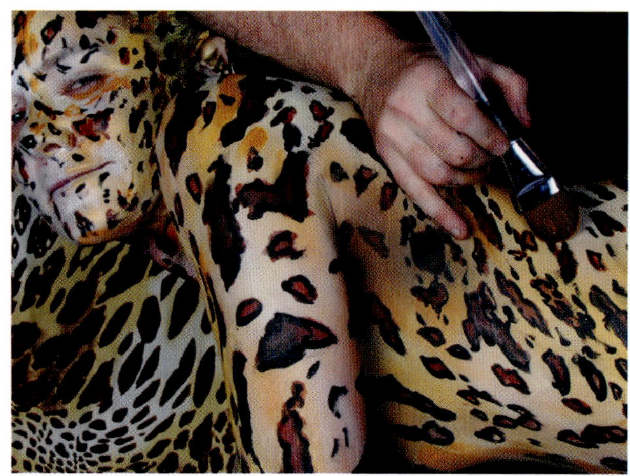
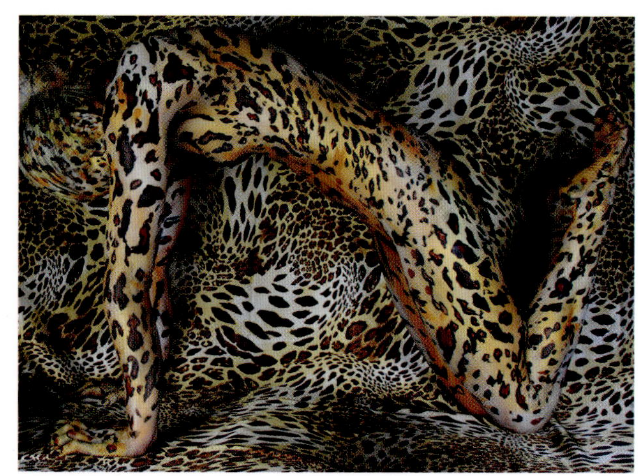

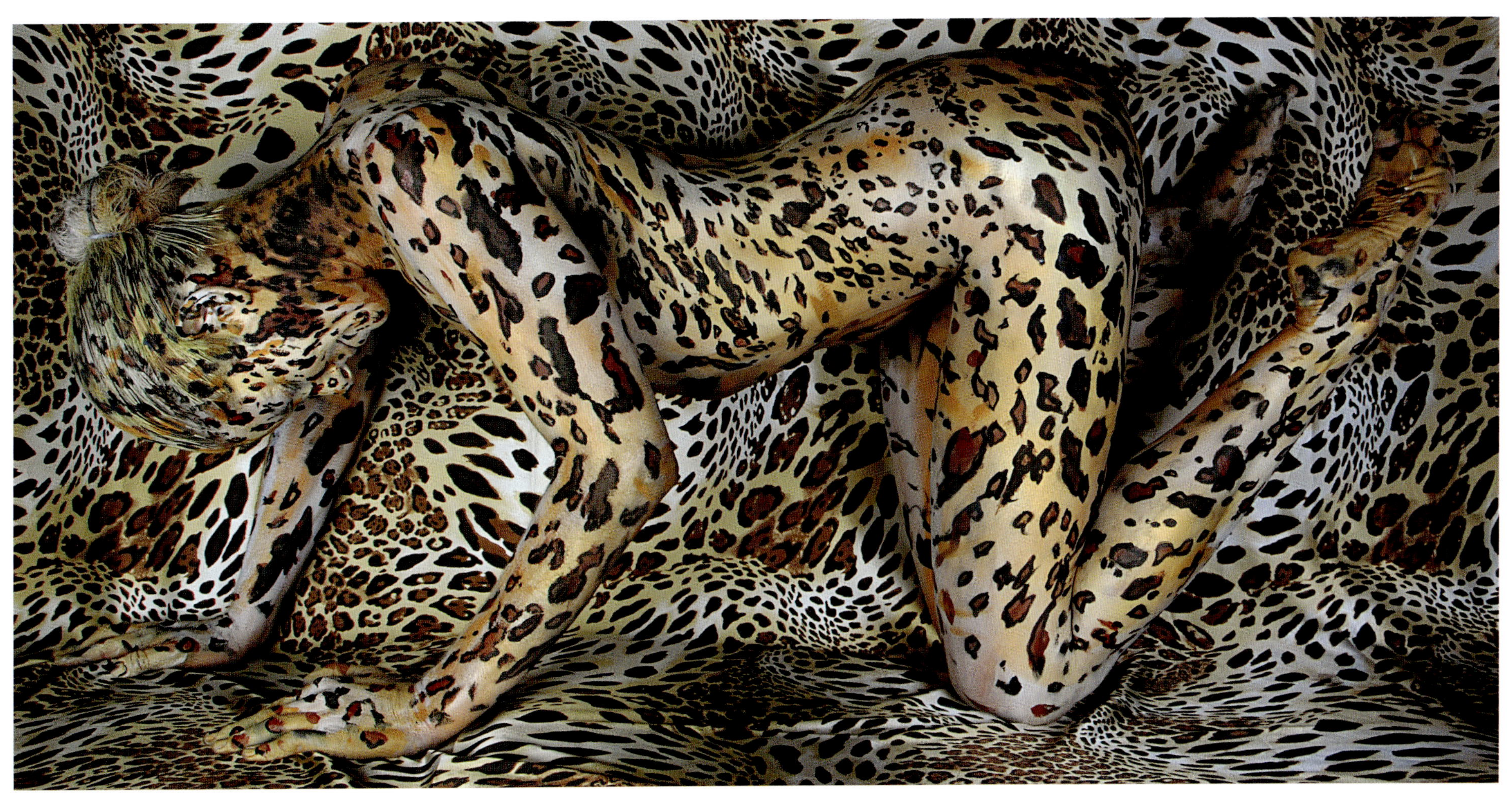

Rose

By any other name.... I fell in love with this pose as soon as it happened in front of my eyes and my camera's hungry lens. The element of the model's hand crossing over and emerging in the center of this composition delights me so. I love working hands and feet into my compositions whenever possible. This pose offered so much potential in such a compact and intriguing way. I decided on the subject as it seemed to lend itself to the pose so naturally. When I use simplistic subject matter, I often try to complicate and balance the image with a more complex and challenging pose. Here I want the viewer to feel comfortable for a moment and then be a bit puzzled by her pose and the questions it offers.

Model: Amanda
Photographer: Craig Tracy

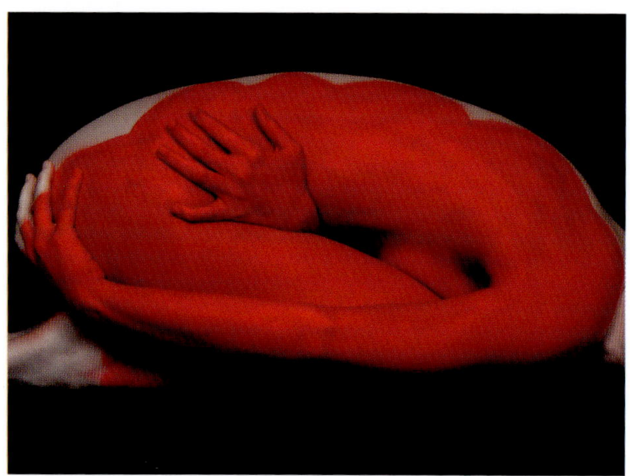
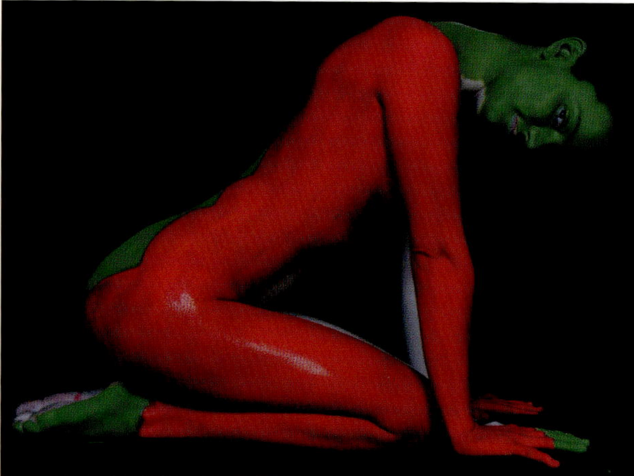
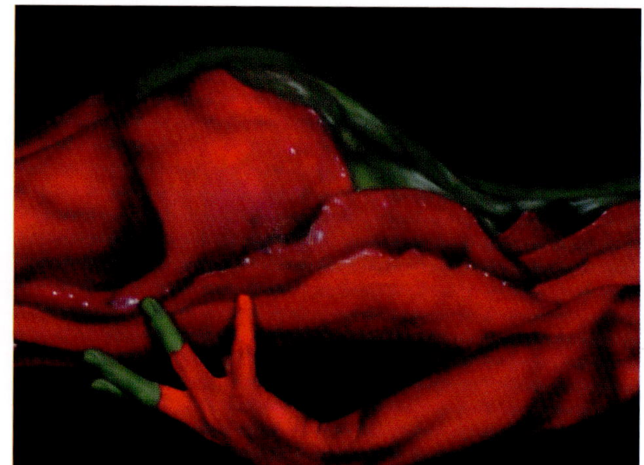

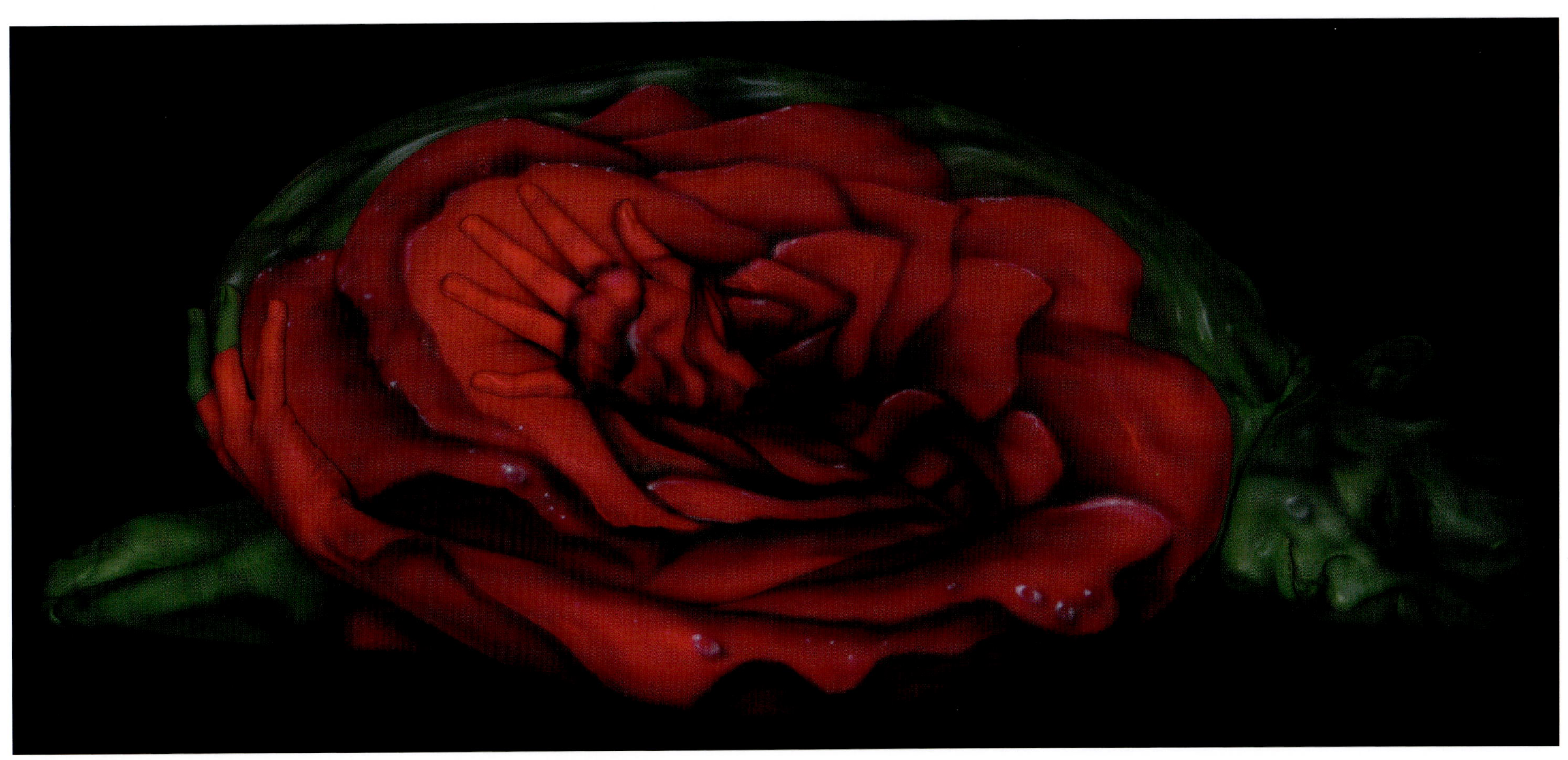

The Gift

When I work with an expecting mother, I prefer them to be in their eighth month so as to maximize their size and ever-evolving shape. The pose possibilities are limited to the comfort of the model, and I do my best to make the painting substantial and comfortable. I design away from the natural urge to see the image as emotionally endearing. I try more for a mature complexity that connects the mother to her unborn child. With *The Gift* we are presented with metaphors and explorations of thought, the natural and the man-made. As with working with newborn babies, working with expecting mothers is a privilege for me and I'm honored to have the opportunity to create with them.

Model: Samantha
Photographer: Craig Tracy

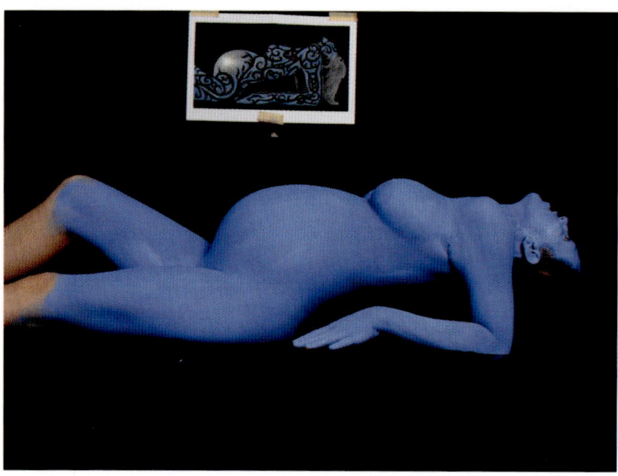
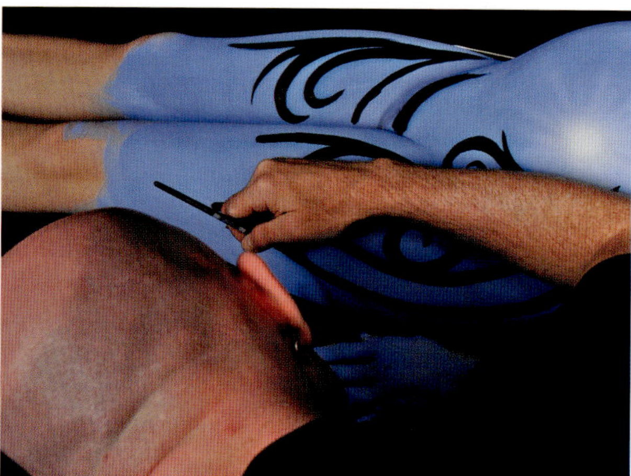
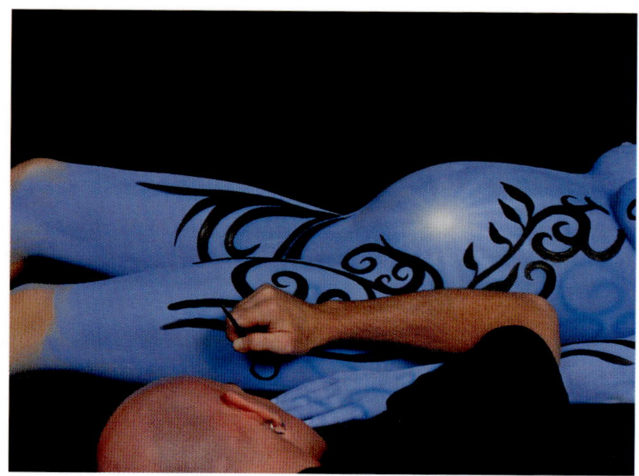

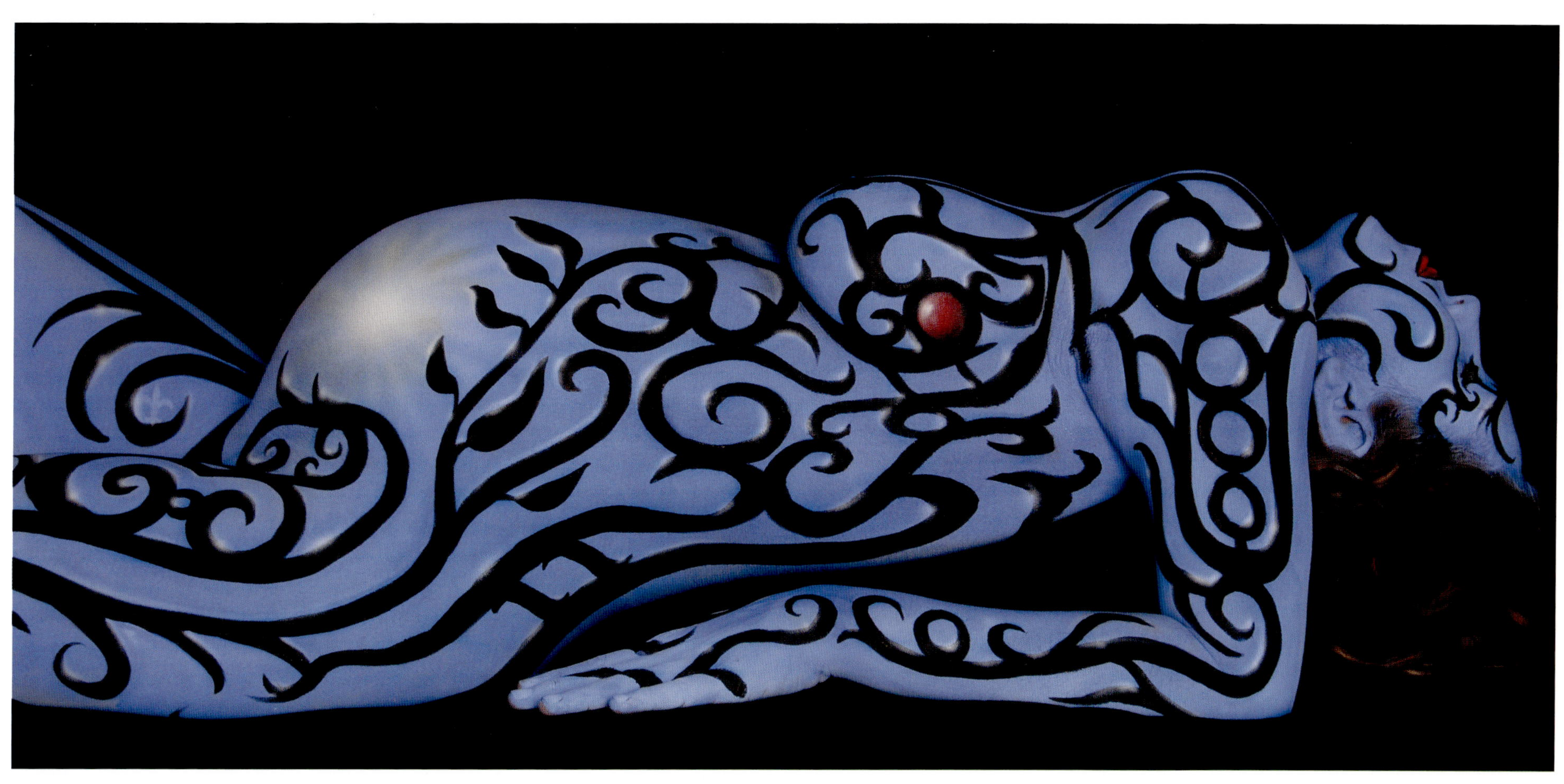

Ember

There's a deeply primitive and visceral human connection to fire in all of its majesty. Ember hopes to capture the warmth and timeless visual fascination to all that glows and dances in the darkness. I found that the pose used here was as unique as the individual that held it. Painting on human beings allows for so much, that no other surface can come close. *Ember* was a result of this model's persistence and determination to become one of my works. I love the passion shared between the desire and the execution in such cases, and the fulfillment of both a dream and a vision.

Model: Amber
Photographer: Craig Tracy

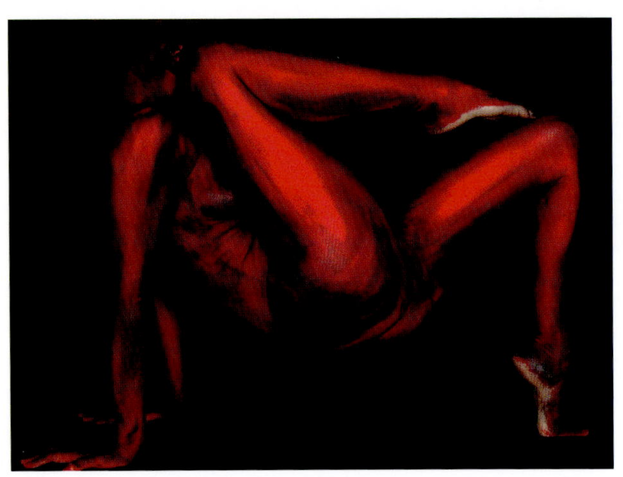 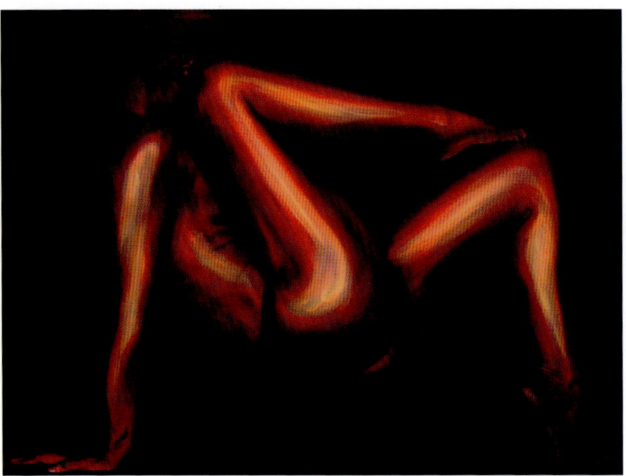 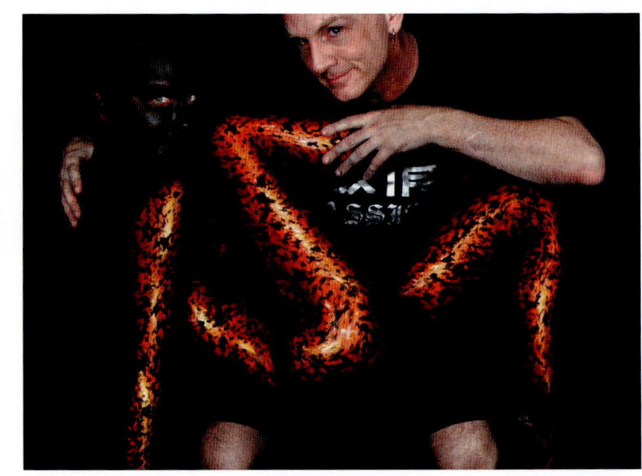

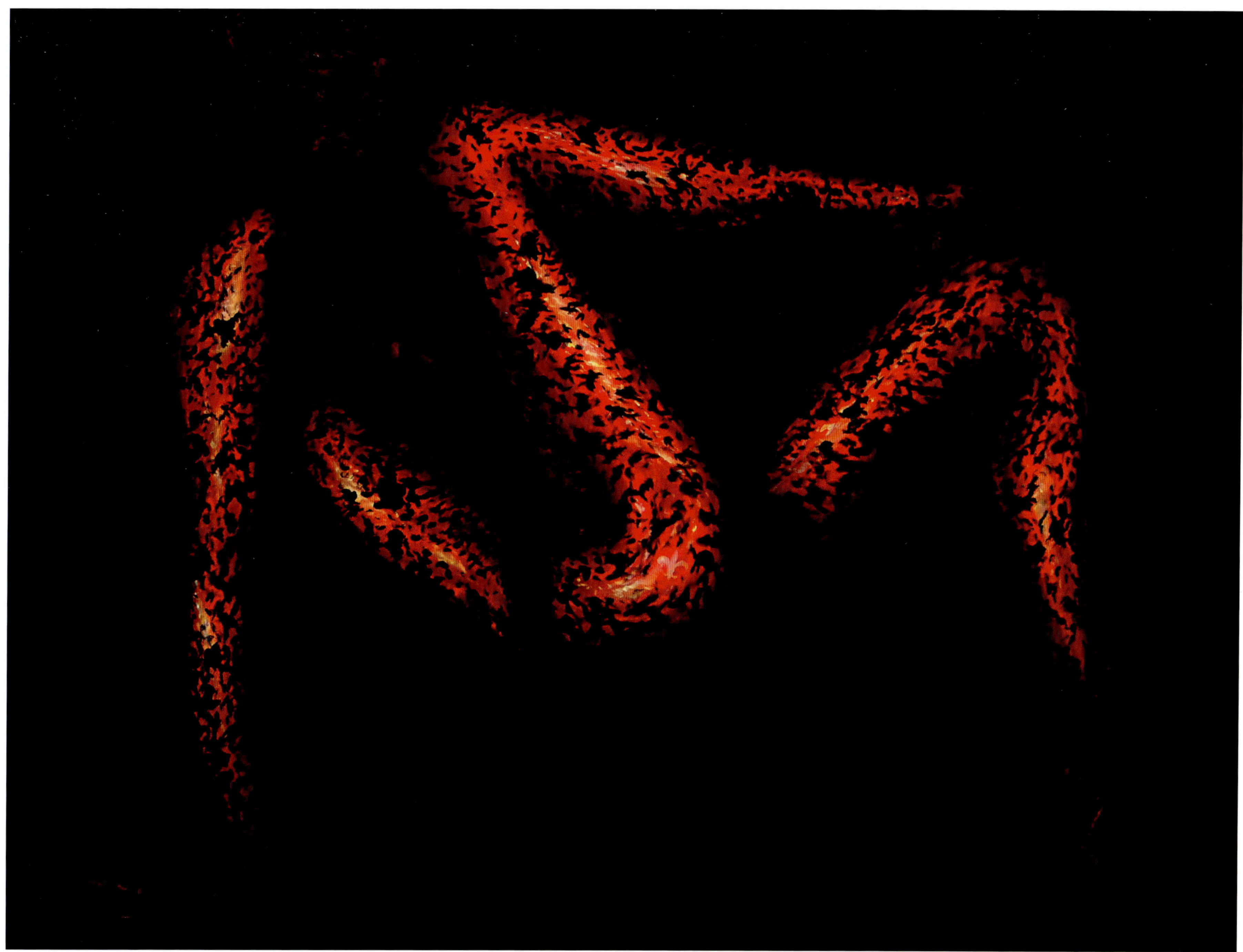

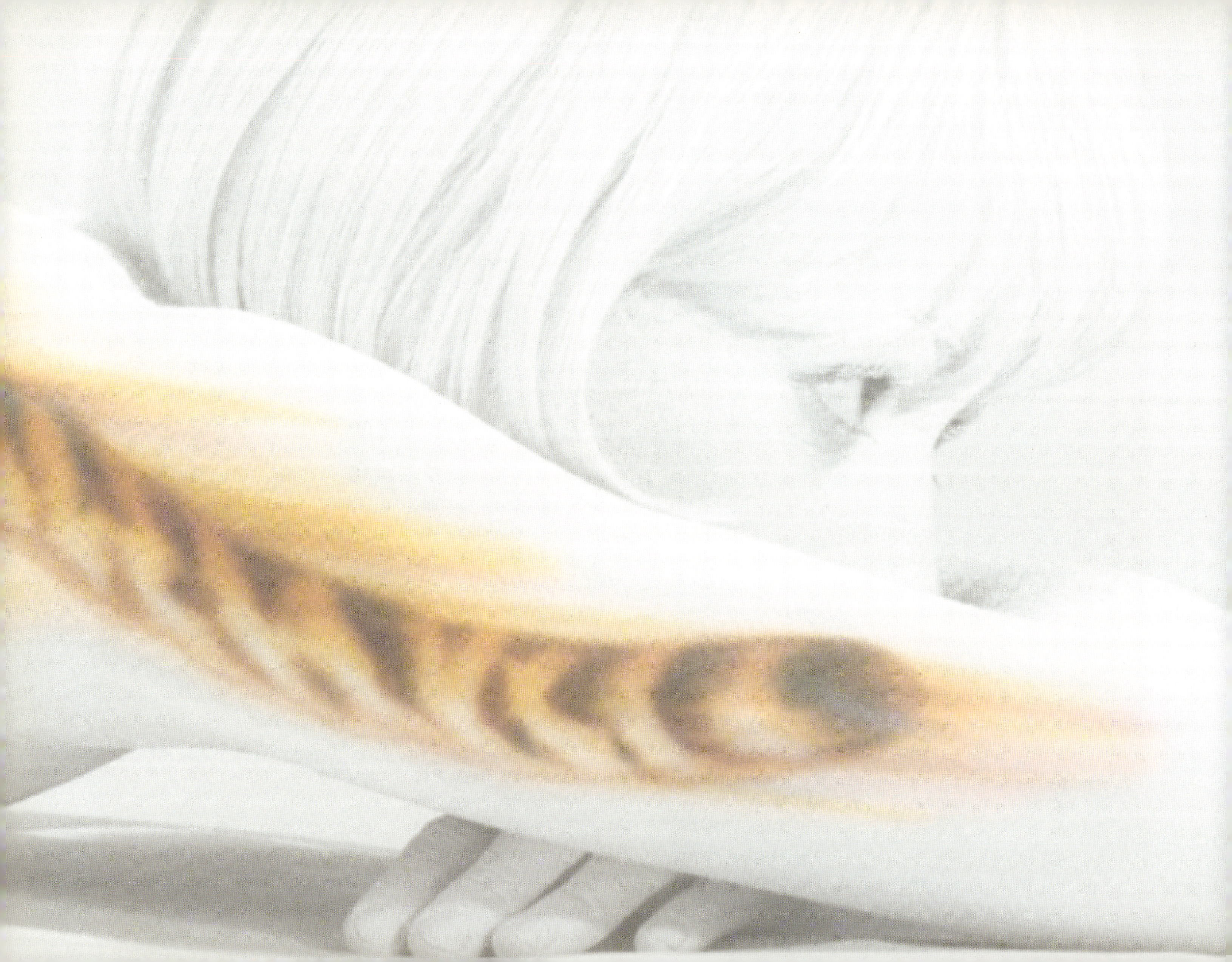

Speed

Considering that my model is an olive-skinned brunette with waist-length hair, one might appreciate this image for its transformative quality alone. Created in the winter month of January, the unheated studio was so cold that I actually painted Cara in the studio's heated dressing room. The geometric icon rendered in the background represents the man-made and the modern in contrast to the foreground's natural and more primitive qualities. This image is to date my personal favorite of my work.

Model: Cara
Photographer: Chris Mathews

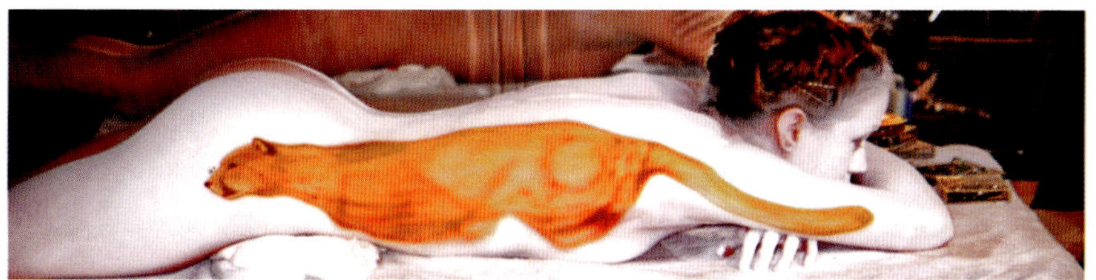

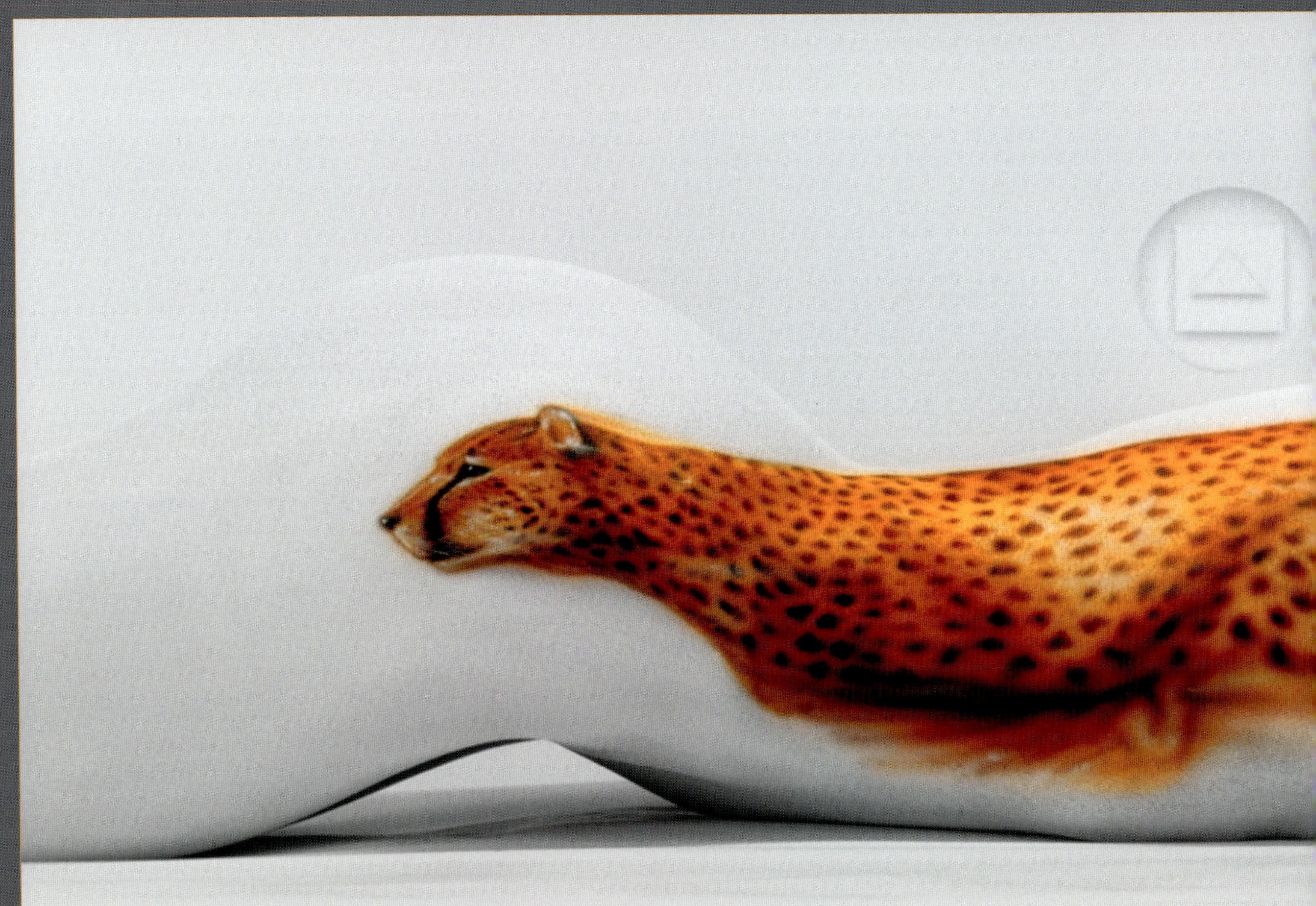

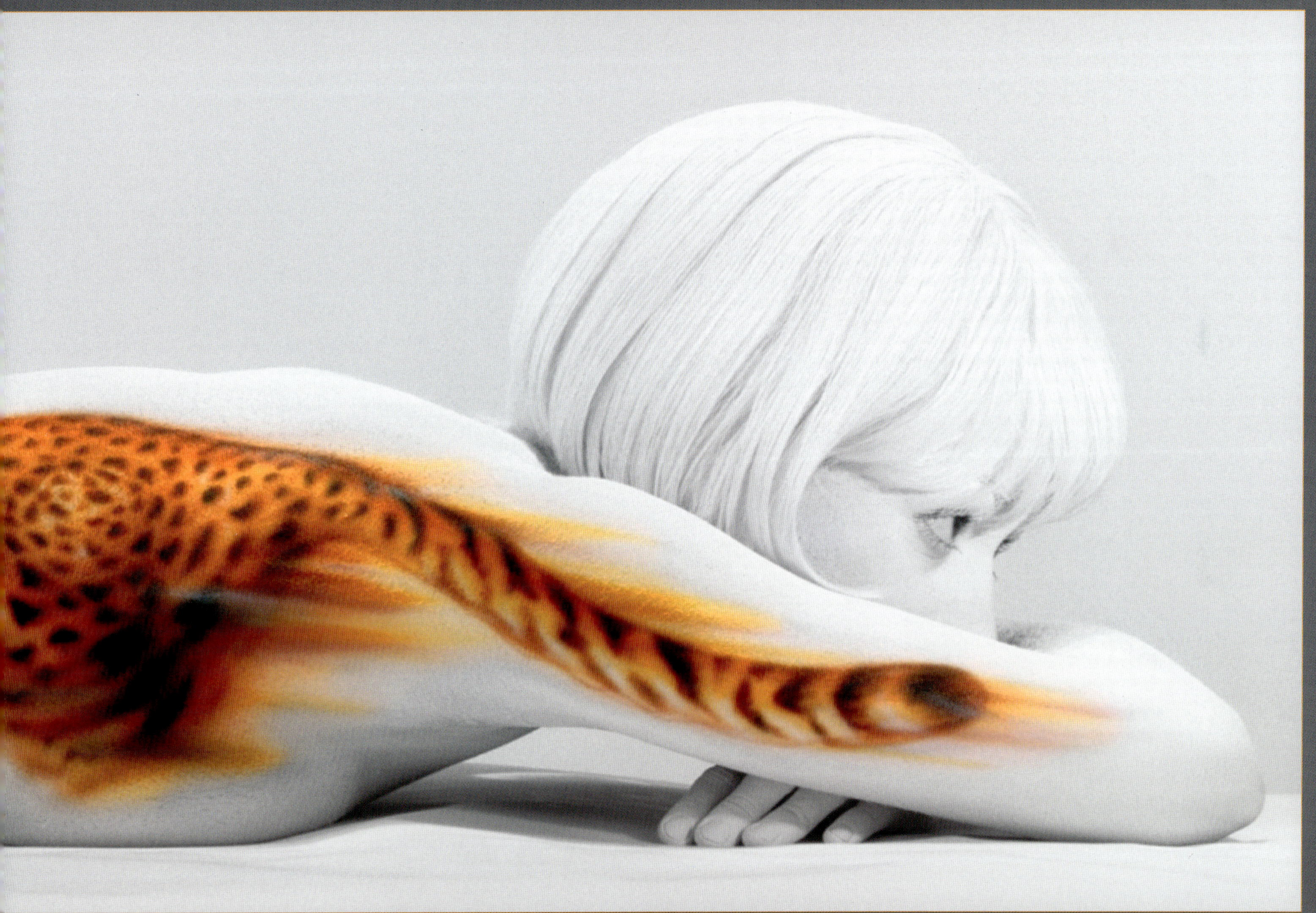

O

My lovely model in this piece has perhaps the smallest waistline that I have ever had the pleasure to encounter. The design itself was inspired as an extension of her amazing figure. All shadows in this image are painted and are not a result of lighting. Also note that because I absolutely love color, I've included multiple colors in some less obvious places.

Model: Olga
Photographer: Mark Giaviano

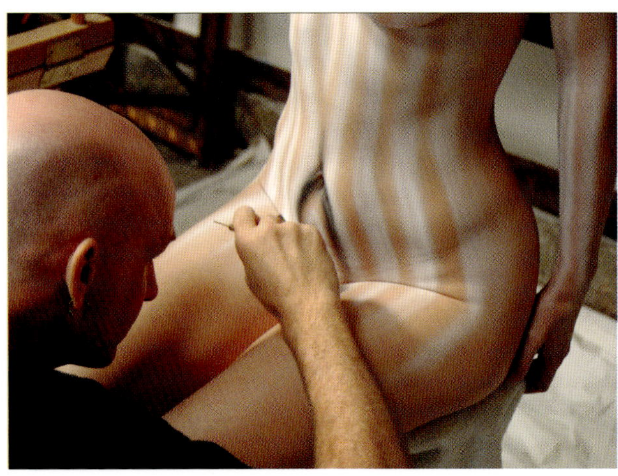
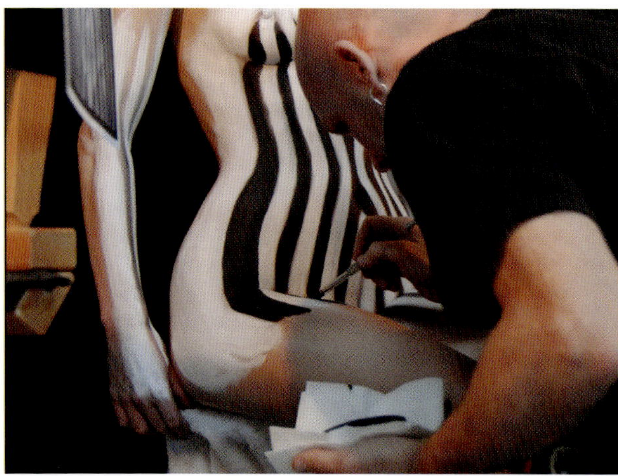
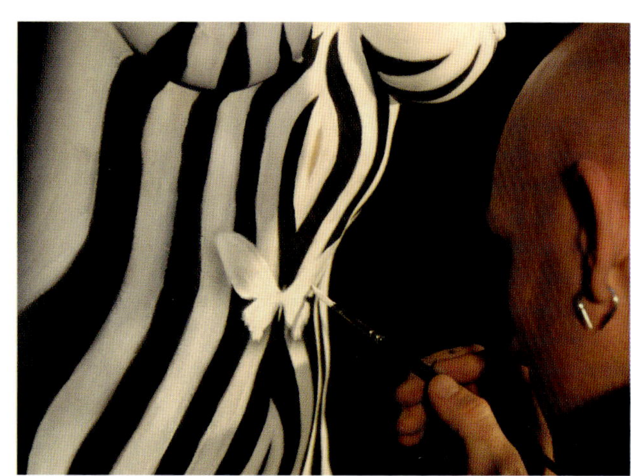

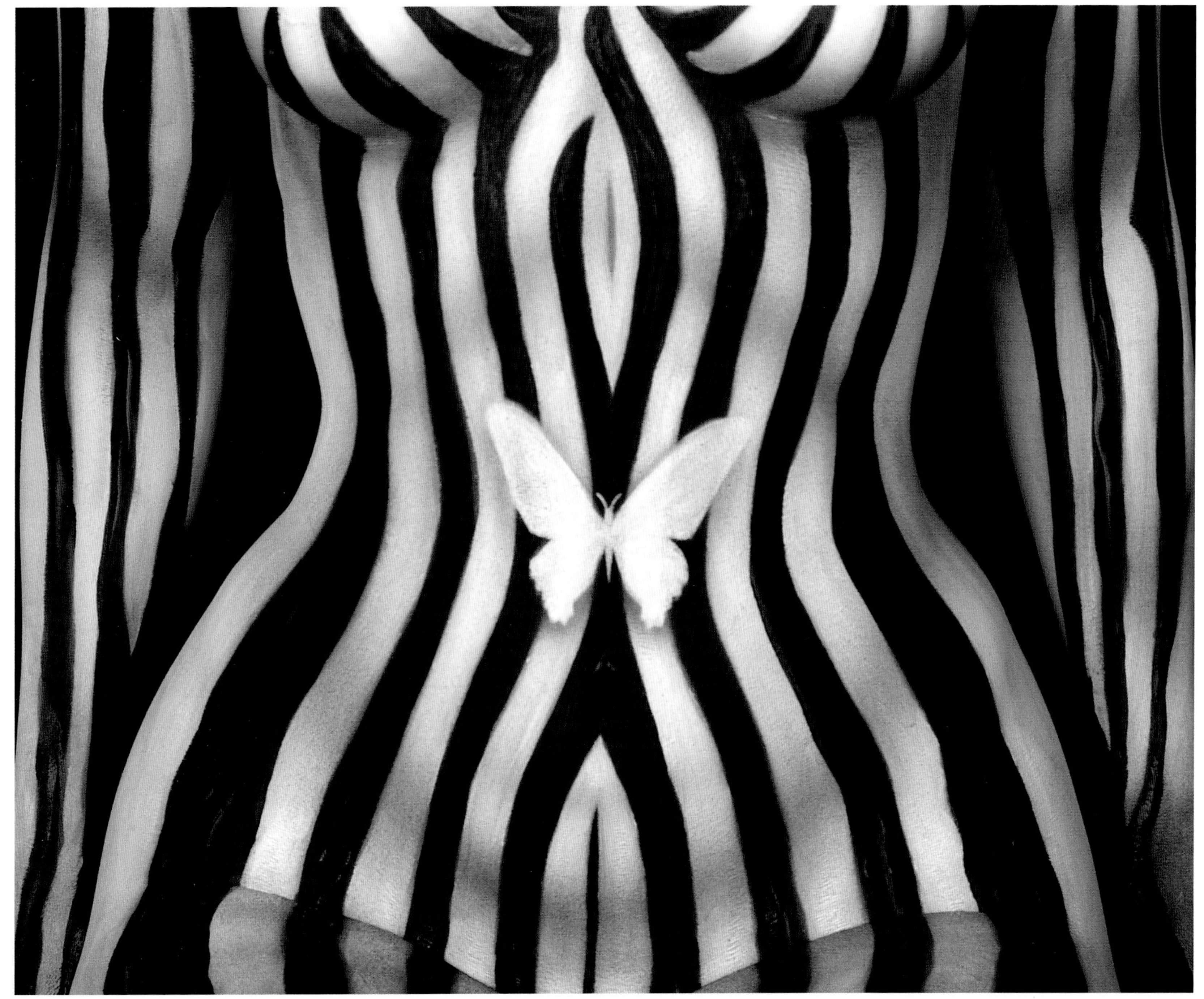

Clown

With this image I was able to combine three of my favorite elements: the female form, the hammerhead shark, and the decorative pattern found on a very small fish called a Mandarin. The title of the image, *Clown,* is a result of the very unintentional clown face that can be seen on the shark's head. I noticed it early in my concept sketch; I liked it, and allowed it to remain, hat and all. Some mistakes are just too perfect.

Model: Stacy
Photographer: Craig Tracy

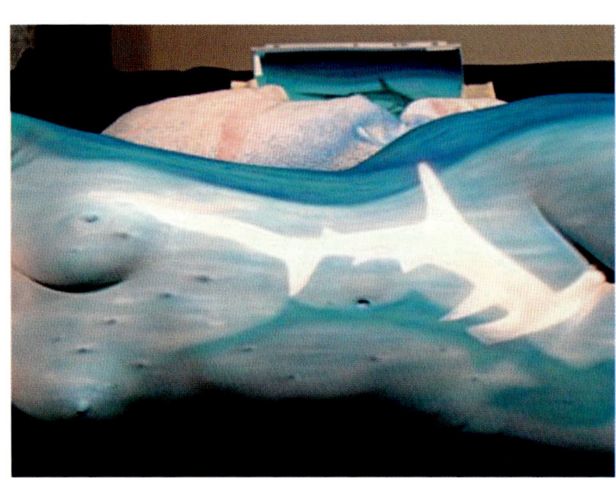 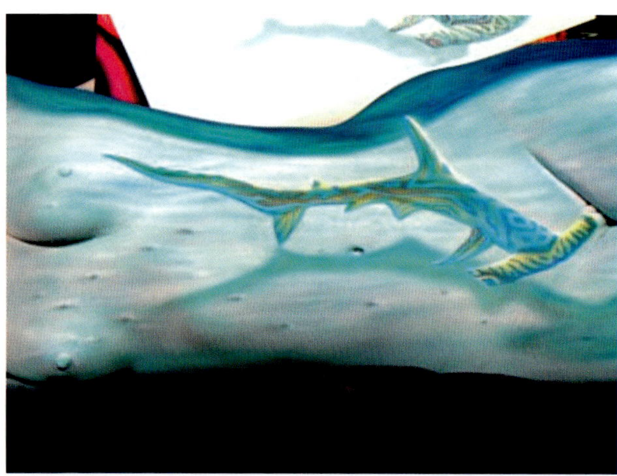 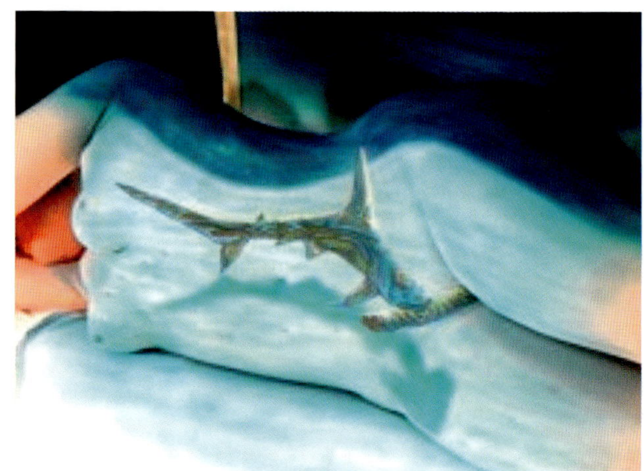

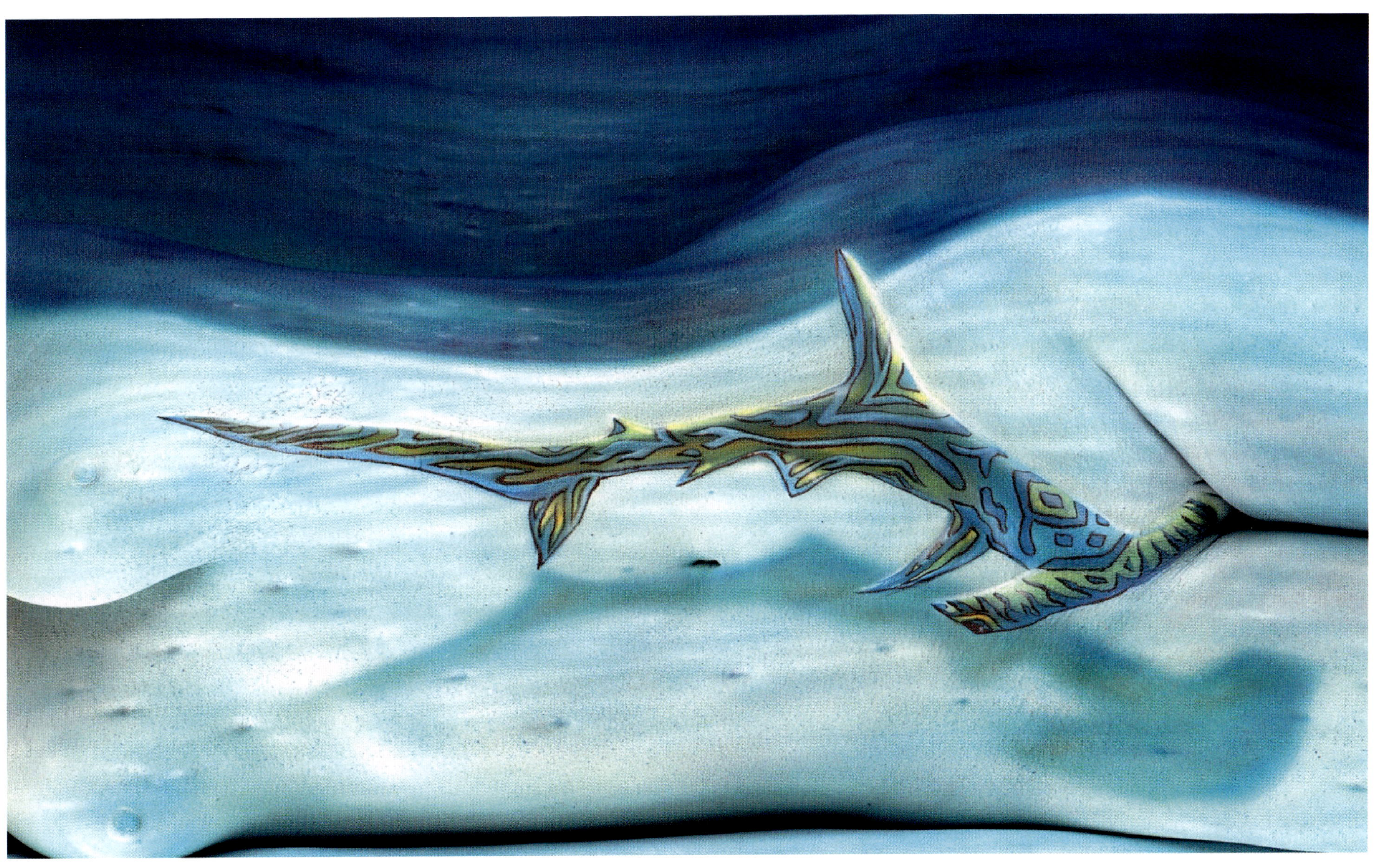

Blessed

Working here with the family as a harmonious unit, I try to convey love and tenderness with both the pose and my use of color. It's very rare to be able to bring new parents and their precious newborn all together into my studio long enough to create a painting that truly is worthy of the effort required. I'm delighted with *Blessed* and its final outcome. I'm also grateful that I'm trusted and respected enough to work with families at such a beautiful and special time. Three to five weeks old is my preference in working with newborns. It is in that very limited time that they are both young enough and old enough to model with such grace and comfort.

Models: The Harris Family
Photographer: Craig Tracy

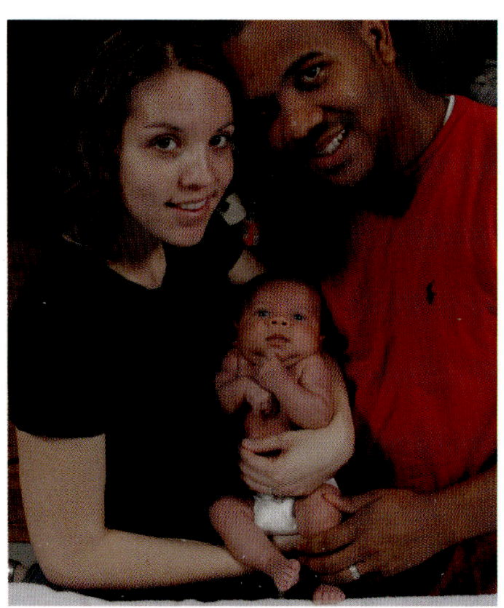
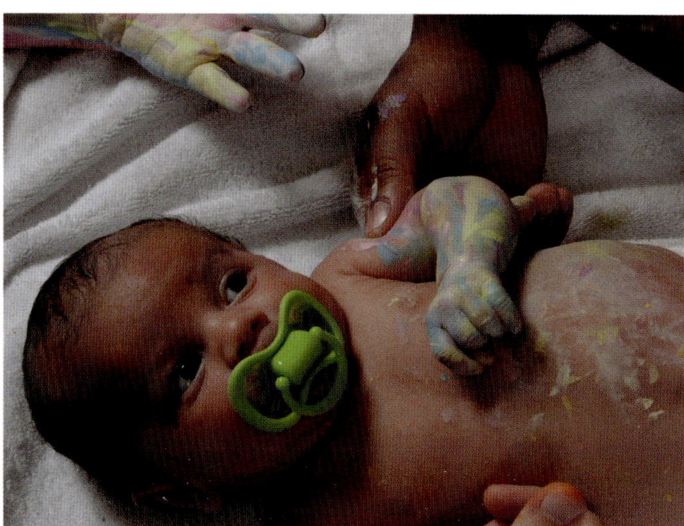
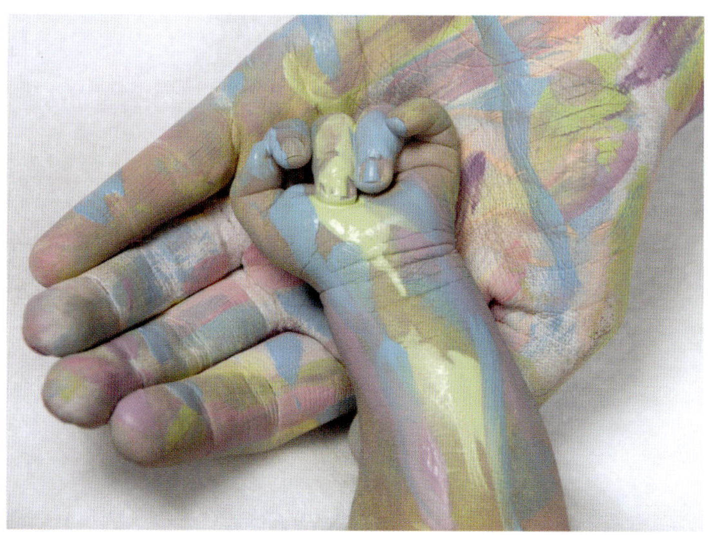

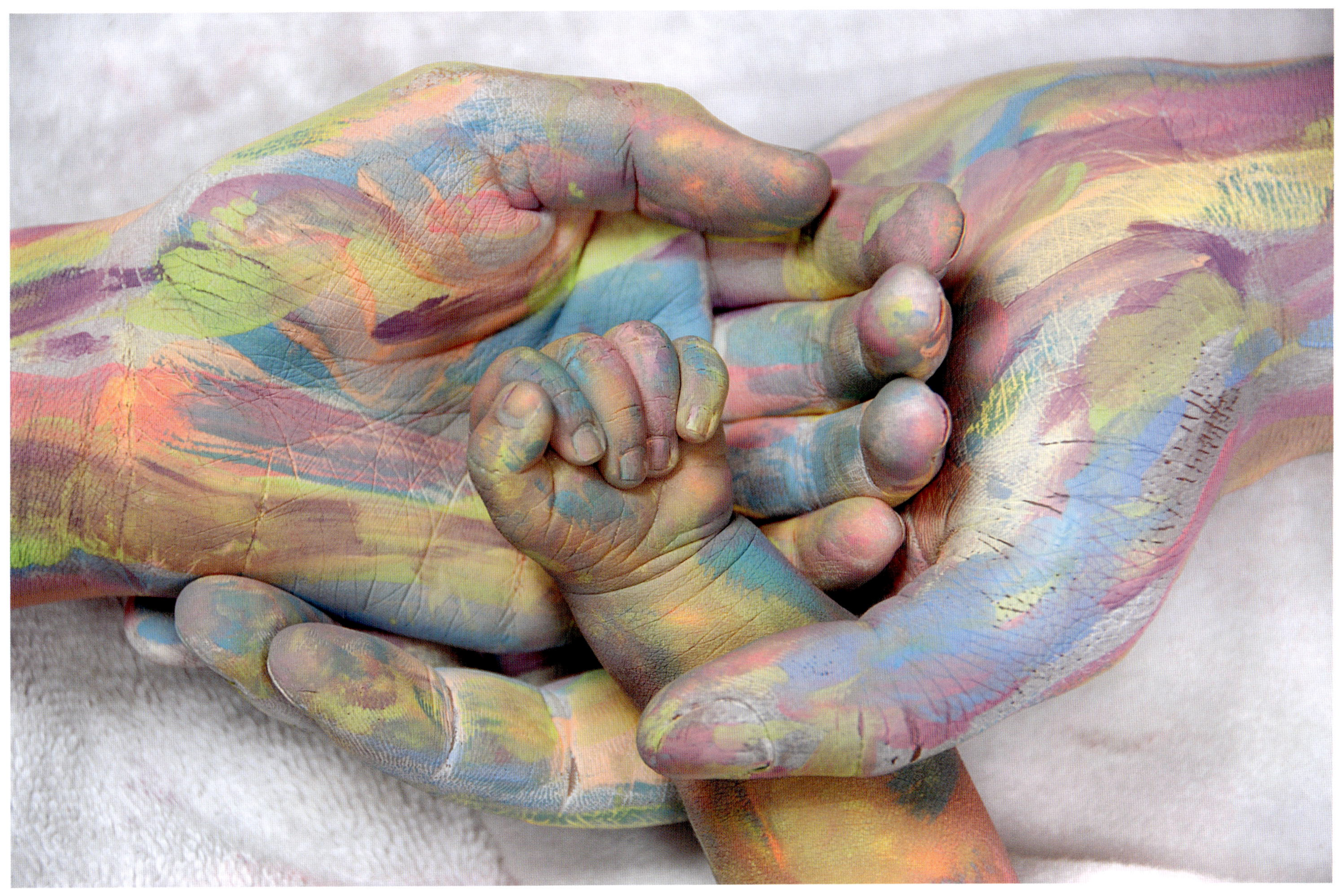

Tweefwog

All elements of this painting merged with grace and splendor. Once completed, this image confirmed within myself that what I was trying to accomplish artistically was valid and worthwhile. I embellished a bit with the addition of violet in this otherwise green on green image. Unfortunately, I don't have a video clip from this project due to the simple fact that I was too "green" myself to bring the camera. This was only the second fine art bodypainting that I had ever done. To this day it is still one of my favorites.

Model: Stacy
Photographer: Chris Mathews

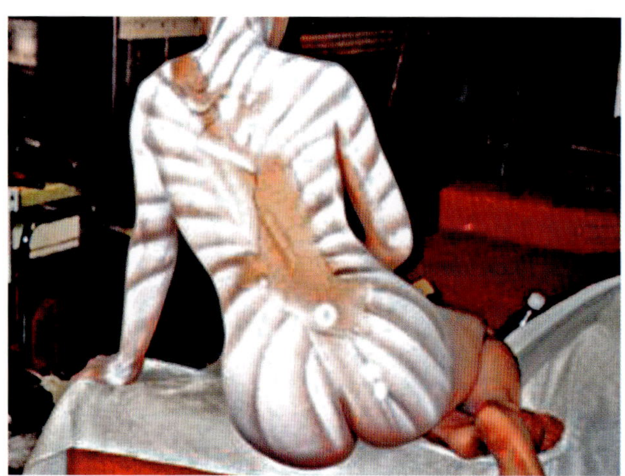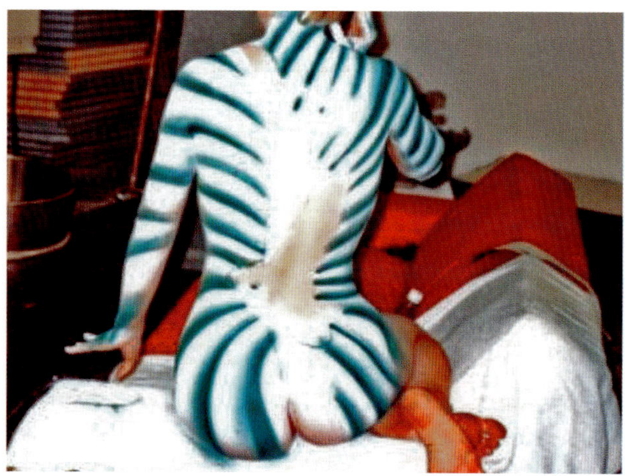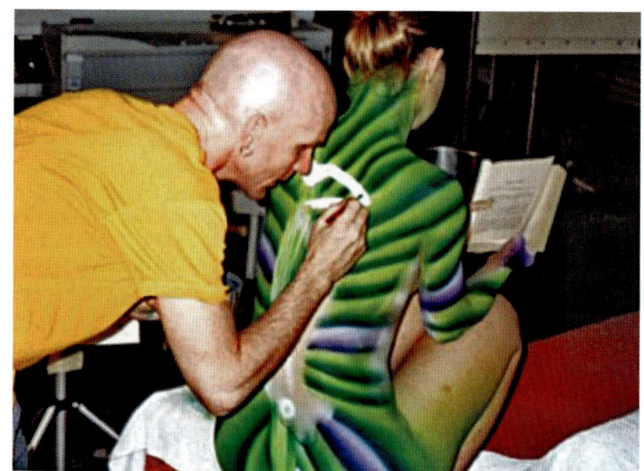

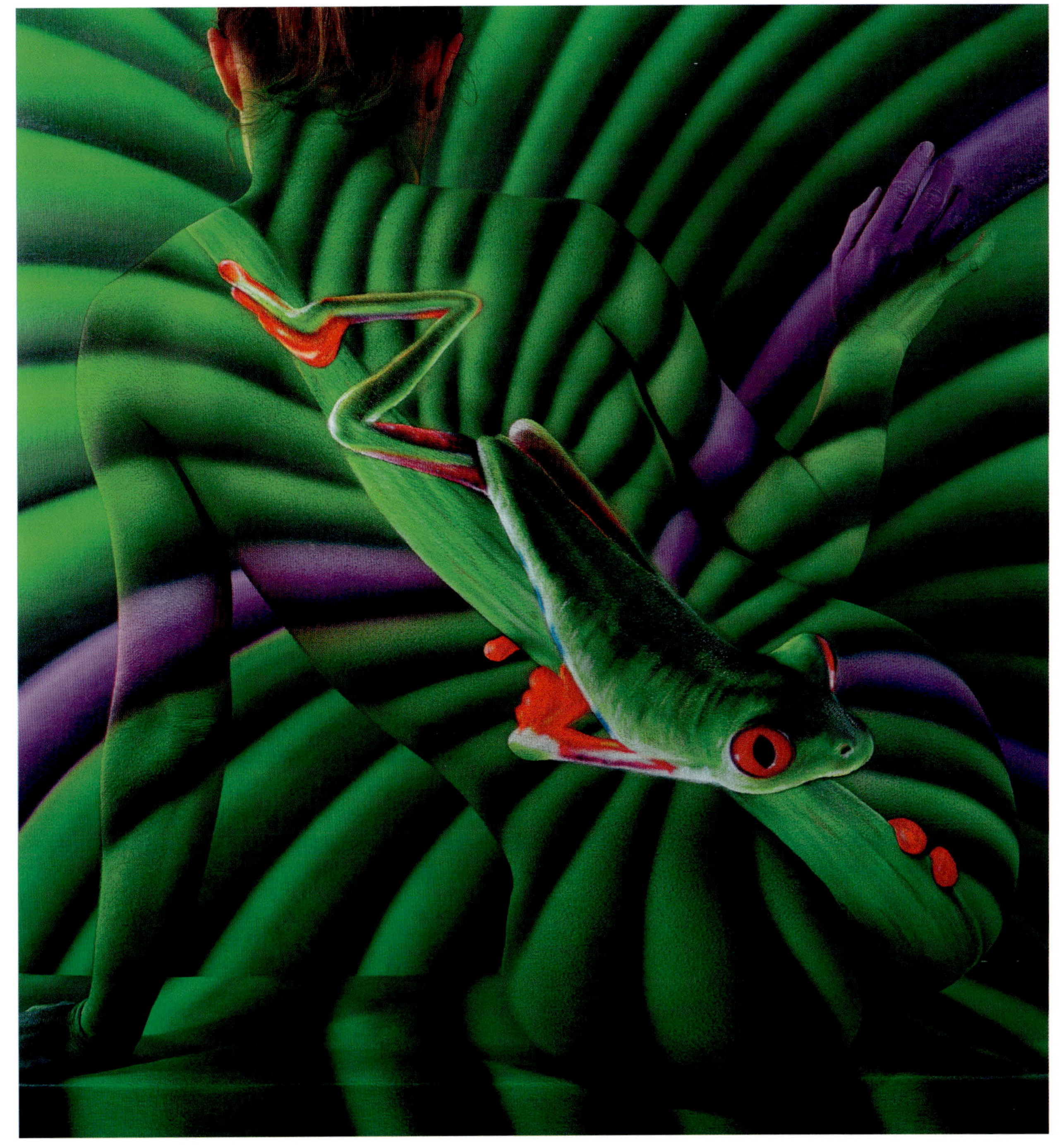

Three Weeks

Each day has its own feeling, has its own flavor, and in this case, its own color and shape. Day to night and night to day, each changing and telling its own individual tale. I love this image for its style and joy. I love it for its distinction and its dance. Twenty-one days. Twenty-one nights. Three weeks distilled into one sweet visual moment. I love this image.

Model: Mea
Photographer: Libbie Allen

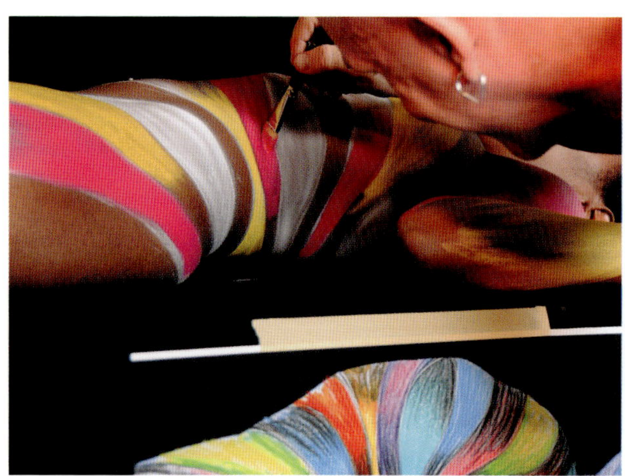
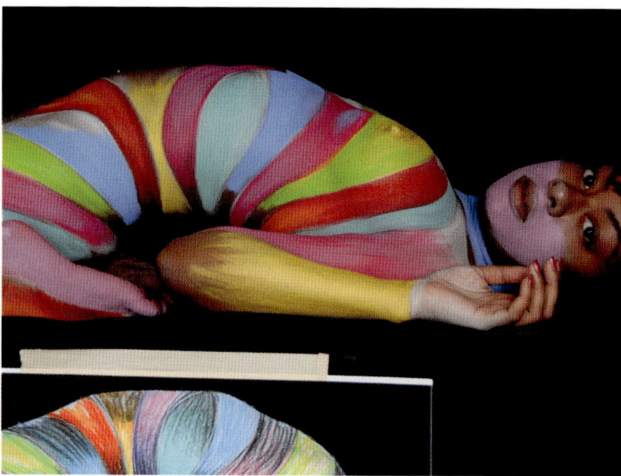
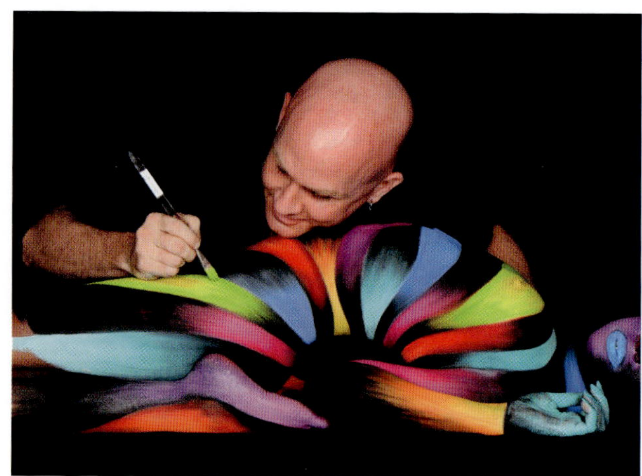

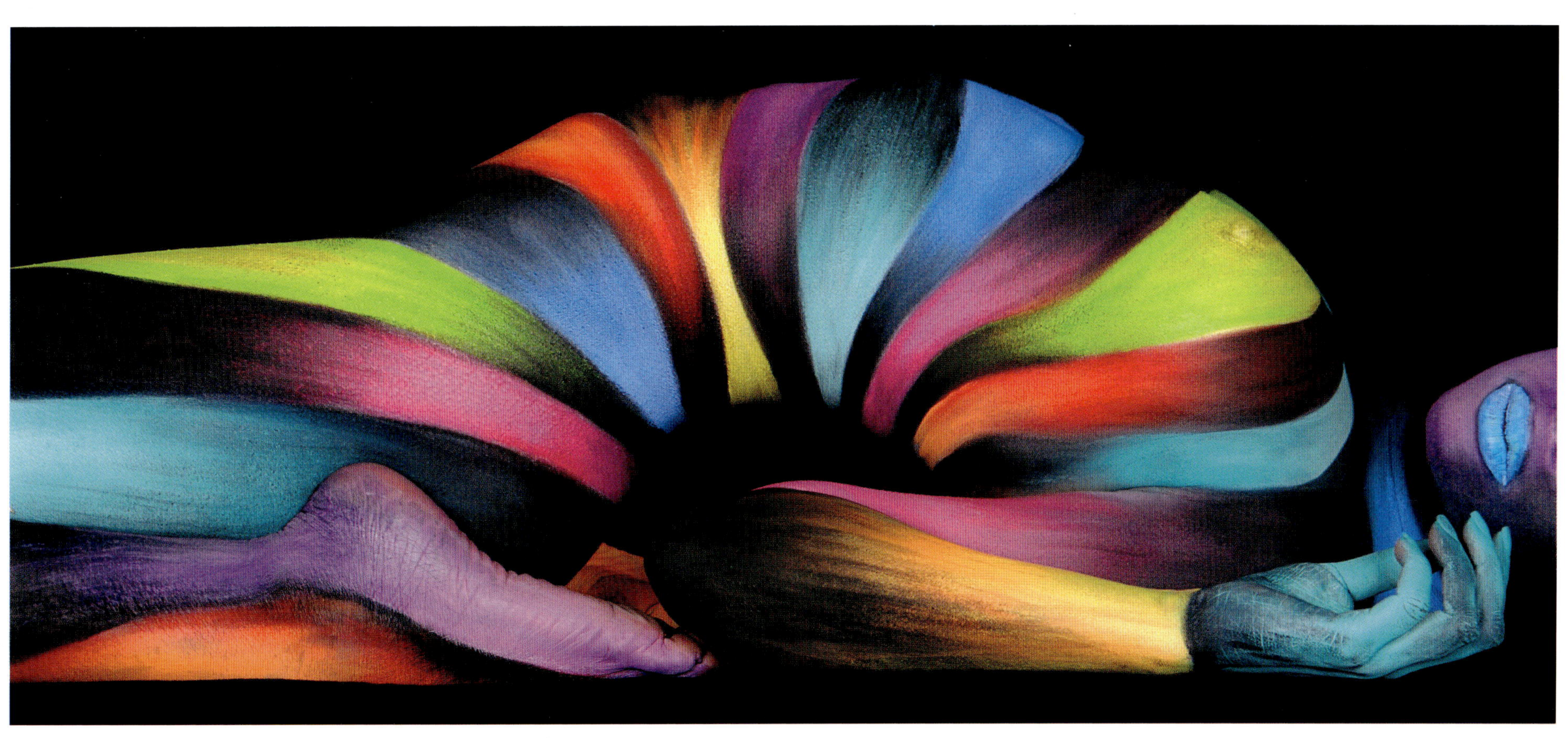

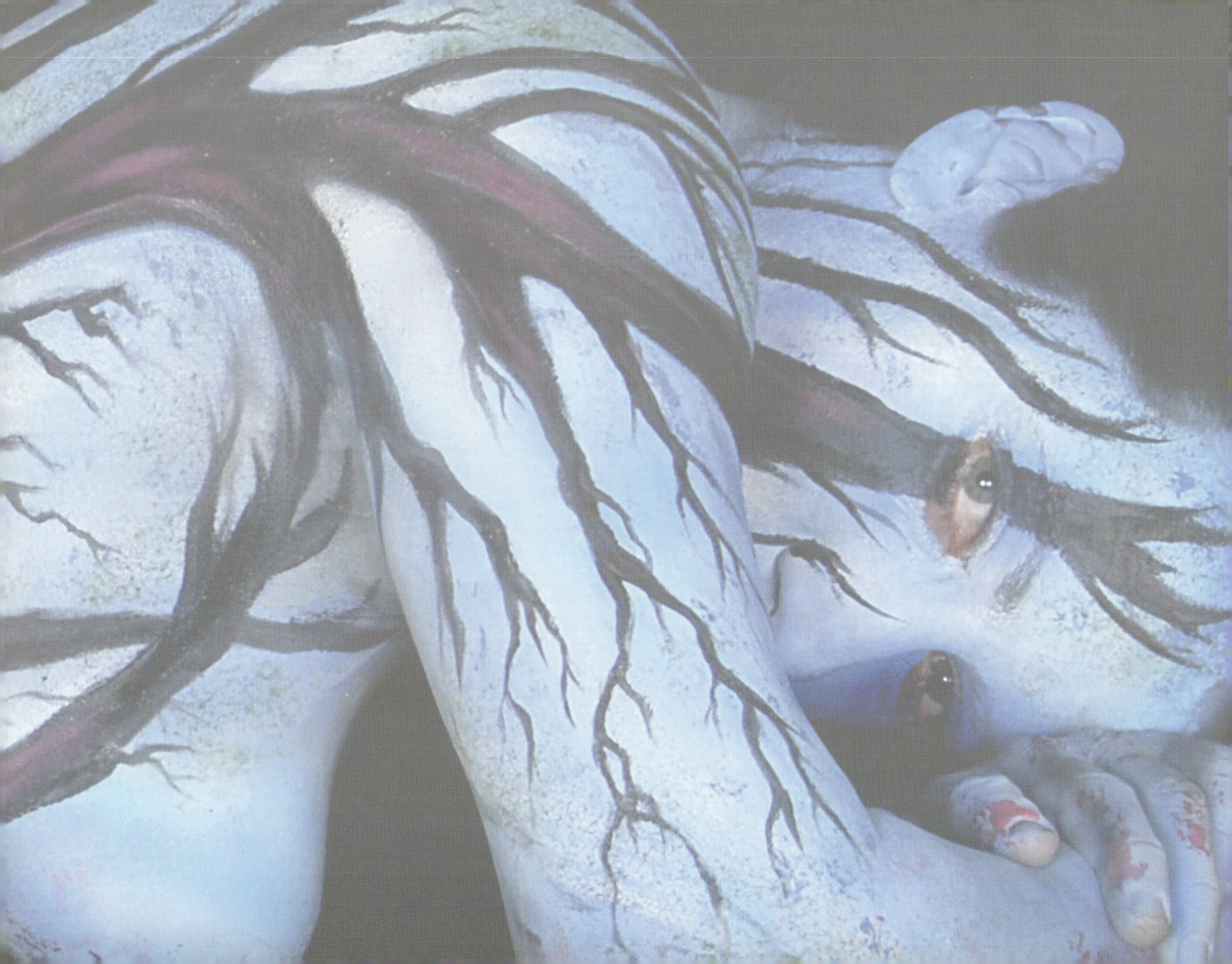

Kindred Spirit

The composition of this piece was designed organically and required little effort or thought. These lines flowed from my hands as though I were merely the interpreter between vision and reality. A mix of paintbrush, airbrush, and sponge was used to keep things interesting. I often use mixed media when painting a body. Meg was the perfect model for this piece and the image created here speaks of her growth, strength, complexity, and mysterious self.

Model: Meg
Photographer: Craig Tracy

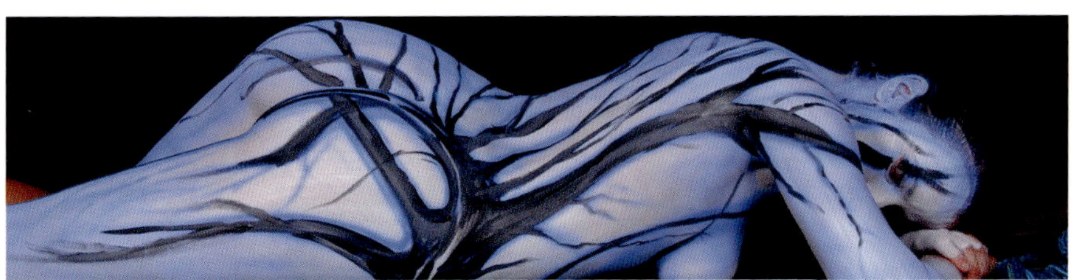

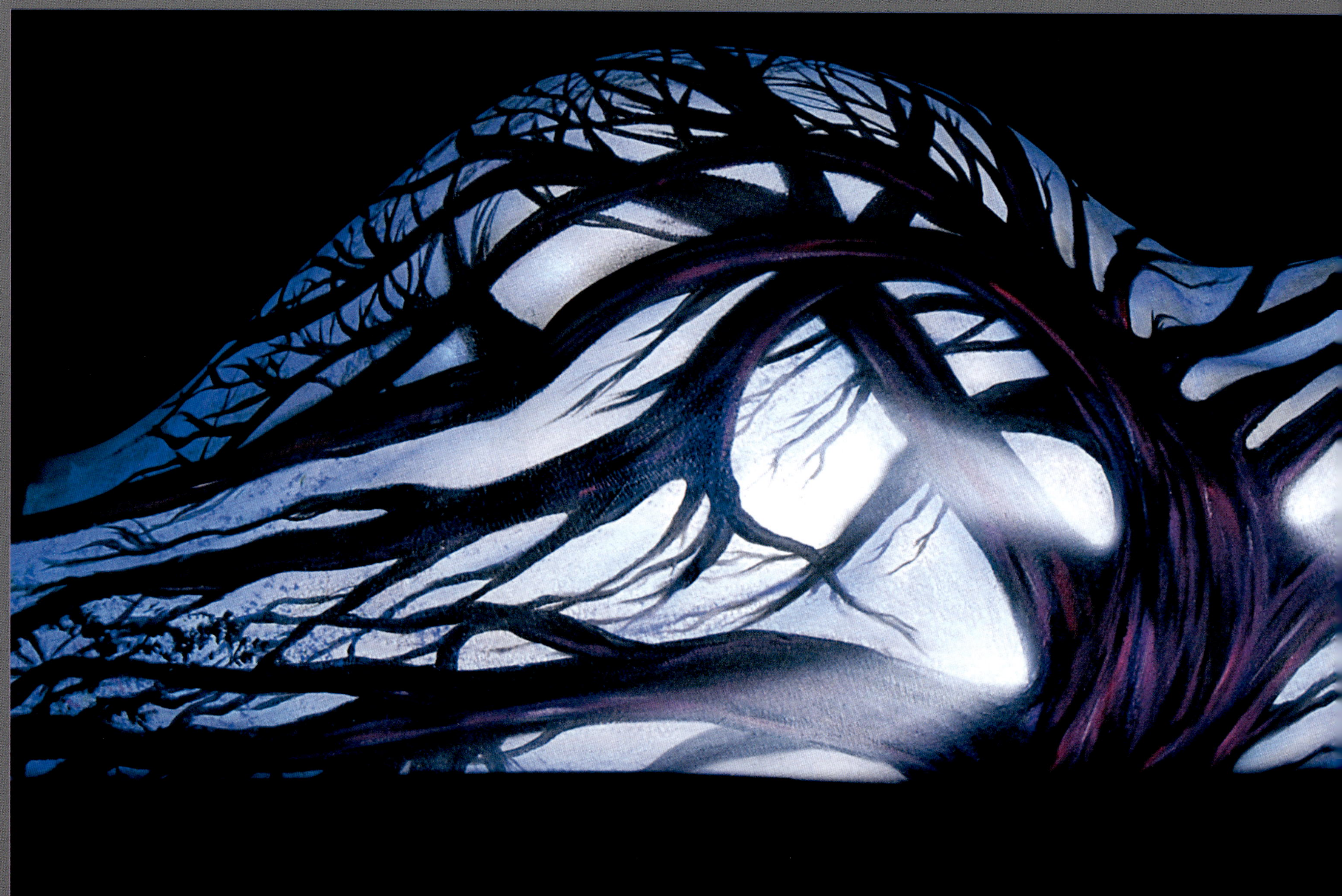

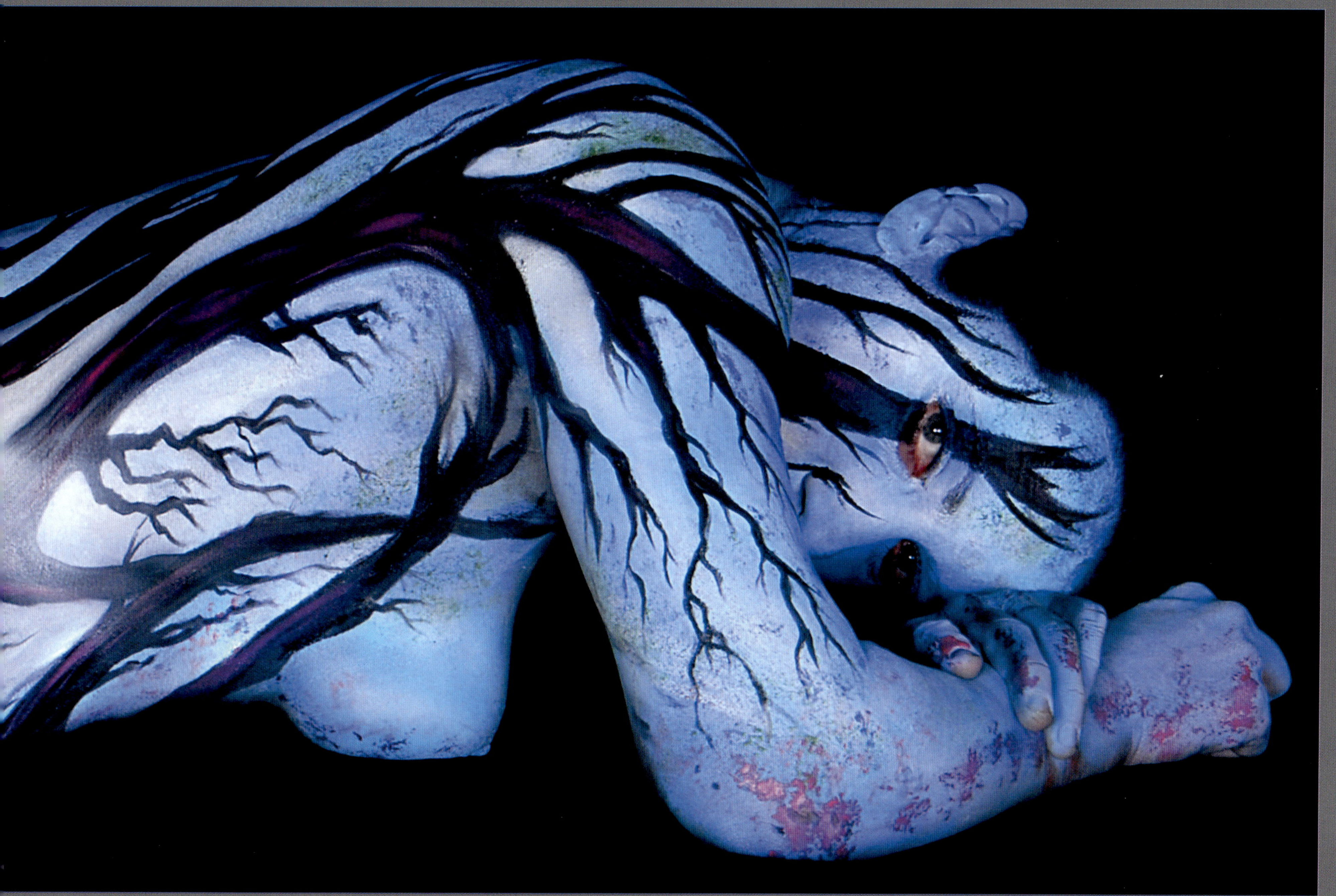

Salvation

This unique bodypainting was created to increase awareness and benefit a cause that is near to my heart. Tigers have always been my favorite animal and when asked to aid in the effort to protect, repopulate, and re-wild this, the most endangered tiger in the world, I immediately said yes. Only 100 South China Tigers are reported to remain alive and if my bodypainting can help increase that number by one, then I'll have lived with purpose. This painting was also inspired by the beautiful photograph by renowned photographer Thomas Mangelsen.

Models: Mary, Lauren, & Jessica
Photographer: Mark Giaviano

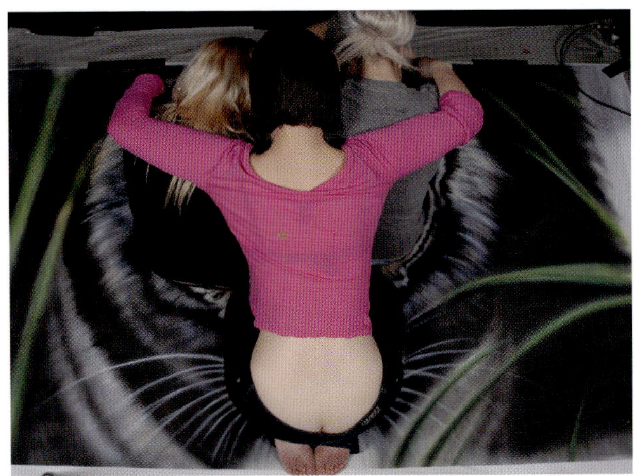
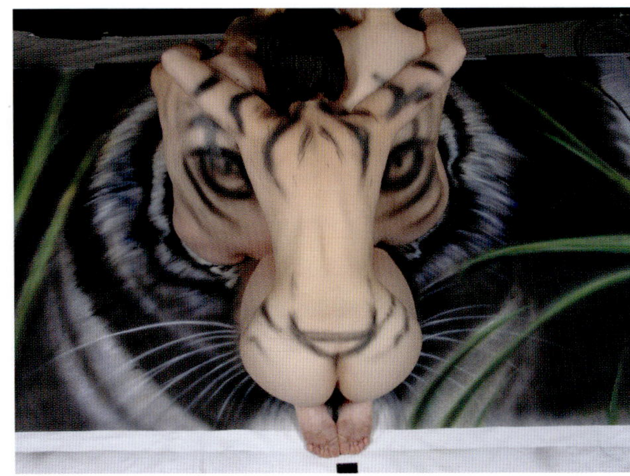
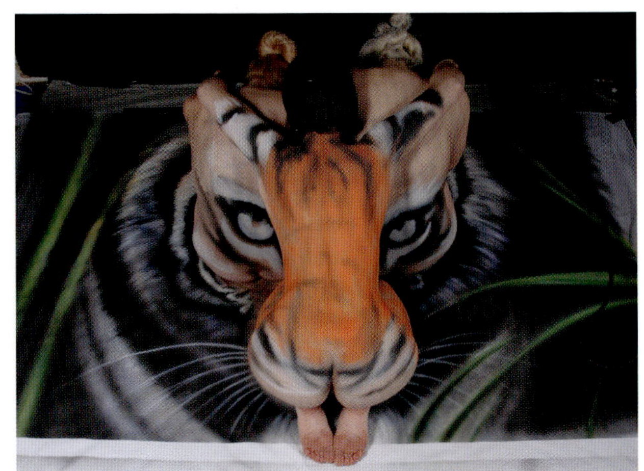

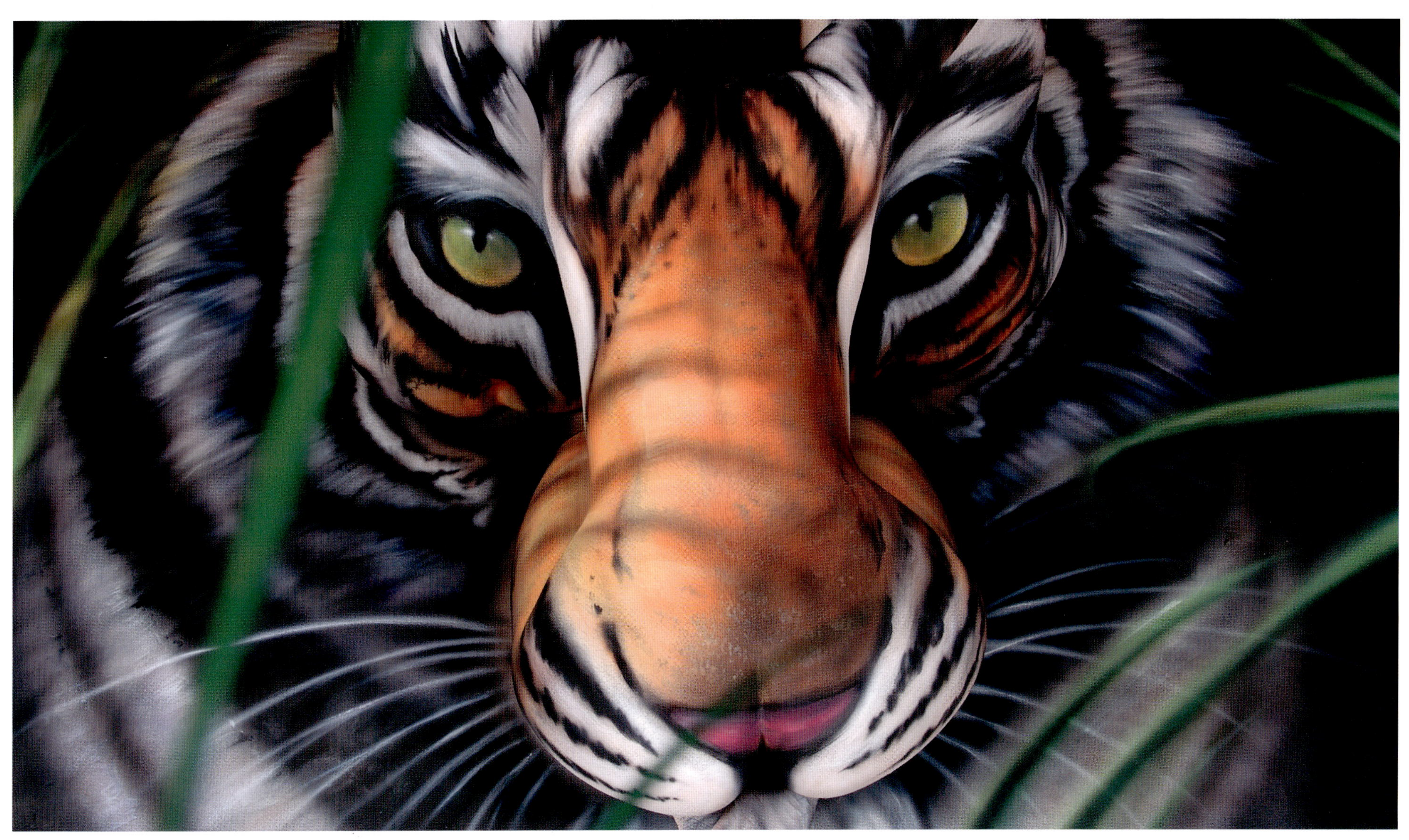

Pieces

Hand-cut puzzle pieces complement the composition in a painting that was first inspired by the pose and then by my lovely model. I consider this painting to be one of my semi-spontaneous images, as I had designed certain elements in advance but I also allowed other aspects to unfold as the painting progressed. Most of the shadows seen in this image are painted and not lit, as is the case in the vast majority of my finished works.

Model: Dani
Photographer: Craig Tracy

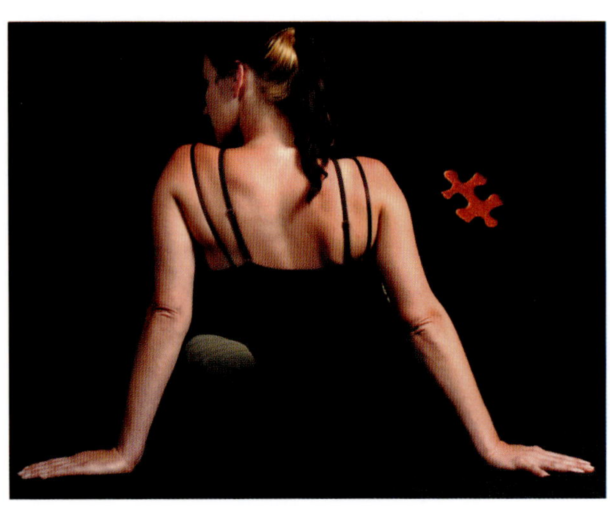
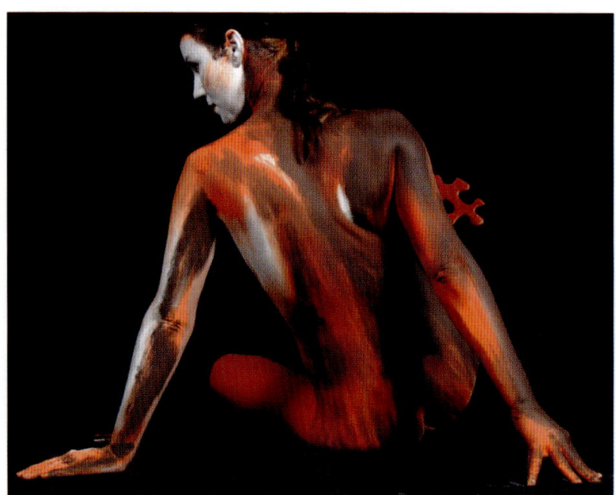
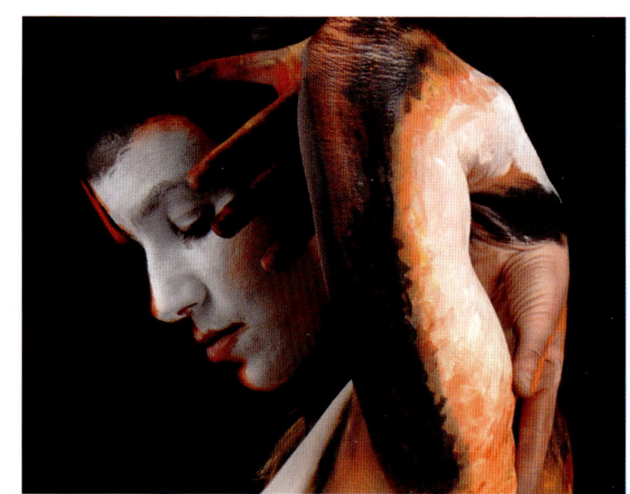

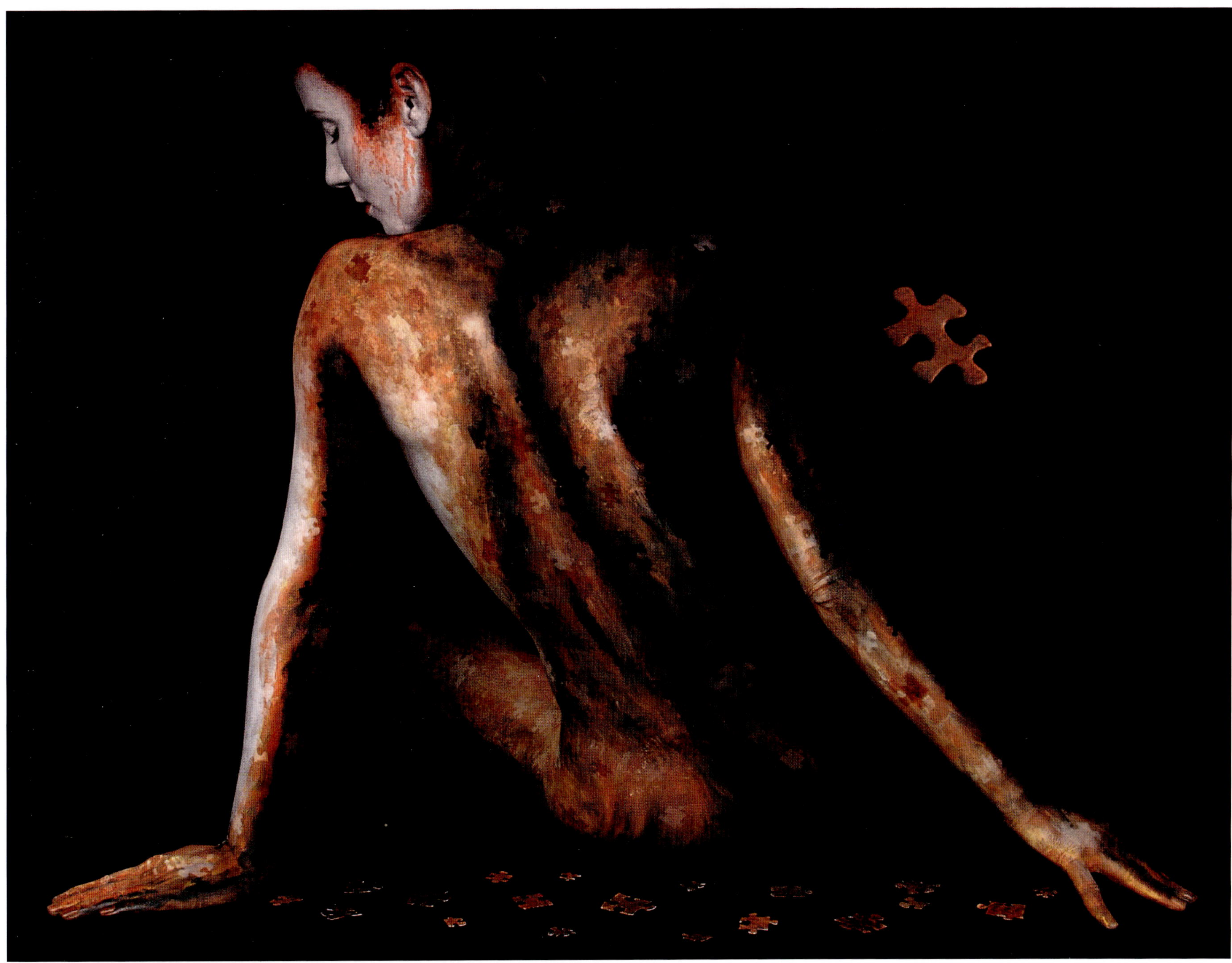

The Artist

I had attempted this painting twice before. Both, unfortunately, ended with humbling futility. I've learned to have a secondary plan when painting precious newborns. Plan B is what I had made of my first two attempts. Both were special and both were successful but I still needed to realize my original vision. *The Artist* is a mini miracle and the much needed closure and completion of the concept. I'm so very pleased with the result of that very special day in my studio.

Models: Leslie, Justin, & Baby Sydney
Photographer: Craig Tracy

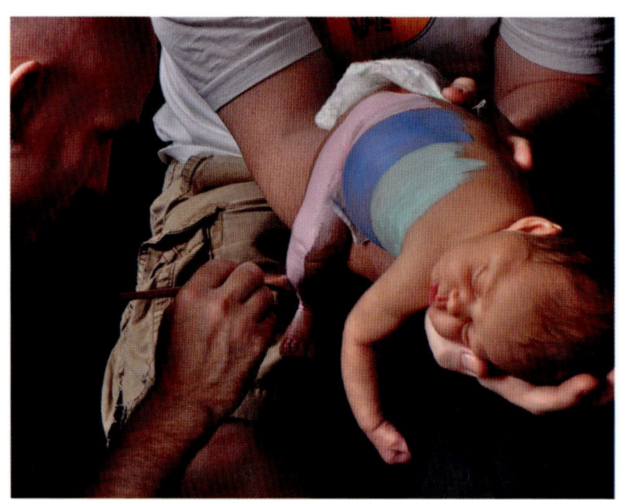 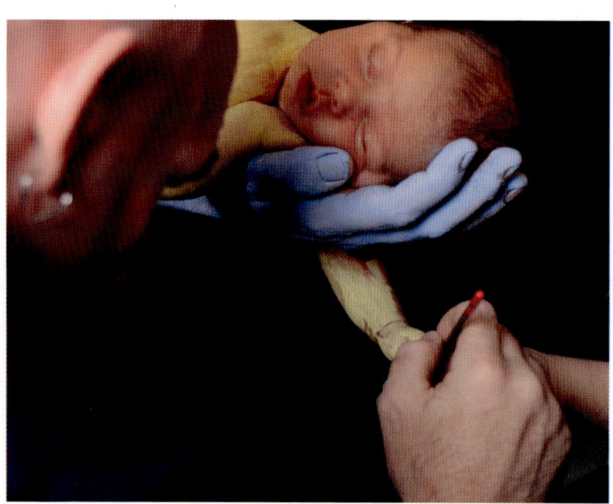 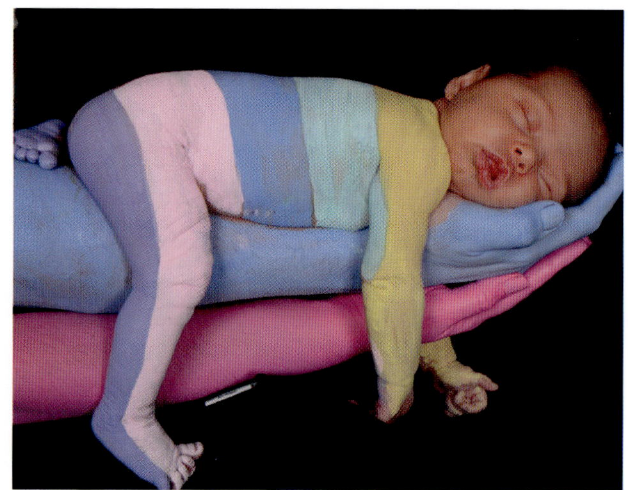

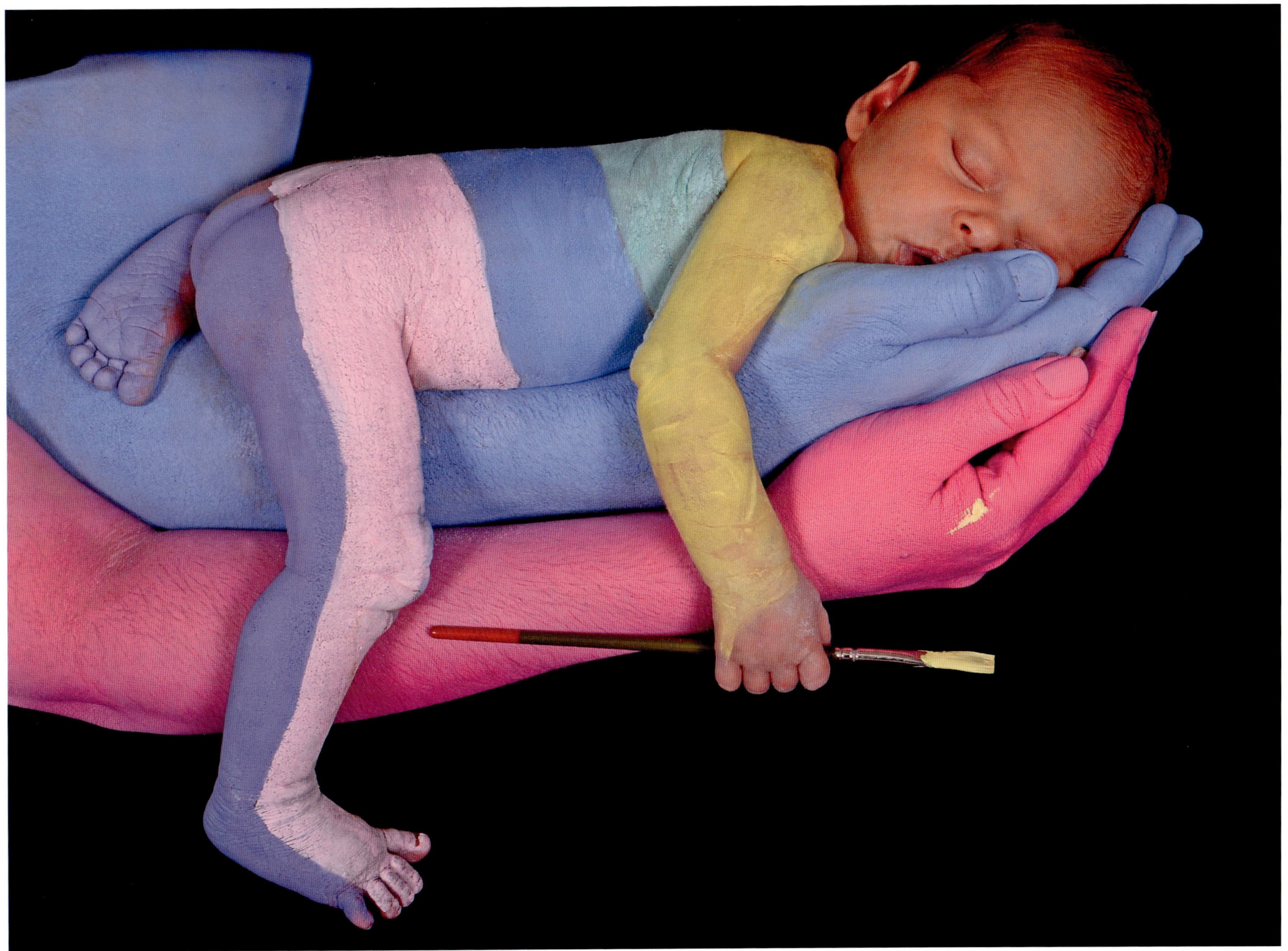

Renda

Renda deals with a combination of elements from the ancient hieroglyphic to the circuitry of the very modern computer, electricity, and femininity. Cold and metallic is merged here with the warm and seductive. Lips, lashes, and fingertips dance with color while the purity of her hands boldly frame the undeniable face of a goddess. This was the very first time that I allowed lips to be painted as lips in one of my designs and the five panel composition felt like the most natural solution to what otherwise would have been an abundance of negative space.

Model: Renda
Photographer: Libbie Allen

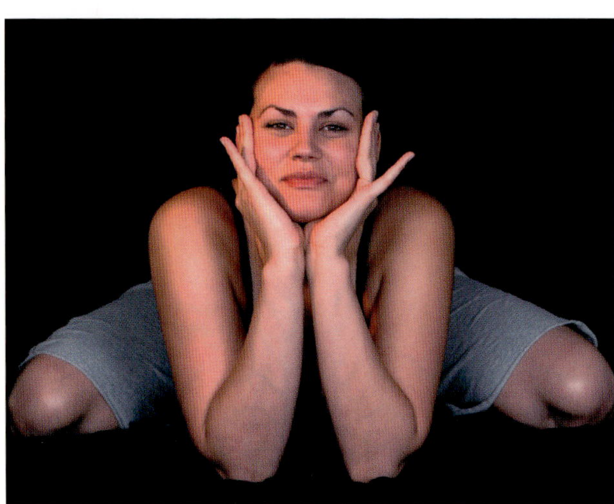 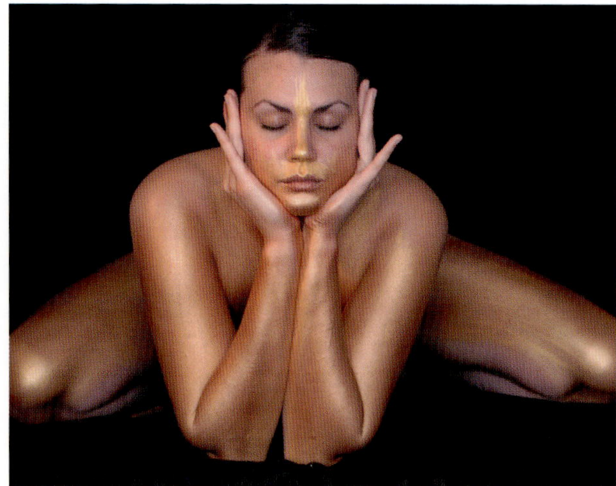 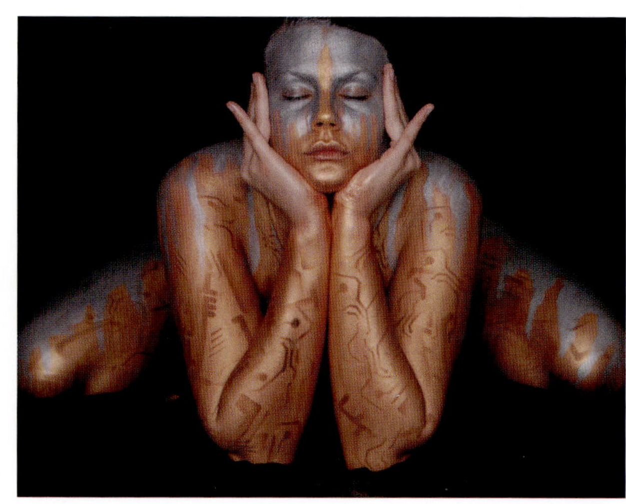

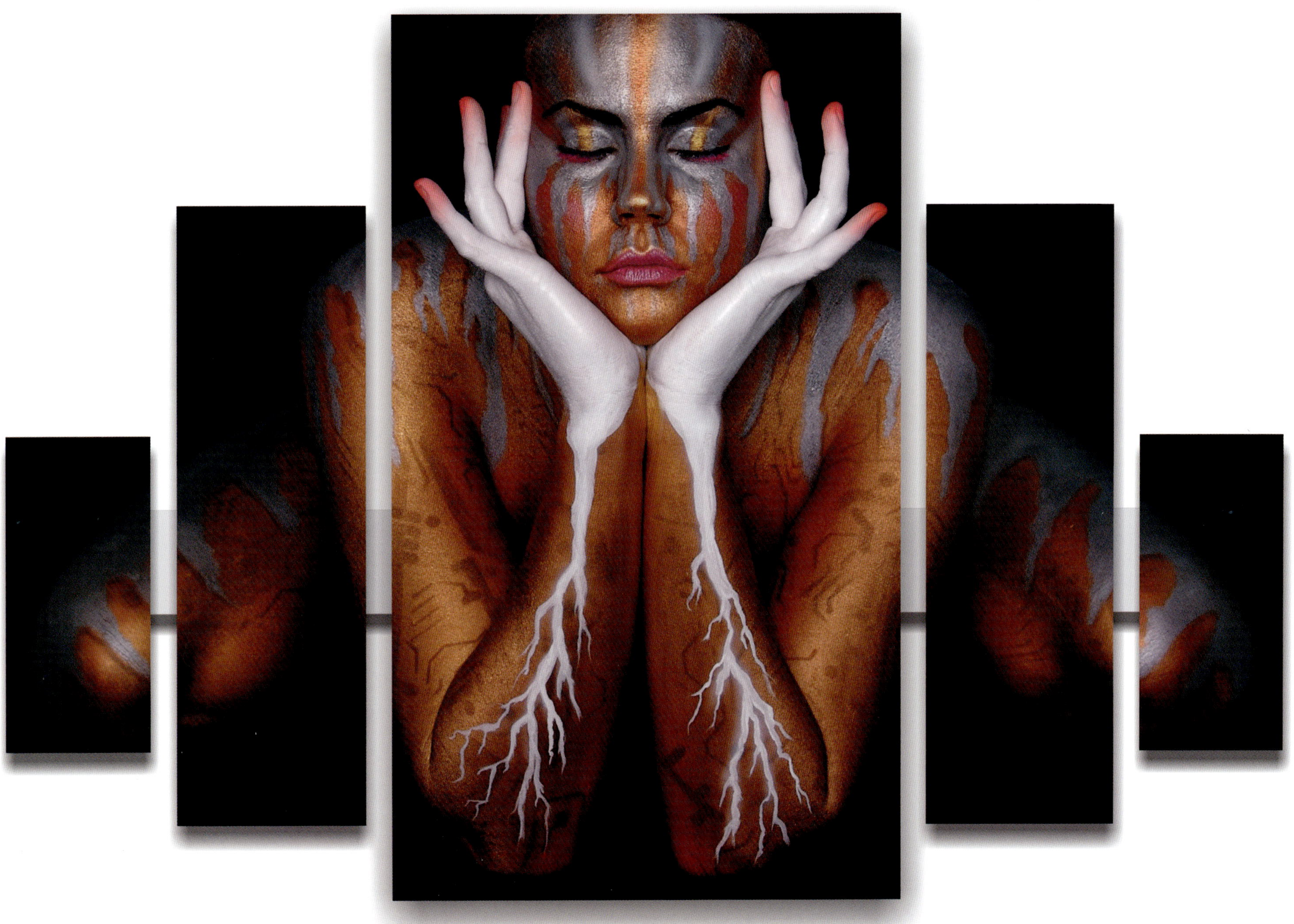

Tricksy

Painted live during a gallery show in Anaheim, California, *Tricksy* is a fantasy creature inspired by color and feminine dreams. Fuchsia and teal cascade one after the other in succession to dance magic into the feeling of this image. Its design was born just twenty-four hours before I first touched paint to skin. Its semi-spontaneous nature made it as fun to paint as it is to view and it wouldn't surprise me at all if I paint a few more that have a similar feeling or vibe.

Model: Brittany
Photographer: Craig Tracy

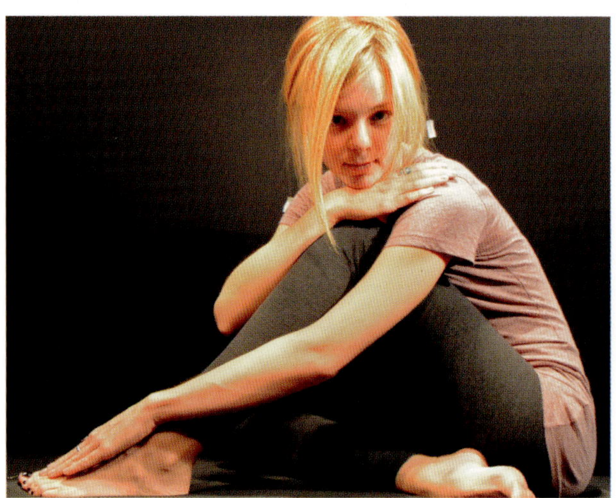 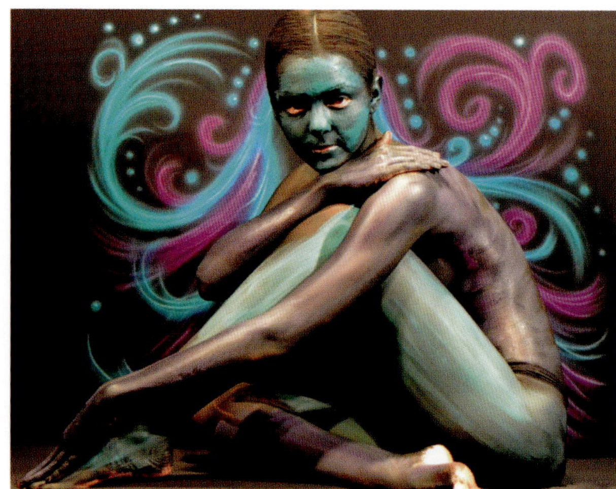 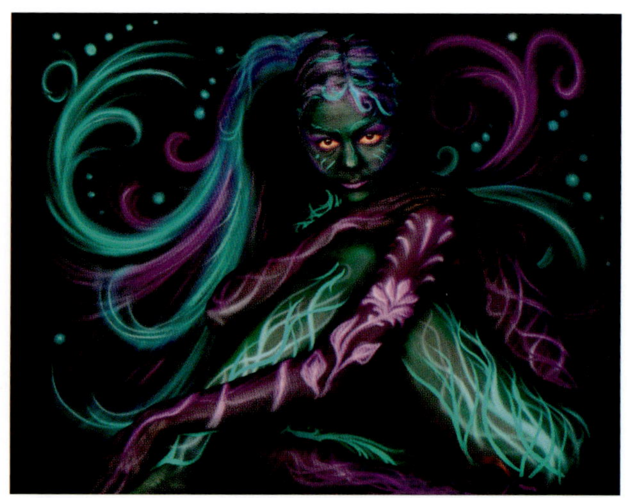

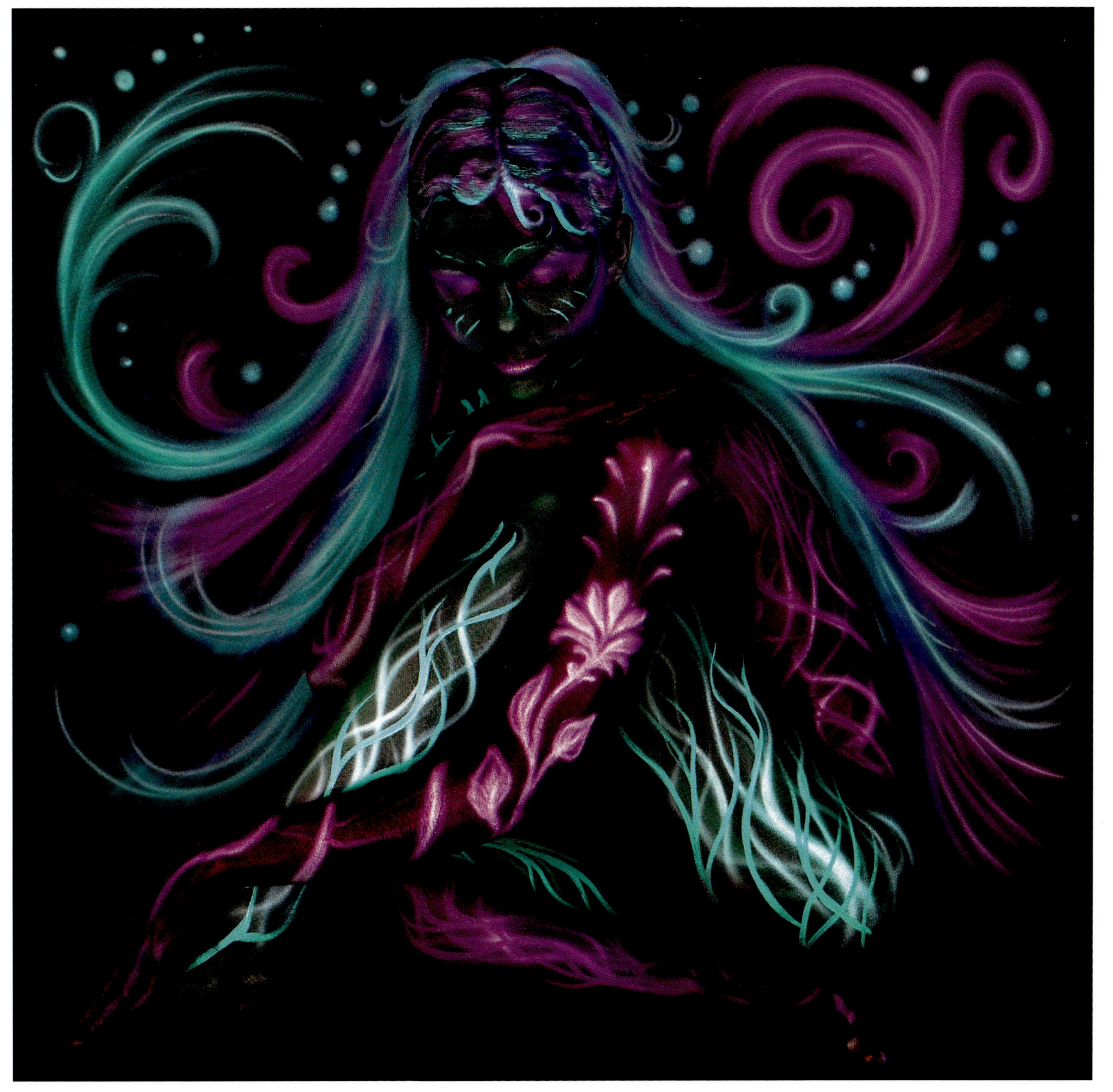

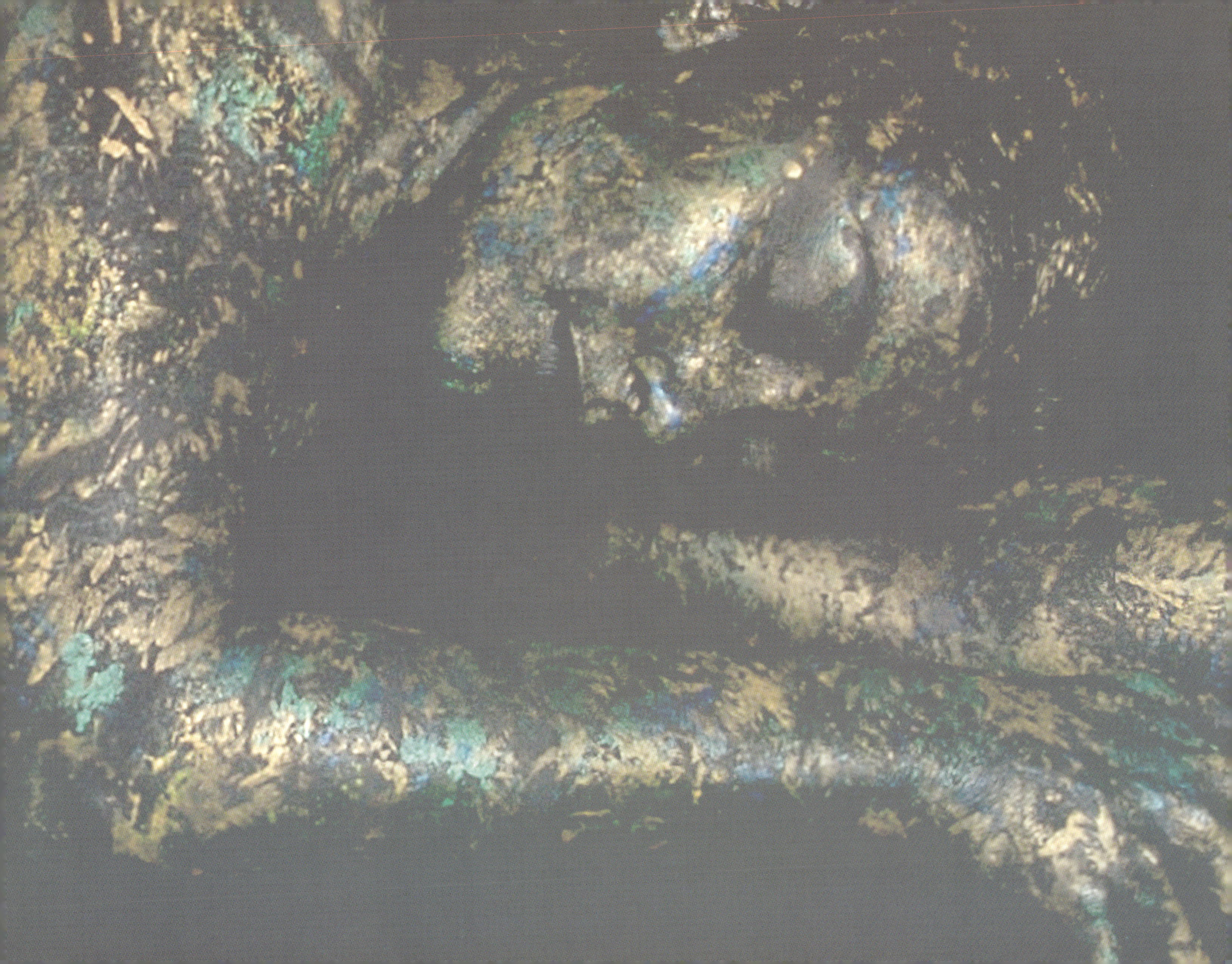

One Seventeen A.M.

I had fallen in love with this pose before I had ever met my model or designed this painting. Another of my portfolio images titled *Yes* also comes from this painting session. Paintbrush, airbrush, and sponge were all used here with sponge being the most obvious. The title comes from the exact time that I captured this most unique creation.

Model: Natalie
Photographer: Craig Tracy

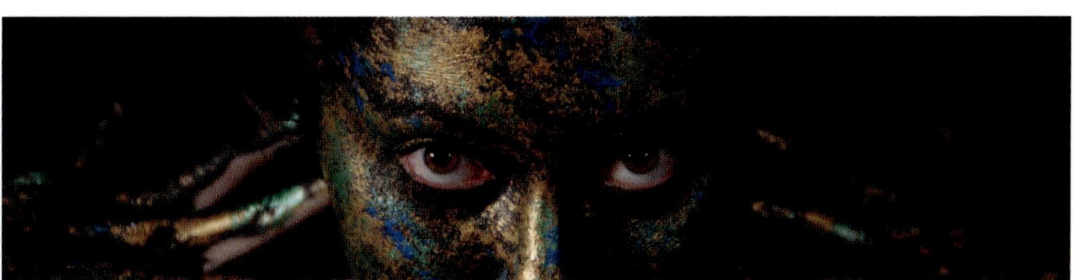

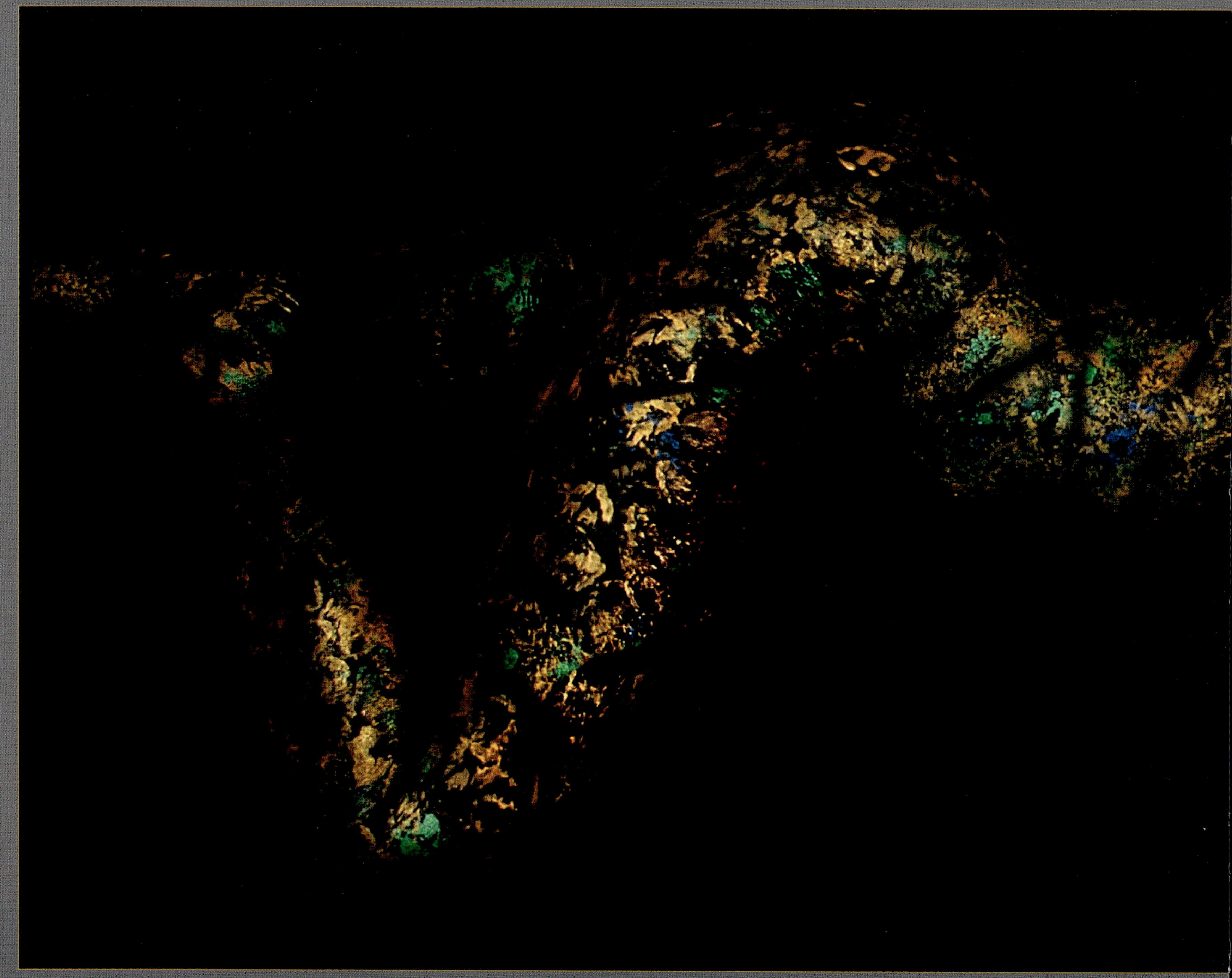

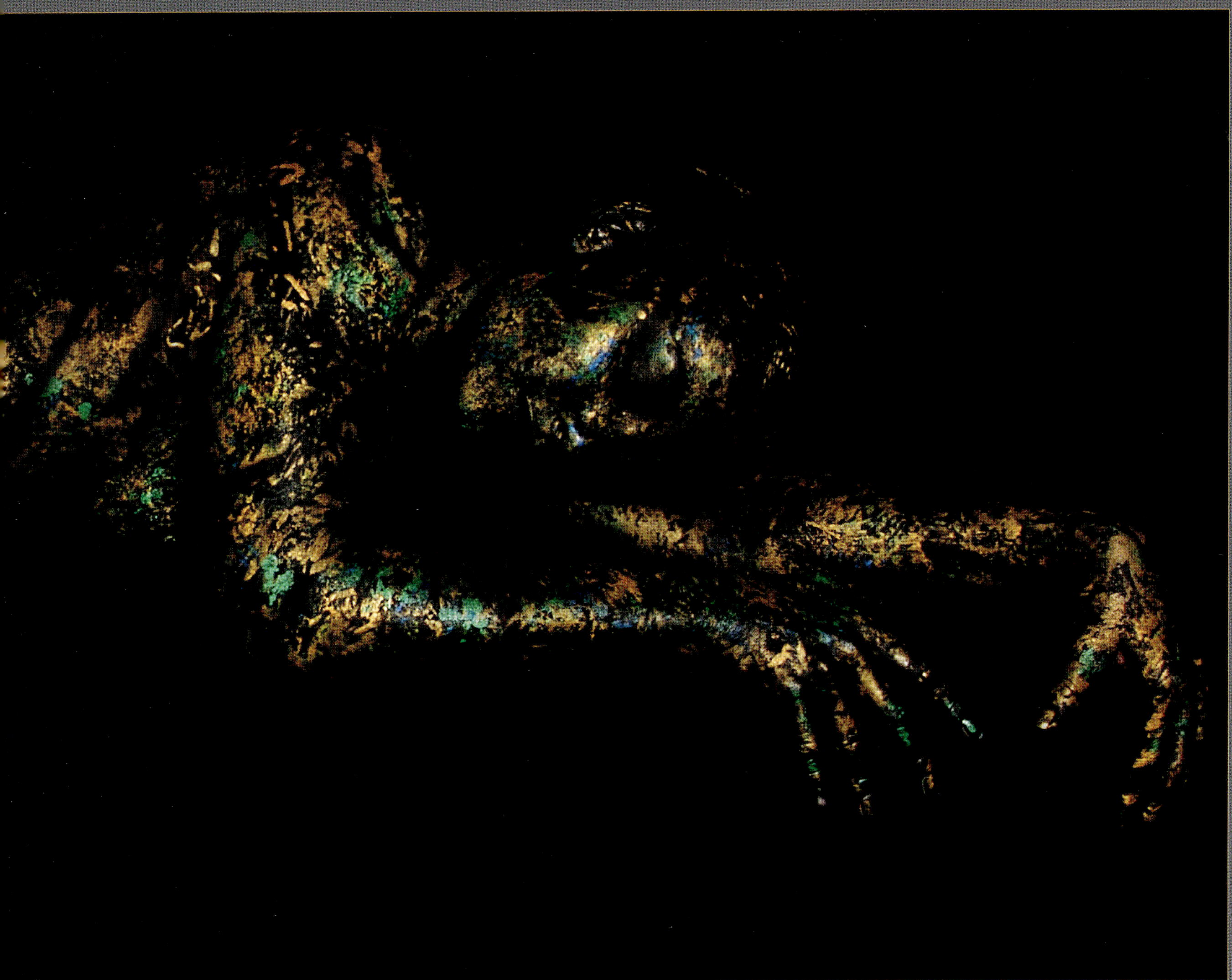

Firm

Spontaneity has a definite place in my work and *Firm* is a prime example. This painting was never planned or even imagined, but rather born from my attempt to make something substantial from what otherwise was frivolous and playful. Four complete bodies were painted that very late night in my studio in what was an impromptu jam session including the artist as model. I directed this image out of frustration with all that had come before it. This image is a personal favorite.

Models: Craig and Bean
Photographer: Craig Morse

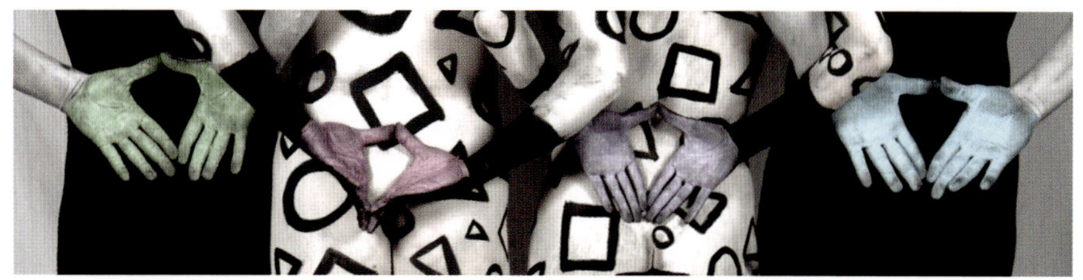

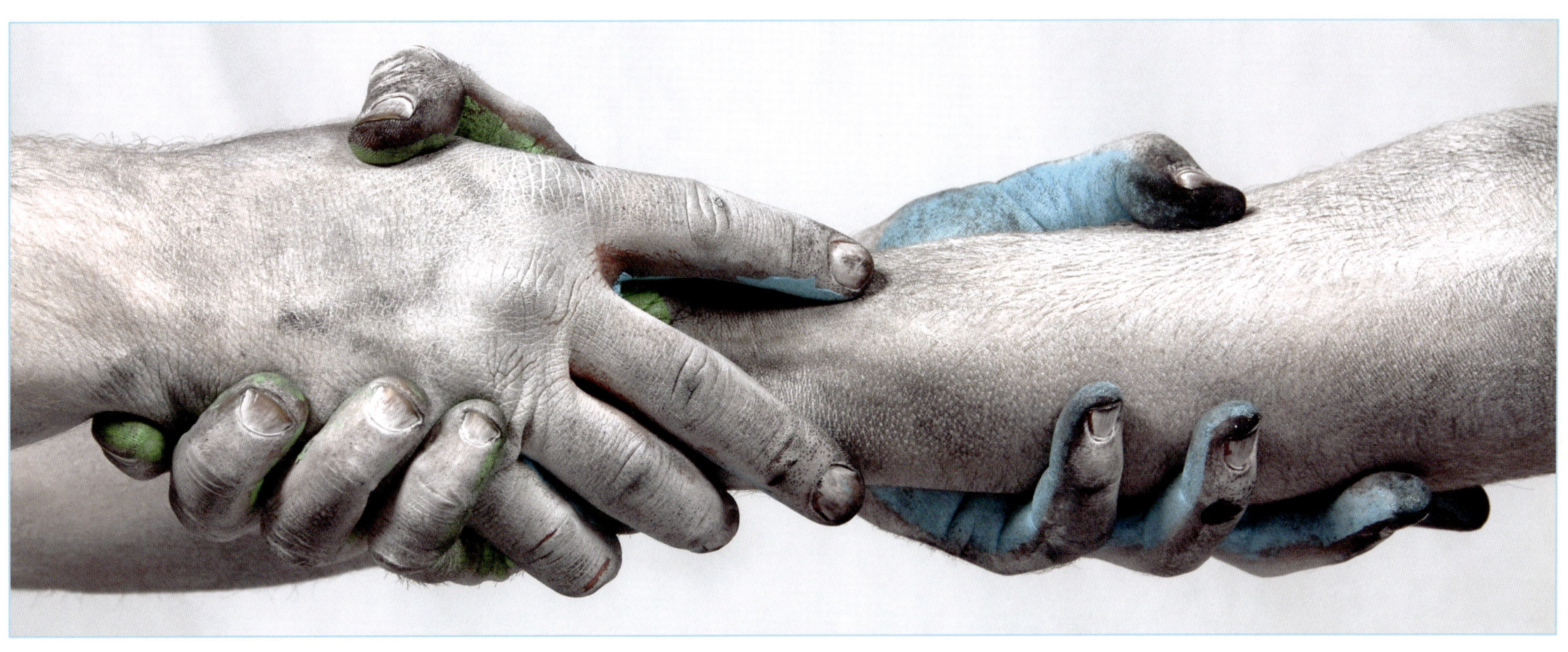

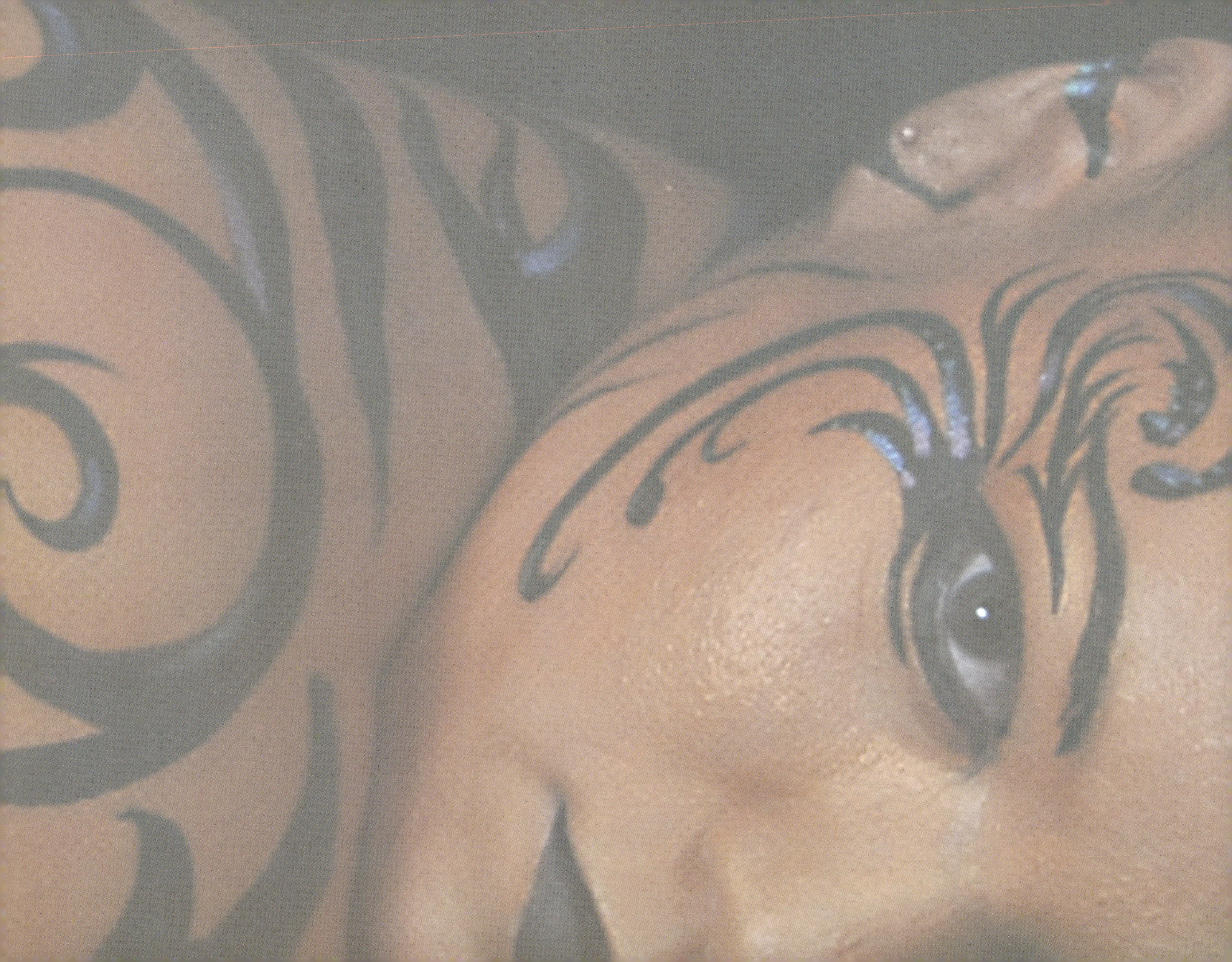

Chosen One

I met my model for this piece several years before we ever worked together. Her unique shape offered me both challenge and dynamic possibilities. With each of my paintings I try to explore uncharted territories with regard to style, design, technique, color, and shape. *Chosen One* balances, provokes, and delights us with a fluid feminine ease.

Model: Carla
Photographer: Craig Tracy

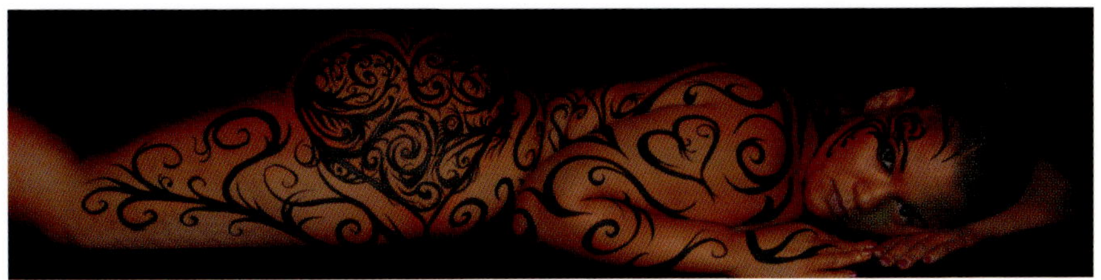

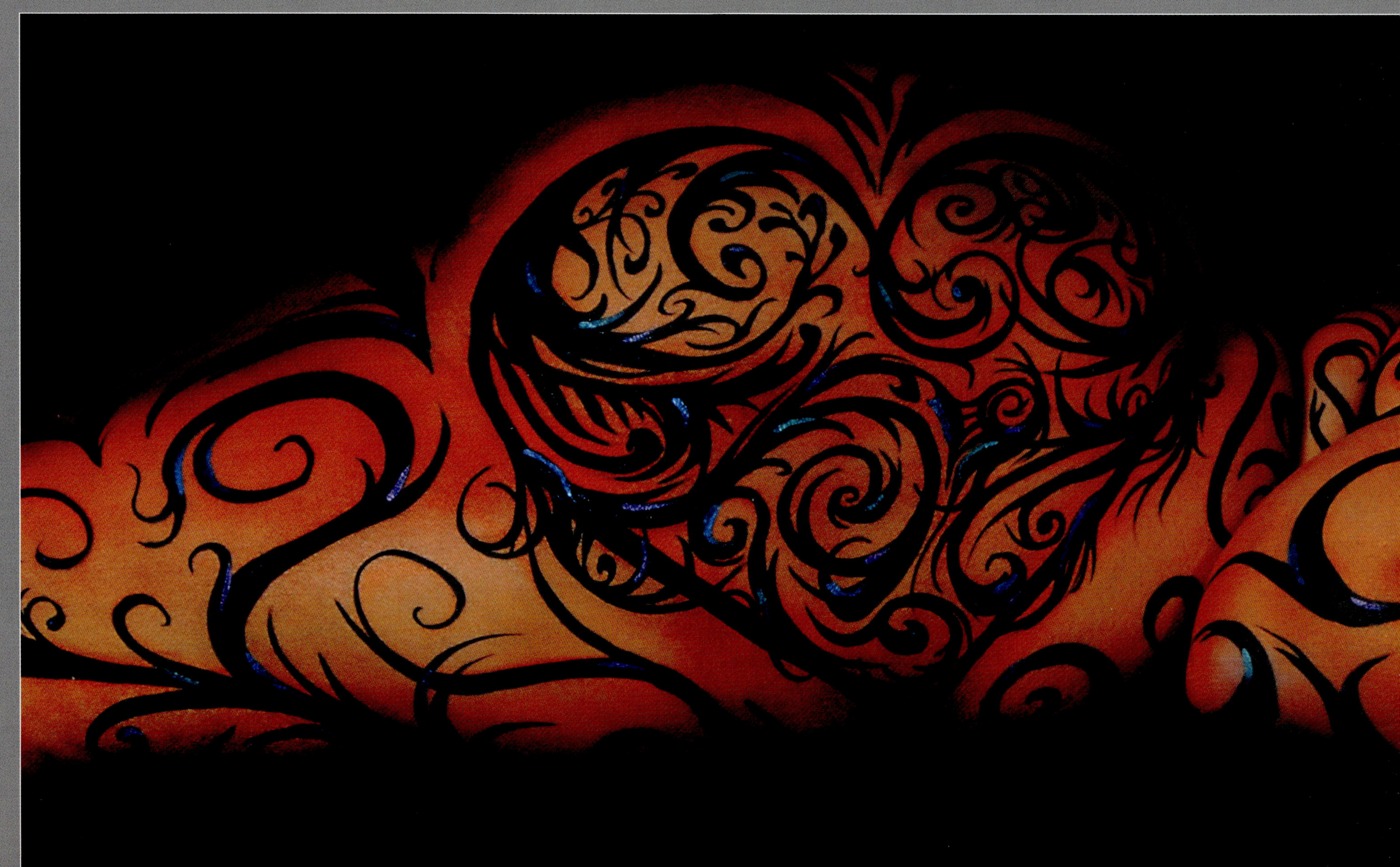

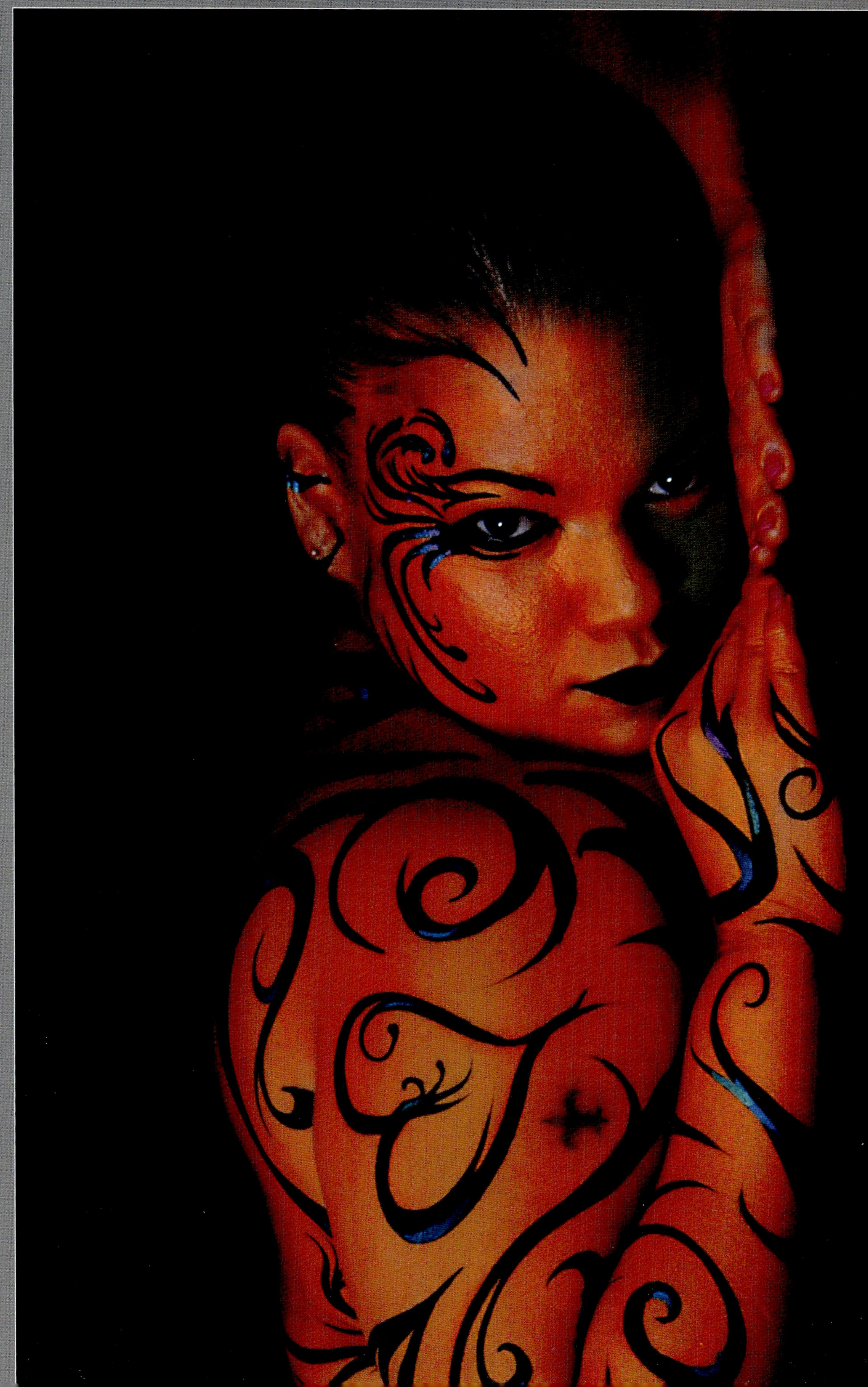

Gaia

This image was painted live during a gallery show that I did in Prince George, British Columbia, Canada. I wanted to create an image filled with vibrant color to contrast the then early winter white and grey of Prince George. My love of trees has lead me to painting them more than any other single subject. *Gaia* deals with the living and the dead, the young and the old, the dark and the light, the rooted and the transient.

Model: Carmen
Photographer: Craig Tracy

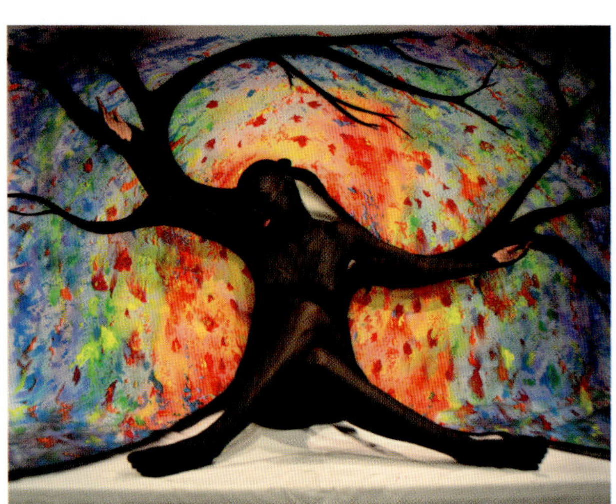
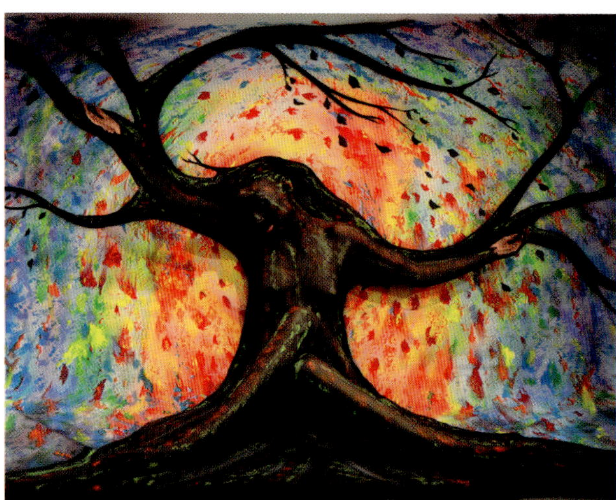
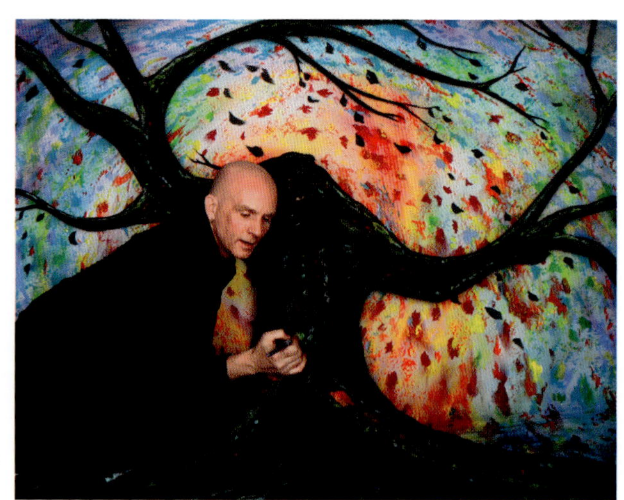

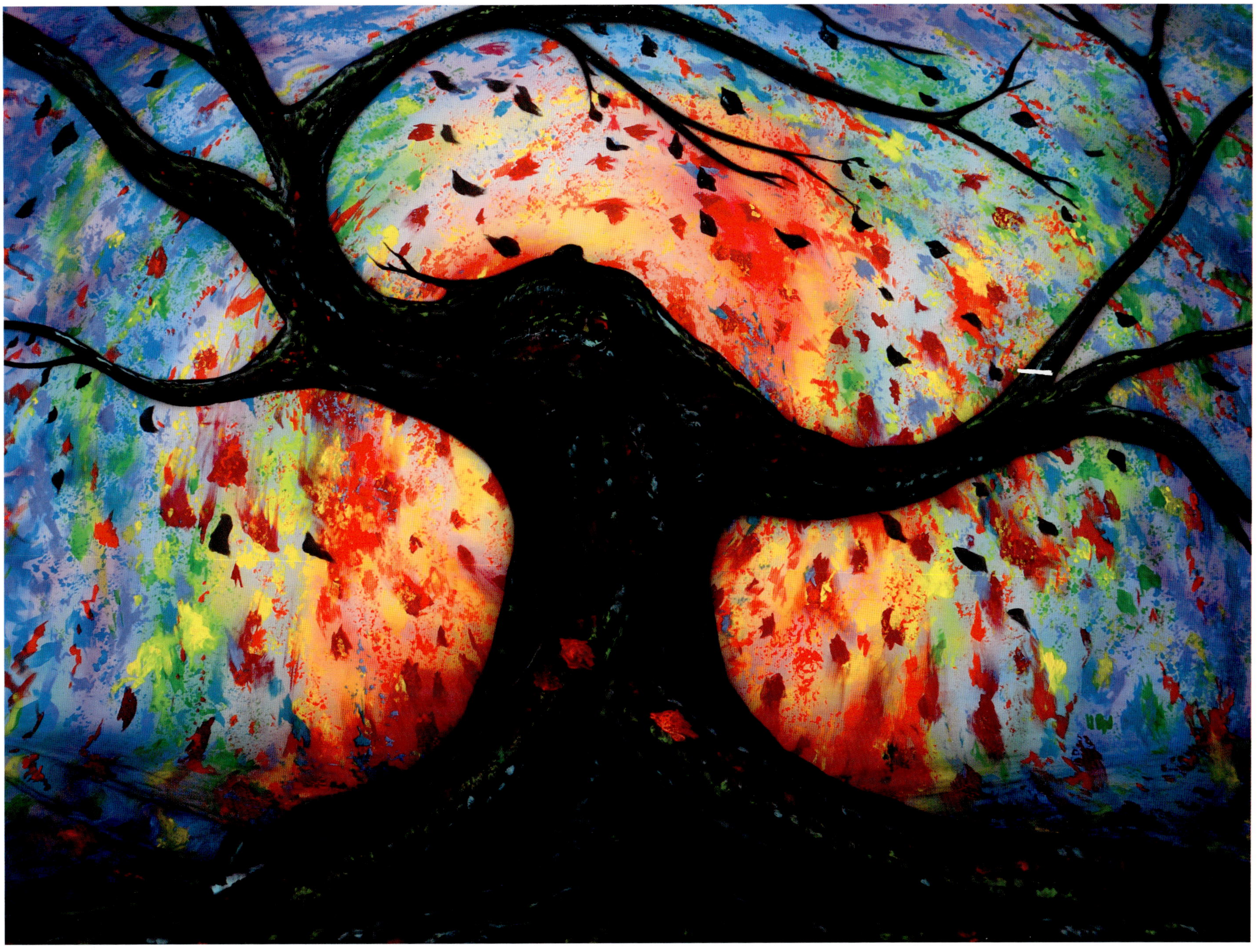

Maureen

Maureen is a commissioned painting where I worked closely with my clients to create a painting that we all love. The majority of the painting was influenced by decorative elements in her home combined with a Venetian-inspired painted mask. Using multiple panels for my final image allowed me to minimize negative space in the composition, and it allowed the client to comfortably hang the image perfectly on a curved wall accompanying her grand staircase.

Model: Maureen
Photographer: Craig Tracy

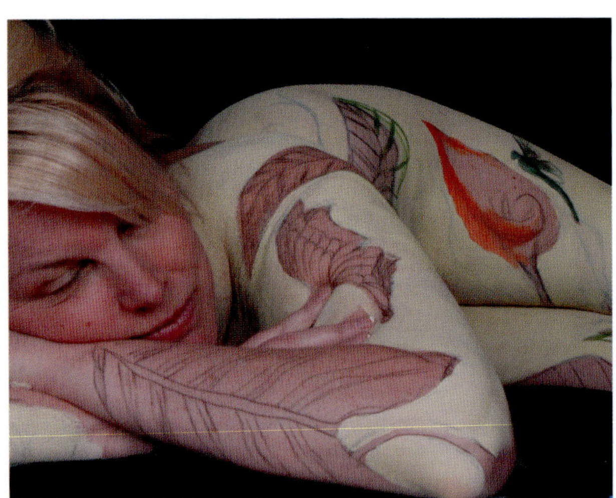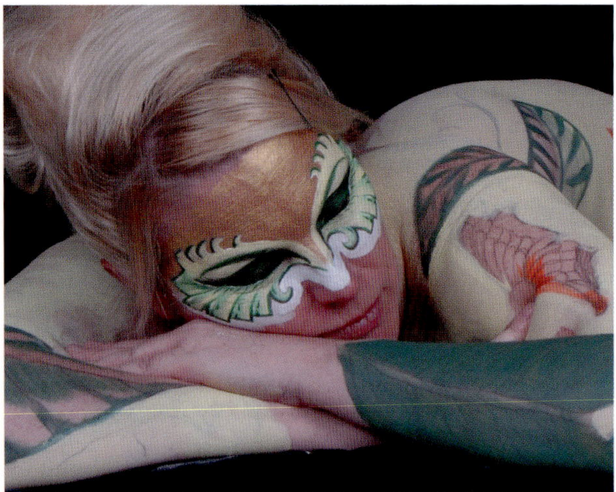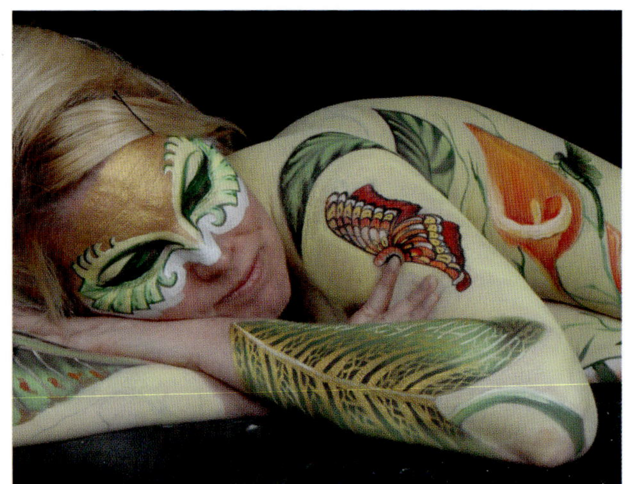

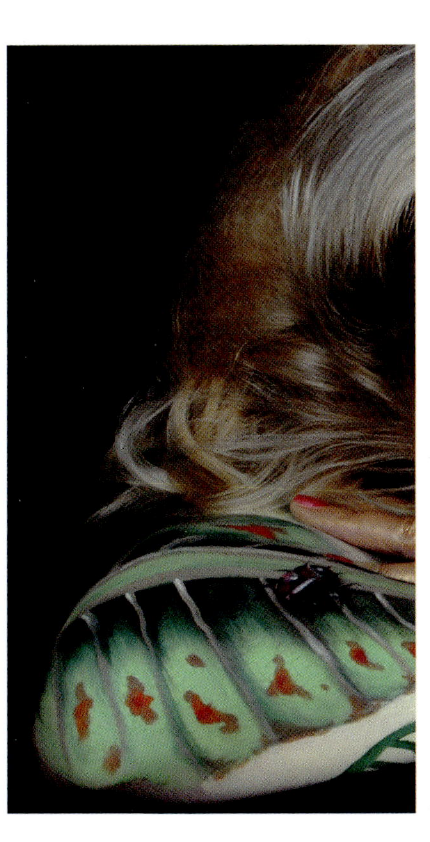
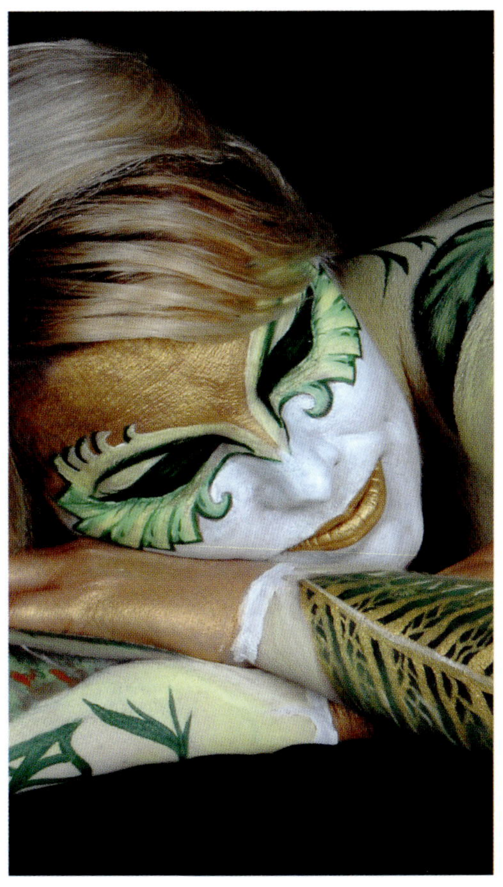
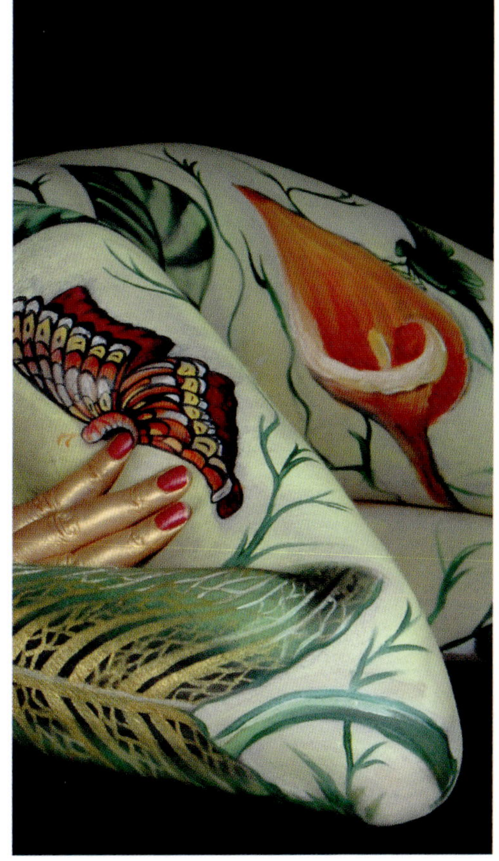
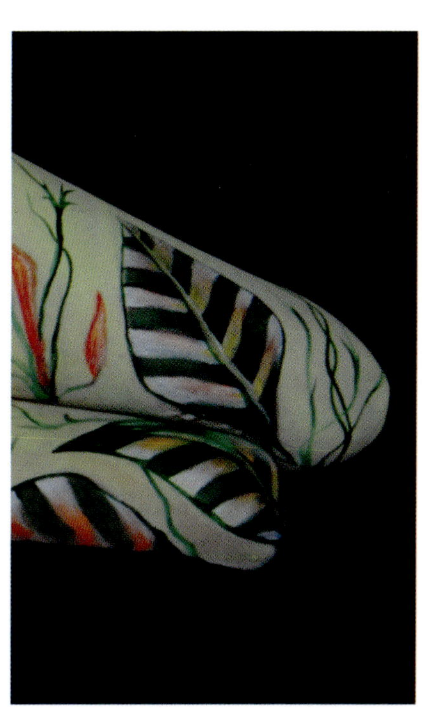

Spirit

Bodypainting is often a challenge for the model as well as the artist. *Spirit* required the perfect collaboration of both. The image was inspired by the pose that was so beautifully held by my model. For many years I had wanted to paint something that dealt with the wildness of horses and this was well worth the wait. I've again added subtle touches of color even though the image is primarily black and white. Abstract and surreal, *Spirit* is certainly one of a kind.

Model: Erika
Photographer: Craig Tracy

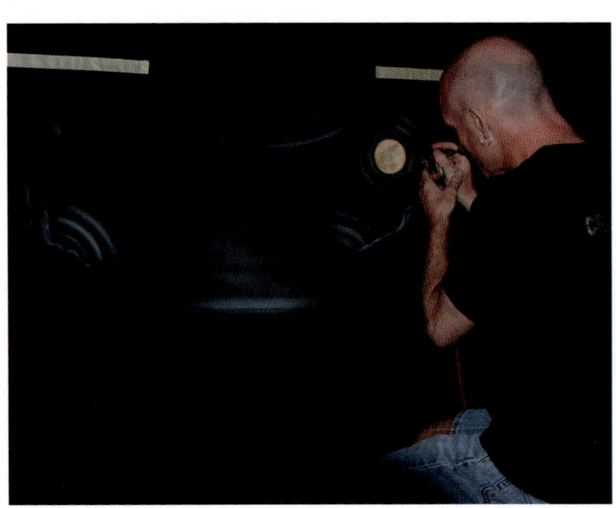
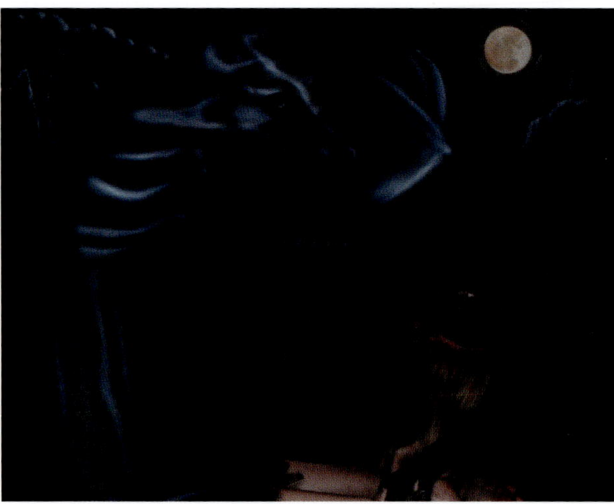
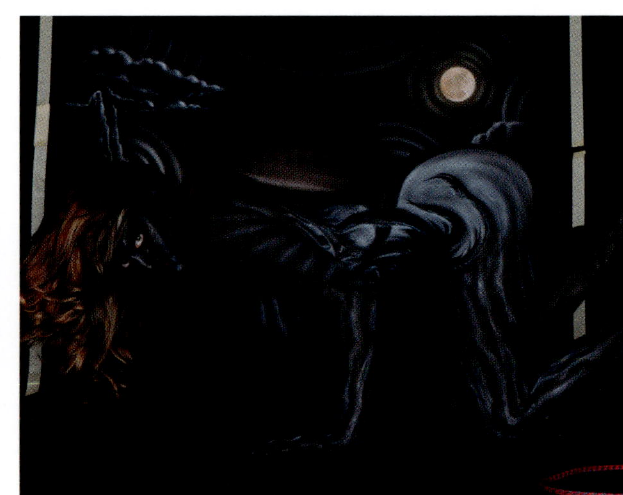

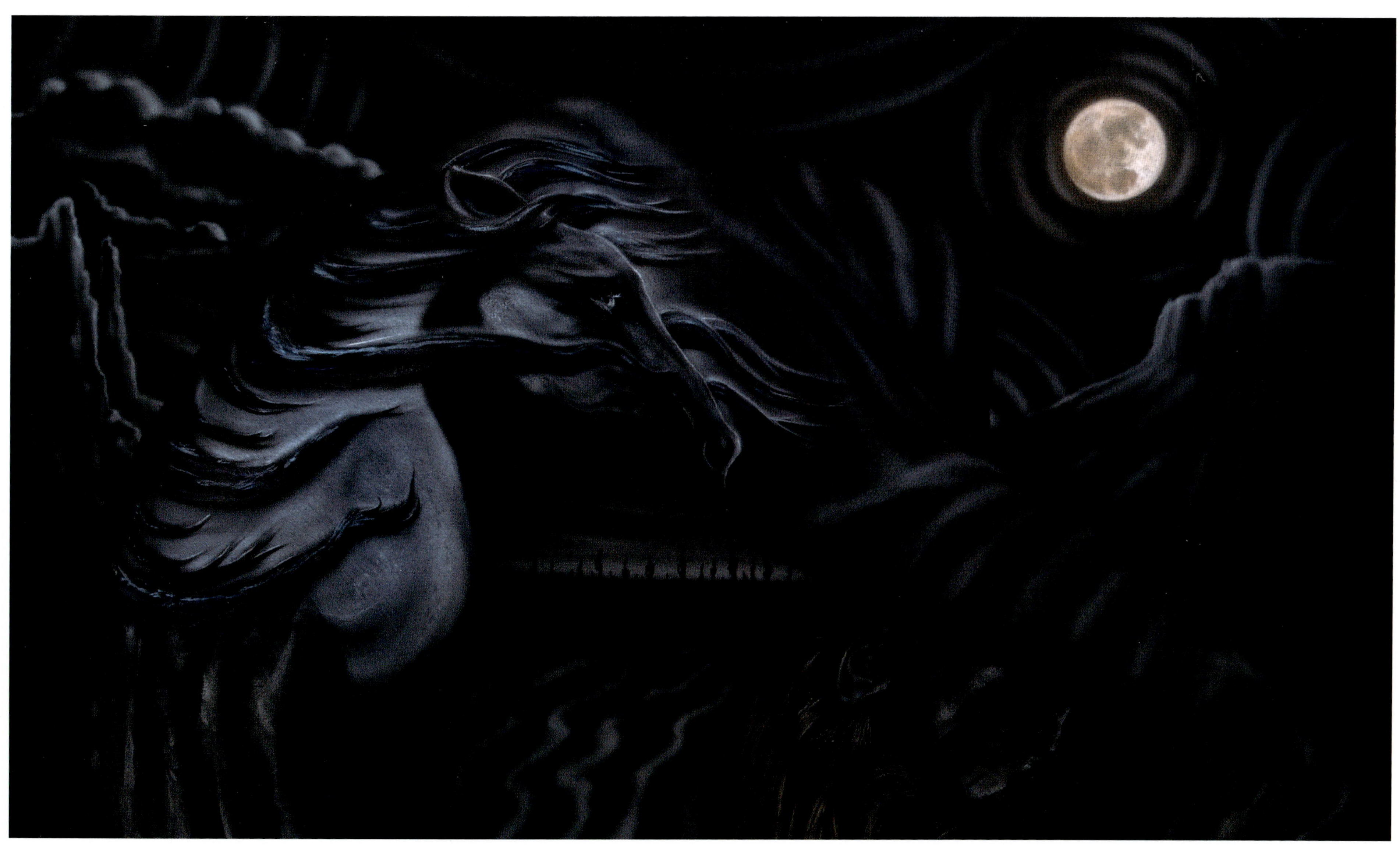

A Special Thanks

To all of the models, photographers, printers, assistants, framers, friends, family, inspirations, gallery consultants, teachers, and clients who have helped nurture and support my unique perspective, I wish to include you all in my thanks here. I truly and deeply appreciate your involvement in my life. And thanks go to: The Tracy and Bowsky families; MOM; Philip Michael; Eric Paul; Ashley, my love; little Miss Maggie; Ferenc; Giesla and the Pro Color team; Kayce; Robert G.; Karala; Chuck S.; my high school guidance counselor, Mrs. Helen Hibbets; Alex B., for having the coolest festival possible (www.worldbodypaintingfestival.com); Filippo Ioco (www.iocoart.com); Jeral Tidwell (www.humantree.com); Bella Volen (www.bella-volen.com); Scott and Madelyn (www.livingbrush.com); Big Daddy Smith and his team; my assistant on this project, Tilly Finley; the very diligent and insightful Sorche Fairbank; the good folks at Schiffer Publishing; the lovely people of New Orleans and the French Quarter; Boris; U2; and last but not least, YOU!!!! Thanks so very much.

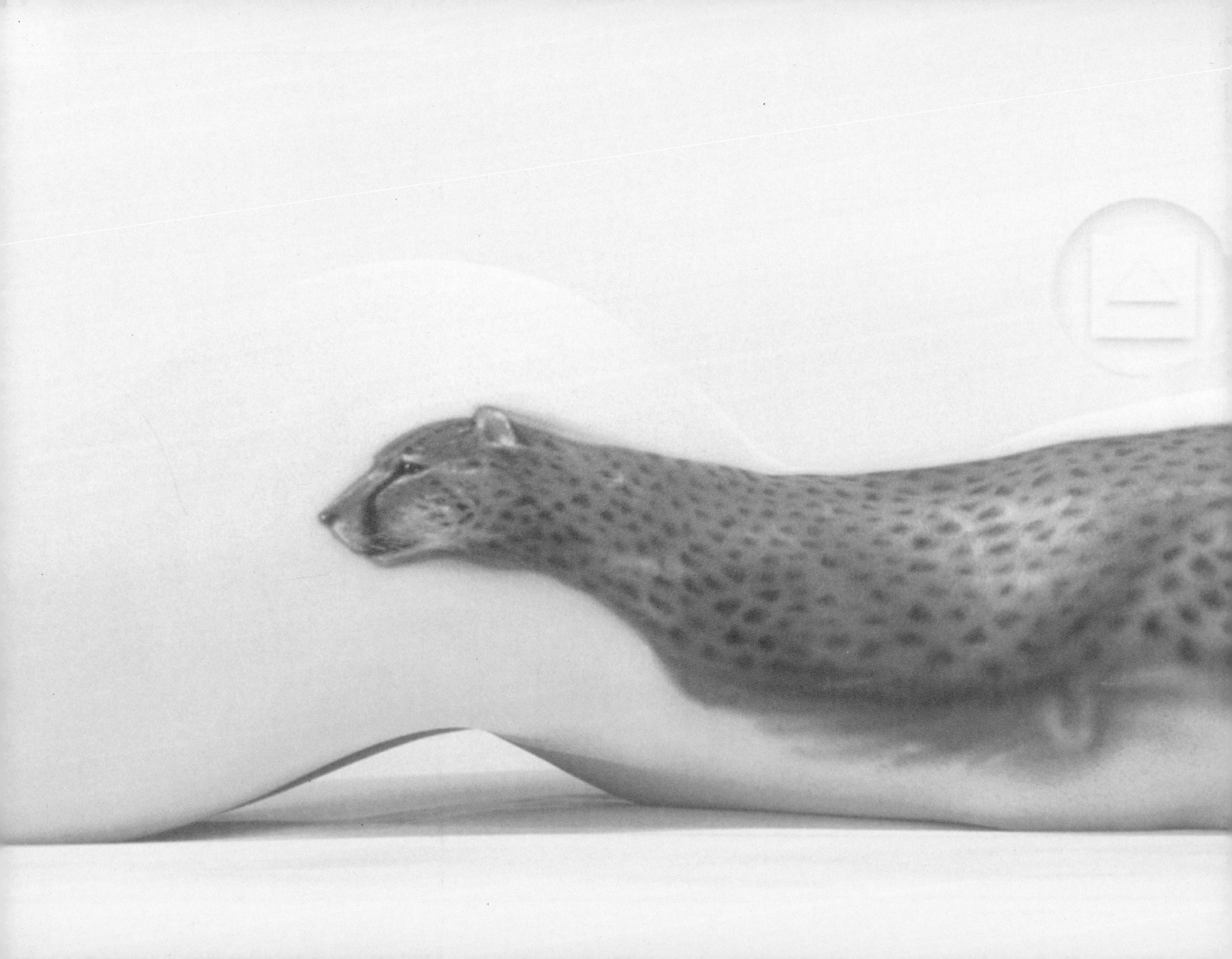